# The Frail Elderly

# The Frail Elderly

## PROBLEMS, NEEDS,
## AND
## COMMUNITY RESPONSES

### Carole Cox

AUBURN HOUSE

WESTPORT, CONNECTICUT • LONDON

**Library of Congress Cataloging-in-Publication Data**

Cox, Carole B.
    The frail elderly : problems, needs, and community responses /
Carole Cox.
      p.  cm.
    Includes bibliographical references and index.
    ISBN 0–86569–031–6 (alk. paper).—ISBN 0–86569–228–9 (pbk. :
alk. paper)
    1. Frail elderly—Services for—United States.  I. Title.
HV1461.C74   1993
332.6—dc20       92–38000

British Library Cataloguing in Publication Data is available.

Library of Congress Catalog Card Number: 92–38000
ISBN: 0–86569–031–6 (hc) 0–86569–228–9 (pbk)

First published in 1993

Auburn House, 88 Post Road West, Westport, CT 06881
An imprint of Greenwood Publishing Group, Inc.

Printed in the United States of America

The paper used in this book complies with the
Permanent Paper Standard issued by the National
Information Standards Organization (Z39.48–1984).

10 9 8 7 6 5 4 3 2 1

To my parents, Morris and Bebe,
and in memory of my grandparents.

# Contents

# Preface

The dramatic expansion of the elderly population in this country, as well as in many other countries, is a relatively recent phenomenon which has ramifications throughout society. Although the majority of this older population continues to live and function well in the community, the sheer growth in the size of this population implies that increasing numbers of older people are at risk for becoming dependent upon others for some type of assistance. Those in need of such support, whether due to physical, mental, or social limitations, are commonly referred to as the "frail elderly."

Although frailty is not intrinsic to aging, many factors place the elderly at particular risk of experiencing limitations in their functioning that can threaten their autonomy. In order to effectively meet the needs of this population, it is essential to understand the nature and meaning of frailty and the ways in which the community responds to it.

To be frail does not alter one's interests or desires. The frail elderly, just as their peers and others in society, desire to live in their own homes in the community as independently as possible. Unfortunately, in many instances the limitations that affect their functioning also limit the extent to which this desire can remain a reality. Policies and services that can enhance independence among the frail tend to be inconsistent in their availability and application. Variations in the interpretation and definition of frailty further contribute to a fragmented system of support. Consequently, many older persons in need of some assistance remain vulnerable in the community or are forced to move into more sheltered settings.

This book examines the ways in which communities are responding to the needs and problems of the frail elderly. Perhaps reflective of the varying interpretations of frailty and the absence of any consistent policy to deal with the problems of the frail, responses on the national level remain restricted and often fail to reach many of those in need. However, the needs of this population are not going unnoticed. Much creativitity and innovation are occurring at the state and local levels as well as in programs in other countries. These diverse models can provide ideas for the development of comprehensive programs of services for the frail elderly.

As the book discusses the problems faced by the frail elderly and the ways in which communities are responding, it will hopefully stimulate thought and discussion on measures that may best address their concerns. With the population continuing to age, there is an urgent need to do so, for the challenge posed by the frail elderly is one that cannot be ignored.

I would like to express my appreciation to Beth Nelson for her assistance with the manuscript and to Mary Carol Murphy of the National Council on the Aging and Donna Folkemer of the National Association of State Units on Aging for help in obtaining valuable materials for the book. My appreciation also goes to the many program administrators who shared their expertise and resources with me; I hope I have done your programs justice. I am particularly grateful to Abraham Monk for giving me the motivation and impetus to undertake this project.

My appreciation must also be given to my husband, Colin, for his technical expertise and assistance, and to my daughters, Amanda and Susannah, for their comments and patience throughout this long process. Finally, I would like to thank John Harney of Auburn House for his continued support.

# The Frail Elderly

*Chapter One*

# Overview

This century has witnessed major advances in the prevention and treatment of disease. Consequently, the rate of mortality from acute illnesses has declined while the average life span has continued to increase. In addition, the large number of births prior to 1920, coupled with a declining birth rate since the mid-1960s, has contributed to an increasingly older population. Between the years 1985 and 2030, the 65 and older population is expected to more than double and will comprise 21 percent of the population, with the 85-plus population nearly tripling (Special Committee on Aging, 1989).

This demographic shift necessitates dramatic changes in social policy and services to meet the needs of this aging population. Most of these older individuals will continue to reside in the community. However, this group will place new demands on society in accordance with the limitations caused by their restricted functioning. The national attention being given to long-term care is recognition of the fact that the needs of these elderly already have been noticed. These dependent elderly pose a challenge to many segments of society, and, indeed, as frailty affects increasing numbers of older individuals and their families, it assumes the characteristics of a major public health problem.

Aging is not synonymous with illness or incapacity, but it is associated with expanding rates of dependency. These dependencies result primarily from chronic illnesses, which are more common among the elderly than younger cohorts. Although chronicity does not necessarily connote frailty, impairments increase with the number of conditions, and older individuals are most likely to have multiple chronic illnesses (Guralnik et al., 1989). The majority will require at least minimal assistance in order to continue functioning in the community. Without help, independence is threatened.

The population of frail elderly requiring assistance is expected to grow so that by 2030 the nursing home population will reach 5.3 million and 13.8 million elderly in the community will need help with the activities of daily living (U.S. Bipartisan Commission on Comprehensive Health Care, 1990). Although advances in health care may reduce the likelihood of developing certain illnesses among the elderly, the projected increase in life expectancy is expected to lead to more years spent disabled prior to death (Guralnik, 1991).

Needs for assistance increase dramatically with age. Whereas only 5.9 percent of all persons in the community 65 to 68 have difficulty with one activity of daily living necessary for independence, the proportion increases to 38 percent of those 85 and older (Leon and Lair, 1990). Although chronic physical conditions are the major factors causing these limitations, cognitive changes also contribute, particularly among the very old. Those 85 and older are more than twice as likely to have Alzheimer's Disease, which, as it progresses, severely jeopardizes the capacity for self-care.

On the individual level, the burden of frailty is primarily felt through its restrictions on functioning and the potential loss of independence. But society also suffers from the burden of frailty. Estimates of the annual cost of health care for frail older persons range from $54 billion to $80 billion, and by 2030 this cost could be $132 billion (Department of Health and Human Services, 1991). Moreover, this sum is an underestimate of costs in that it does not include all of the other services and assistance, formal and informal, that these frail individuals require.

The costs of frailty to society cannot be measured solely in economic terms. A true measure of the costs must also consider the toll it places on families. The bulwark of support for the frail elderly is provided by relatives with little input from the formal service system. The demands associated with this caregiving can be extremely stressful with the needs of the caregiver often paralleling those of the frail relative. However, without this immediate support from the family, the ability of many frail to remain in the community would be severely curtailed. In many instances, it is the support of the informal caregiver that prevents institutionalization.

The frail elderly require assistance with their functioning in order to remain independent, but these needs cannot be attributed solely to physical or mental impairments. Social and environmental factors can also contribute to frailty insofar as they limit functioning. Isolation and decreased socialization can decrease morale while also emphasizing to the individual the seriousness of the impairments. The impact of the environment on frailty can be particularly severe. Thus, an individual may be able to adequately cope in a home with special adaptive devices or with the assistance of a relative, friend, or formal worker. Without these supports, functioning may be difficult or impossible, placing independence in jeopardy.

Identifying and separating the contributions of each of these factors— physical, social, and environmental—to frailty is imperative to the design of appropriate interventions. Moreover, this task is complicated by the effects of interactions among these variables on the functioning of the frail elderly and by the ability of these interactions to easily compound the severity of the impairment.

However, it is also because of these numerous interactions that responses to the needs of the frail for assistance can be so effective. Interventions in one area can have major ramifications in another. For example, increasing mobility can affect socialization, which in turn enhances mental well-being. Changing the home environment can improve the ability of the frail older person to perform the normal activities of daily living, which subsequently reduces the need for further assistance.

As is true of effective responses to all public health problems, appropriate responses to the problems of the frail elderly cannot be restricted to only one arena or strategy. Frailty must be perceived and dealt with in terms of its many dimensions. As it affects and permeates many critical aspects of the older individual's life, it necessitates broad and far-reaching interventions.

The majority of the frail elderly live in the community and desire to remain there. For both economic and humanitarian reasons, this desire should dominate our search for responses to the needs of this population. Widening doorways or putting a bathroom in the downstairs of a house can be more cost-effective than providing support for several years in a nursing home. Society is therefore faced with the challenge of responding to the frail so that their capacities for independence are enhanced rather than diminished.

A major step in approaching the issues of frailty has been taken by the National Institute on Aging (NIA). In 1991, the NIA allocated $41.9 million for research related to physical frailty, including its prevention and treatment. This focus provides a necessary framework for addressing the problems associated with frailty; however, as this book will discuss, responses and interventions must be made on many levels. New policies and a network of responsive services based on a comprehensive view of frailty are also required.

## THE DISTRIBUTION OF FRAILTY

Frailty is not evenly distributed throughout the aged population. Data from the National Medical Expenditure Survey (NMES) provide striking descriptions of those with functional impairments in the community (Leon and Lair, 1990). Both minority group status and gender are important characteristics to be considered with regard to the prevalence of frailty.

Blacks 65 and older more often report limitations in their activities of daily living (26.9 percent) than do whites (19.1 percent) or Hispanics (14.1 percent). Older women consistently report more limitations in functioning than elderly men, even among those 85 and older. It is important to note that income status interacts with these variables in that those on Medicaid have significantly higher rates of functional impairment than those on Medicare or with private insurance. Poverty rates—and therefore Medicaid eligibility—are highest for elderly black females living alone.

The living situation of the elderly also reveals a strong association with frailty. Data from the NMES show only 7.9 percent of elderly individuals living with a spouse to be impaired in comparison to 13.3 percent of those living alone and 15.6 percent of those living with a relative. Those living with a spouse appear to be the least impaired or to not recognize their impairments. Those living alone or with a relative are likely to need more assistance with their daily functioning.

Further examination of data on the frail in the community suggests that they are most likely to be widowed women living alone, 85 and over, living near or below the poverty line (Manton, 1988). This does not mean that older males are not affected by illness or impairment but that there are differences in the type of care that they require. Males require more medically acute care for more limited periods of time than do women. Women, on the other hand, require less intensive care that tends to be ongoing.

The relationship of gender to frailty is further supported by data from the 1982 Long Term Care Survey. Survey findings show functionally impaired males to be significantly more likely to be living with a spouse than impaired females (Macken, 1986). Forty percent of impaired females lived alone in comparison to only 14 percent of functionally impaired males.

These findings suggest that it is impaired elderly women living alone whose independence is most at risk. Without a spouse or support system to provide care and with few resources, the ability of these women to remain in the community is doubtful.

## CHRONIC ILLNESS AND FRAILTY

Chronic illness is not synonymous with frailty, but many of the chronic illnesses afflicting the elderly can cause disabilities which restrict the ability to live independently. As the incidence of chronic illness increases with age, that of acute illness declines. Data from the "Supplement on Aging" included in the 1984 Health Interview Survey show that more than four out of five persons over the age of 65 have at least one chronic condition, and the majority have multiple conditions (Dawson et al., 1987). The most prevalent chronic conditions are arthritis, heart disease, hypertension, and sensory losses. As these conditions become progressively worse, they can severely limit functioning.

The same data also show that, between the ages of 50 and 75, coronary heart disease and cerebrovascular disease account for the majority of disability. After the age of 75, degenerative processes such as arthritis and dementia begin to account for an approximately equivalent percentage of disability. However, it is important to note that despite the high incidence of chronic illness among the elderly, the majority of the elderly claim that they are not restricted in their activities.

In a study conducted using a sample of 113 elderly community residents between the ages of 74 and 95, Ford et al. (1988) examined the relationship between chronic illness and disability and found that arthritis and rheumatism accounted for 34 percent of the disability. The next most disabling conditions were stroke, visual impairment, heart trouble, and dementia. Diabetes, hearing impairment, and hypertension were the least disabling with regard to the individual's ability to carry out the tasks of daily living.

Using data from the 1984 "Supplement on Aging," Verbrugge et al. (1989) found that cerebrovascular disease, hip fracture, and visual impairment were the three conditions with the highest impact on activities. But the prevalence of disorders is not necessarily associated with their effects on the lives of the elderly or their functioning. Arthritis, which is ranked first in prevalence of chronic conditions, has less effect on functioning than cerebrovascular disease or visual impairment. The findings also show that disability cannot necessarily be implied by the number of chronic conditions and that it is essential to specify what the conditions are.

Other research suggests that specific joint and muscle impairments are primary contributors to frailty in the elderly. Disability is likely to result from conditions that affect hand functions related to such basic tasks as dressing, bathing, and eating and those that affect the lower limbs, thus restricting shopping, housekeeping, driving, and food preparation (Jette et al., 1990). Limitations in these activities imply that assistance is required in order for the individual to remain in the community.

Important gender differences exist in the rates of these disabling conditions. Arthritis, which includes over 100 different inflammatory and degenerative changes in the bones and joints, has a higher incidence rate in females for every age group until age 85, when it afflicts approximately half of both men and women (Ford et al., 1988) with prevalence rate highest among black women 65 years and over (National Center for Health Statistics, 1987). The pain and discomfort caused by arthritis can lead to further disability as individuals are forced to restrict their activities. These restrictions can cause joints to become inflexible, further exacerbating the effects of the disease.

Osteoporosis, characterized by the chronic loss of bone mass, is a major debilitating problem for 24 million persons. Half of all women over age 45, and 90 percent of women over age 75 have some degree of osteoporosis (Special Committee on Aging, 1989). This condition leads to an increased risk of hip, neck, and wrist fractures and is a major cause of disability among older women.

Hip fracture caused by osteoporosis is responsible for over 100,000 new cases of long-term disability each year with almost half of the incidents occurring in those over 80 (Department of Health and Human Services, 1991). Half of the patients able to walk before a hip fracture are unable to walk independently afterward (Miller, 1978). Because the incidence of osteoporosis-related fractures increases with age, the potential for affliction and frailty in the aging population is enormous.

The rate of hypertension similarly increases with age, and the rates are higher for women than for men at each age and highest for black females. For the elderly, hypertension is the single greatest risk factor for increased coronary heart disease and cardiovascular disease (Kannel and Gordon, 1978). Cardiovascular disease, which can deprive brain cells of blood, is a primary cause of strokes among the elderly. The effects of strokes include aphasia (the loss or impairment of speech), paralysis, and/or blindness.

## SENSORY IMPAIRMENTS

Impairments in vision and hearing commonly accompany the aging process. The incidence of blindness in one or both eyes and of other vision problems, including cataracts, increases with age.

Elderly individuals with visual decline report significantly more limited physical functioning, more limited social functioning, poorer morale, and higher depression scores than those with good vision (Branch et al., 1989). Being forced to curtail usual activities can affect many spheres of the older individual's life that are associated with independence and well-being.

The relationship of hearing loss to frailty and restricted functioning is less conclusive than that of vision. Hearing deficits usually occur gradually, so that the older person is able to adapt to them. However, as the loss becomes severe, communication may become difficult or impossible, causing the elderly individual to retreat from social activities. Even hearing aids may not compensate for extreme hearing loss. Some findings suggest that the consequence can be withdrawal and isolation of the older person due to diminished interactions with relatives and friends (Weinstein and Ventry, 1982). However, other research (Thomas et al., 1983) finds few effects of hearing loss on emotional or social integration in elderly individuals who are otherwise healthy and independent. On the other hand, the effects may be most severe on those who already have diminished functioning.

The debilitating aspects of sensory losses highlight the complexity of factors contributing to frailty. Impaired sight or hearing can severely impede the ability of the elderly to function in the community, and these effects may be most pronounced in the absence of social supports.

## MENTAL HEALTH AND FRAILTY

Physical impairments are not the only risk factors with regard to disability and frailty in the elderly. Attention must also be paid to the impact of mental health problems, particularly depression, on the functioning of older adults. Depression affects 15 to 22 percent of the elderly community (Gurland, Cross, and Golden, 1980). The apathy, indecisiveness, withdrawal, and sense of helplessness associated with depression are conducive to frailty, as these symptoms affect the older individual's motivation and capacity for self-care.

A survey of physical functioning in over 11,000 patients found that depression strongly affected the ability of the older patient to carry out the activities of daily living (Wells et al., 1989). The disabling effects of depression on bathing, climbing stairs, dressing, socializing, walking, and working were comparable to those of serious heart condition and greater than those of most of the chronic conditions of angina, arthritis, back problems, coronary artery disease, diabetes, gastrointestinal problems, hypertension, and lung problems.

## HEALTH CARE

### Medical Services

Given their high rates of chronic illness, it is not surprising that the elderly make more physician visits and have longer and more frequent hospital stays than younger age groups. In fact, most of the utilization of hospitals is due to acute episodes of a chronic condition (National Center for Health Statistics, 1988).

Due to the complexity of their problems, elderly patients in hospitals have longer stays. Heart disease, malignant neoplasms, eye problems, fractures, and particularly hip fractures for women are the primary reasons for admissions, and frequently these conditions occur in conjunction with other problems. The average length of stay in hospital is longer for the elderly, averaging 8.6 days for those 65 and older, as compared to 6.4 days for all ages (National Center for Health Statistics, 1988).

In a study focused on the hospitalization of the disabled elderly under Medicare's Prospective Payment System, the length of hospital stay has been found to decline for those disabled elderly with only mild impairments while it has remained the same for those with medically acute conditions (Liu and Manton, 1988). Moreover, there has also been a decrease in the rate of hospital admissions for Medicare patients. This decrease has been attributed to a reduction in unprofitable admissions (those elderly who remain in hospital for excessive days), changes in medical technology, and the movement of some services from inpatient to outpatient settings (Des Harnais et al., 1987). Although these findings are encouraging on a cost basis, there is little information available on what happens to those who would be unprofitable to the hospital due to their risk of excessive stay.

It should be noted that the use of health care by the elderly is not uniform throughout the country. The rural elderly are particularly vulnerable in the present health-care system. A shortage of physicians as well as treatment facilities in rural areas means that the rural elderly frequently suffer from poor preventive as well as tertiary care. Rural elders experience a higher rate of arthritis, cardiovascular disease, diabetes, and hypertension than do the elderly in urban areas (National Resource Center on Health Promotion, 1991). Poverty, isolation, poor transportation, and a reluctance to discuss personal and financial matters contribute to the rural elderly's being denied appropriate health care. Consequently, the ability of many of these elderly to function in the community is seriously threatened.

## Mental Health Services

Given the fact that depression can be a major contributor to frailty, the role of mental health services in meeting the needs of the elderly community must also be examined. Unfortunately, such services remain underutilized by the older population. Findings from a survey made by the American Psychological Association found that only 2.7 percent of services were to individuals 65 and older (VandenBos et al., 1981).

These findings were replicated in two other studies. An epidemiological survey of mental health problems among the elderly in Baltimore, Maryland, found that 4.2 percent of those 65 to 74 had sought mental health treatment during the preceding six months in comparison to 8.7 percent of the younger population (German et al., 1985). Data on the patients treated in community mental health centers similarly reveal that only a small percentage are elderly (Flemming et al., 1984; Swan et al., 1986).

With these limitations on community mental health care, it may be anticipated that many of those in need of treatment do not receive it or are forced to move to an institution due to an inability to cope in society. In fact, a majority of those in nursing homes have mental disorders and disorientation that limit their capacity for self-care (Rovner et al., 1986; U.S. Senate Special Committee on Aging, 1989).

In a study of mental morbidity that closely examined the etiology of each subject's illness, 80 percent of the residents in the eight nursing homes studied were found to have some mental illness at the time of admission with 60 percent accounted for by dementia (German et al., 1992). However, about half of these demented patients had complicating problems which were treatable. It is therefore possible that some of these elderly residents could have remained in the community if appropriate services and supports had been accessible.

## PREVENTION OF FRAILTY

There is mounting evidence that frailty can be prevented or the effects of impairments reduced. As an example, research on physical exercise suggests that it can be an important means of preventing disability in the elderly. Maintaining muscle strength is fundamental to the performance of many of the tasks of daily living such as getting out of bed, walking, or rising from a chair. In addition, weakness in the lower body and diminished strength increase the risk of falling and the risk of injury from a fall (Work, 1989). Although the evidence is still inconclusive, there are some data which do suggest that exercise, particularly weight-bearing exercises, can be important factors in reducing falls among the elderly and thus in reducing the risk of serious disability.

An inherent hazard associated with aging is the development of a sedentary lifestyle, which leads to a more rapid decrease in leg muscles. Exercise programs continued over time can counteract this decrease by increasing muscle mass and bone density. Of particular importance are exercises which increase strength as a means to increasing muscle mass.

Even the oldest of the old, those 85 and over, have been found to significantly increase their strength through weight-lifting exercises (Shephard, 1987). According to Shephard, participation by the elderly in three one-hour exercise classes per week may reduce the cost of acute and chronic treatment, mental health treatment, and extended residential care by more than $600 per year for each older person.

In addition to exercise programs, health promotion and health education activities can also play important parts in reducing the incidence of impairments associated with chronic illness. Programs that educate the elderly about the risks of falling and how to prevent falls can be important means of preventing frailty. Unfortunately, health education and promotion programs have tended to focus on younger persons, perhaps in accordance with the belief that change in the older population is difficult to achieve and is unlikely to have any real impact.

However, studies show that health education targeted to older persons can alter behavior patterns and increase participants' sense of well-being (Cox and Monk, 1989a). Changes in diet and nutritional intake as well as exercise patterns were observed among participants in health education programs offered at senior centers. An equally important finding was that the participants, regardless of their physical limitations, enjoyed the program, felt that it was stimulating, and believed that it gave them more control over their own health.

Health education activities, as they focus on functioning and positive health practices, can counteract attitudes and belief systems in which frailty is viewed as an unavoidable risk, even for those with impairments. Duffy and MacDonald (1990) found that older persons who have healthy lifestyles and engage in activities that promote their health are functionally more healthy than their peers. Moreover, the highest exercise levels were found among the oldest and most impaired group, those 85 and older. These findings support the view that impairment does not need to be equated with frailty.

The prevention of mental impairments conducive to frailty is potentially even more complex than the prevention of physical ones. However, because many spheres of the older individual's life may contribute to mental health and depression, there are innumerable areas for intervention. In addition to physical change and losses, environmental and social deprivations can also trigger mental problems. Poor housing, isolation, and the loss of loved ones and relationships are all factors which may contribute to depression. Many types of interventions, ranging from counseling to environmental change, may be beneficial in preventing stress, which can contribute to frailty.

## THE PERCEPTION OF FRAILTY

Most older individuals appear to accept and cope with impairments and adjust to their limitations. However, for some, disabilities are related to a decline in self-esteem and well-being and the perception by themselves and others of frailty. As older individuals begin to identify themselves as frail, they become increasingly vulnerable to dependency and withdrawal from society which may not be warranted by the actual physical condition. The individual restricted by a chronic condition is at risk for loss of self due to leading a restricted life, being socially isolated, and becoming a burden to those responsible for support (Charmaz, 1983).

Most studies of the effects of disability have focused on younger people, for whom physical limitations are assumed to have the greatest effect on daily functioning since they impose the most severe restrictions. The elderly, for whom impairments are perceived as "normal," and whose interactions are viewed as generally more limited, have received less attention. Therefore, less is known in this age group of the effects of disability and frailty on self-concept and well-being.

There is some evidence, however, to suggest that the effects of impairments on older persons do vary distinctly. In a study of the effects of chronic illness on the self-concepts and functioning of elderly women, Belgrave (1990) found that it did not affect all older women the same. Elderly women living with chronic illnesses defined themselves in three ways: basically healthy but having a problem which had to be dealt with; ill and doing the best they could; or overwhelmed by illness. Those who were able to continue valuable activities in spite of physical problems and those not minding relinquishing specific activities were likely to view themselves from the first two perspectives. Moreover, self-concepts did not alter if the women did not perceive themselves as disabled.

These findings underscore the myriad of underlying factors that contribute to the perception of frailty, many of which have yet to be discovered and described. But the evidence strongly suggests that functional status alone is not a sufficient criterion to predict frailty. Even those dependent on others may not view themselves as frail or even perceive themselves as dependent. As an example, an elderly husband and wife may continually adapt to changing needs and functioning abilities without defining themselves or each other as being frail. In the same way, an older parent may accept assistance from an adult child without identifying him- or herself as dependent. The gradual adjustment and adaptation process within an established framework of mutual assistance and support means that persons may not recognize increased dependency or frailty.

Comprehensive assessments and sensitive interventions can serve to counteract the development of frailty. To the extent that age is viewed as being concomitant with disease and problems are perceived as being incurable, these older individuals are at risk of being denied the same type of interventions given to younger persons. Age bias on the part of professionals combined with poor expectations on the part of the impaired elderly can contribute to a sense of hopelessness and dependency which, in turn, accentuate the perception of frailty.

## THEORETICAL PERSPECTIVES ON FRAILTY

This discussion of frailty underscores its complexity with regard to the many factors which can contribute to its development. Sociological and social-psychological theories can assist in unraveling this complexity as they provide a conceptual framework which links these factors together in a coherent manner. These theories can also identify those who are most vulnerable to frailty as well as provide a framework for the development of specific interventions. These theories offer a further perspective on how these conditions affect elderly individuals.

Continuity theory is particularly pertinent to the experience of frailty. This theory maintains that older persons seek to continue in their usual roles and lifestyles throughout the aging process. Individuals have a coherent structure which persists over time but allows for a variety of changes to occur (Atchley, 1989).

Two fundamental aspects of the theory are internal and external continuity. Internal continuity refers to the persistence of ideas, personality, preferences, and temperament. People seek to maintain a sense of internal continuity since it offers a sense of competence, control, and self-esteem.

External continuity refers to the maintenance of social roles, role relationships, and activities. The maintenance of external continuity is important to strong social supports and, perhaps more significantly, to the maintenance of a strong self-concept. Internal identity appears to remain constant over time in that persons tend to interact with those who support their sense of self and to maintain their sameness. A desire for external continuity also appears to be the norm in that persons continue to use established skills, perform accustomed activities, and interact within the same relationships.

However, both mental and physical impairments can pose obstacles to continuity. The older person whose memory is no longer intact will be thwarted with regard to maintaining internal continuity. The person with physical impairments that make the performance of traditional skills impossible may find external continuity jeopardized. In both cases, reductions in social support systems can further threaten continuity. Unfortunately such transitions in these systems frequently occur simultaneously with the older person's impairments so that discontinuity develops. It is with discontinuity that the older individual becomes susceptible to frailty.

According to symbolic interaction theory, identity is developed and maintained through interactions and reinforcement with others in society (Mead, 1934). Reference groups, those with whom the individual identifies, and significant others, those who are influential in the individual's life, are key actors in the development of self. Through interactions with these sets, proper roles and expected behaviors are learned and self-concept is developed.

Application of this theory to the elderly leads to the conclusion that older individuals with impaired functioning are susceptible to frailty due to the nature of their interactions with others. As these others perceive and treat the older person as dependent, through actions and behaviors which reinforce the individual's limitations, the individual is susceptible to developing a self-concept which personifies frailty. In accordance with this concept, the elderly person is liable to further restrict activities. Frailty may therefore be socially construed as it becomes a part of the individual's self-identity.

Learned helplessness theory offers further insight into the onset of frailty. According to this concept, helplessness develops as the impaired begin to accept the loss of control over their own lives and their dependency. Individuals become increasingly passive, dependent, and helpless and begin to lose confidence in their ability to function (Seligman, 1975). Unfortunately, others, as they offer assistance, only serve to exacerbate this negative self-concept. Rather than focusing on strengths, they tend to focus on the disability with the result being that the disabled elderly perceive themselves as helpless and frail. This percevied loss of control may be inappropriately generalized—in other words, these individuals may fail to act in their own self-interest even in areas in which they still are able.

One further theory with direct relevance to the development of frailty is the social breakdown and reconstructionist theory (Bengston, 1976). This theory delineates many factors in the environment which can act to threaten and destroy the older person's sense of competence. As abilities become less acute, the impaired individual is vulnerable to being labeled dependent. This label is reinforced by others who intervene by offering assistance. Eventually, the older person accepts the label of being incompetent and acts accordingly.

However, using a reconstructionist model, Bengston proposes that this vicious circle can be broken. Thus, as practitioners and informal supports enhance the strengths and coping abilities of the elderly person, confidence can be rebuilt and breakdown halted or reversed. In this way frailty does not have to remain an indelible identity.

All of these theories suggest that frailty can result from social-psychological factors through interactions in the social environment. A devalued self-image associated with a sense of helplessness which is reinforced by others can contribute to the development or enhancement of frailty. However, with proper interventions the process can be halted or even reversed so that the impaired individual is able to maximize rather than minimize abilities. But, the imminent danger is that without counterbalancing influences, well-meaning others addressing the needs of the impaired elderly, may unwittingly underscore the limitations and thus reinforce the frail identity.

These theories of the development of frailty are particularly useful in that they suggest ways in which professionals and others can intervene to counteract frailty or to diminish its effects. Providing opportunities which enable the older person to continue as much as possible in established roles of ways of acting, of utilizing remaining skills and abilities, of strengthening support systems can be critical for the maintenance of well-being.

Disability can impede physical functioning but it does not necessarily have to include the development of a negative self-concept. Focusing on the capacity of the impaired elderly which enables them to meet some environmental demands, rather than on their deficits, can be important in the maintenance of a positive self-concept.

## THE CONSEQUENCES OF FRAILTY

Frailty tends to limit a person's autonomy in that it commonly involves restrictions on the individual's capacity for decision making. Frail elderly individuals who require assistance either from their family or from agencies frequently find that the number of choices available to them regarding their care is limited as a consequence of their impairments. In many instances, depending upon others means relinquishing to others the power to make decisions in many spheres of their lives.

Losing autonomy of action and the ability to function independently is often associated with forfeiting the capacity for self-actualization. The dependency of the frail older person means that he or she is liable to be perceived as no longer having the ability to act with any judgment. Consequently, the frail are at risk for having their decision-making powers revoked or restricted due to perceived incompetence. Obviously, these perceptions can further threaten the individual's self-concept and ability to remain independent.

Frailty connotes dependency and vulnerability, two concepts which conflict with a person's right to autonomy and self-determination. As policy makers, families, friends, and social services personnel strive to meet the physical demands of the frail elderly, they risk infringing on these basic political and social rights. Planning and designing appropriate services and interventions to meet the needs of these persons is therefore an expansive task which necessitates sensitivity to the humanity of the impaired individual.

The consequences of frailty are not restricted to the elderly themselves. As revealed throughout the data on supports to the frail, families provide the majority of this assistance. Providing this support can threaten the well-being of these traditional caregivers. Furthermore, the continued availability of these caregivers is debatable. Shifts in the demographics of the population mean that there are fewer adult children available to care for the burgeoning number of elderly needing assistance in order to remain in the community.

Caution must also be exercised when attributing caregiving responsibilities to the spouse. These spouses are also likely to be elderly and are often themselves at risk for becoming impaired. Their ability to meet the increasing needs of the frail can be sharply affected by their own physical and emotional limitations.

Finally, it is important to remember that frailty is not the norm among older people. Growing old does not necessitate disability and frailty, and "healthy aging is not an oxymoron" (Berg and Cassells, 1990). The majority of the elderly reside in the community and function with little restriction on their activities, and even when restricted, they do not consider themselves frail. But the growth of the older population means that there will be more individuals with chronic illnesses as well as with other types of deprivation that may be conducive to frailty. As the expansion of this population begins to be felt, it is essential to understand what is meant by "frailty" and the factors that affect it.

## SUMMARY

This book addresses some of the major issues confronting the frail elderly. As this introduction indicates, frailty cannot be narrowly defined or predicted. Many factors—physical, mental, and social—can result in frailty, and thus appropriate interventions must be made in accordance with this diversity of causes. The majority of the frail elderly reside in the community, and thus the focus of this book is on the ways in which the community responds to the problems and needs of this population.

Impairment and disability are not going to disappear nor are the demands and needs of the frail. With the expanding of the elderly population, it becomes increasingly important to understand who is most at risk for frailty and why. Only with such knowledge can a comprehensive framework of policies and services directed at both prevention and care be designed.

The ramifications of an aging population and of the needs of its frail members affect everyone and defy simple unitary solutions. The issues surrounding the frail are broad, involving many spheres of life. In order for responses to be effective in meeting the needs of this growing population, they must extend beyond just one field in order to encompass the many variables influencing well-being and independence in later life.

This book addresses the issue of frailty among the elderly in the community. Chapter 2 discusses the way in which frailty is defined and the complexity of the term itself. Policy enactment provides a necessary framework for meeting the needs of the frail, and as Chapter 3 describes, these policies are being designed at many levels—federal, state, and local—yet their effectiveness remains questionable. The community responds to the needs of the impaired elderly via services offered through both the public and private sectors. Chapter 4 describes the major services that can have an impact on the lives of these elderly. Housing for the frail elderly remains an overriding concern, and in Chapter 5 the various available options, including adaptations in the home, are described.

Families provide the bulwark of assistance to these elderly. Chapter 6 presents theoretical perspectives for understanding the involvement of these family caregivers while also discussing the extent of family involvement, its effects on the older person, and its effects on the caregiver. As ethnicity and, in particular, minority group membership can influence both the development and perception of frailty as well as the way in which the family responds to it, Chapter 7 is devoted to an elaboration of this subject.

Much innovation is occurring throughout this country as well as in other countries with regard to the care of the frail elderly in the community. Chapter 8 describes some of these innovations, as they may provide important models for programs and services. Chapter 9 is an attempt to summarize and draw conclusions about the frail elderly and their needs in the community, the effectiveness of current responses, and recommendations for change.

# Chapter Two

# Defining Frailty

Eligibility for the majority of public programs and services as well as decisions regarding the capacity of an older individual to remain in the community are frequently based on a definition of frailty. The definition implies that without supports the ability of the person to function in the community is doubtful. Consequently, the definition of frailty and its outcome, with regard to being defined as frail, can have significant impact on an individual's life. Frailty is thus a term which must be accurately and sensitively interpreted so that it unequivocally identifies those in need of assistance. However, as will be discussed in this chapter, there are varying definitions of frailty and subsequent measures of assessment.

For most programs the definition of frailty is synonymous with functional impairment, functional dependency, or functional disability. These terms are used interchangeably, referring to multiple conditions that affect the functioning of the older person and his or her capacity for independence. An individual may be functionally impaired due to hearing loss, functionally dependent due to an inability to use transportation, and functionally disabled due to arthritis which impedes mobility.

Although the three terms measure different capacities, common to each definition is a reduction in the ability to carry out normal activities associated with living in the community. However, the actual effects of the loss on the individual can vary distinctly in interaction with many other variables that also affect the capacity to function. Thus, in themselves, these types of functional changes do not connote frailty.

The World Health Organization defines frailty as "any restriction or lack (resulting from an impairment) of an ability to perform an activity in the manner or within the range considered normal for a human being" (World Health Organization, 1980). Given this very broad interpretation, the restriction may be due to any type of impairment and frailty may be associated with a multitude of causes.

In the early 1970s, as the needs of specific groups of elderly became apparent, the Federal Council on Aging, as a means of drawing attention to the concerns of the frail in the community, defined them as "those, usually but not always, over the age of 75, who because of the accumulation of various continuing problems often require one or several supportive services in order to cope with daily life" (U.S. Department of Health, Education, and Welfare, 1978). The definition continues by specificing that frailty also involves the "loss of a social-support system to the extent that the person is unable to maintain a household or social contacts without continuing assistance from others" (p.15). This definition underscores the fact that frailty is not only the result of physical impairment or disability but is also strongly influenced by the existence of support networks and the capacity of the individual for social functioning. Furthermore, increased age is perceived as increasing the risk that problems that require support will become more pervasive.

Under the Older Americans Act (PL-89-73), the first comprehensive legislative plan for the elderly in this country, frailty is associated with those elderly having the "greatest economic or social need." Social need emphasizes noneconomic factors such as physical and mental disabilities, language barriers, and cultural and social isolation, including that caused by ethnic or racial status, that restrict an individual's ability to perform normal daily tasks or that threaten the capacity to live independently (Coombs, Lambert, and Quirk, 1982).

With these comprehensive definitions of frailty, it might be anticipated that a large proportion of the elderly could be defined as frail due to age and a multitude of conditions that restrict functioning and necessitate support from others. However, as will be shown through a review of current instruments and methods for assessing frailty, the current definitions of frailty, as applied to eligibility for services, seldom encompass more than the capacity for physical functioning.

The emphasis on physical functioning as a main determinant of frailty is underscored by Medicare and Medicaid, two of the main service providers to the frail population. In both systems, eligibility for benefits rests primarily upon physical conditions that affect functioning. Other factors that can restrict the ability to carry out normal daily activities are not generally or routinely assessed in determining eligibility for these programs.

## THE ACTIVITIES OF DAILY LIVING

The assessment of functional impairment or frailty is commonly based upon an older person's ability to perform the Activities of Daily Living (ADLs). These activities are those that are habitually performed and that are required for independent living. The ADLs traditionally include bathing, dressing, toileting, transferring between bed and chair, continence, and eating.

There are several advantages for using these criteria as assessment measures. They are easy to define, are quantifiable, can be based on self-report, and are sensitive to changes in functioning. Moreover, the measures are easy to administer and, therefore, can be applied readily to large populations as a screening device while also being used by paraprofessionals and survey staff. Instruments measuring ADLs are widely used in surveys examining the functional status of community elderly as well as a basis for estimates of the numbers of persons requiring assistance.

The validity of ADL instruments as measures of frailty is supported by findings which show that limitations in functioning are associated with health status. Elderly persons scoring low in their ADLs have been found to have greater needs for health care, particularly long-term care services (Liu and Cornelius, 1988). Restrictions in the ability to carry out these daily activities, therefore, are indicative of an older person's capacity to live independently.

### Measuring the Activities of Daily Living

Originally developed in the early 1960s, measurements of the Activities of Daily Living were used to evaluate treatment and assess the prognosis for aged and chronically ill persons. One of the earliest instruments designed to measure ADLs was developed by Katz (1963).

This instrument, while assessing functional ability in each specitic task, also scales the ADLs in a hierarchial manner according to the effects of each on independence. Requiring assistance in bathing is less limiting to the individual's independence than being dependent for eating or using the toilet. Scores for each item are measured according to whether the respondent is independent or dependent. These scores are summed to provide an overall measure of dependency. Ideally, the measurement is made by a trained observer, but, in large-scale surveys and in determining service eligibility, self-reports from the older person or the caregiver frequently substitute for observation.

The Katz instrument is only one of many used to measure physical functioning. With the growth of the elderly population and the increase in services, newer instruments aimed at measuring eligibility have been developed. In some instances these are unique to specific programs and their service goals, while in other instances the instruments are more widely utilized.

A review of the literature found 43 different indexes used to measure ADLs (Feinstein, Josephy, and Wells, 1986). Some of these instruments are restricted to just five ADLs while others ask about additional activities. These differences are significant in that with more activities being measured there will be an increase in the number of persons who will be classified as "disabled." However, a limitation inherent in all of these scales (which assess frailty solely on the basis of physical functioning) is that they frequently do not measure the extent of dysfunction or adaptation that the older individual has made to the impairment.

As the use of the ADLs as a criterion for disability has grown, the list has been adapted to meet program needs and priorities. As an example, walking was not included in the original list of ADLs, because mobility limitation is not consistently associated with dependence. The use of walkers, canes, and even wheelchairs enables the impaired elderly to function independently. Walking, therefore, does not fit into the hierarchial pattern of dependency. However, in many instruments, walking is included along with other activities such as going outside or getting around inside the house. Expanding the criteria associated with functioning further complicates and diffuses the meaning of frailty. An elderly person may be deemed physically fit according to one instrument but functionally impaired according to another due to problems with mobility or difficulties in walking on the street.

In measuring the degree of disability, instruments also differ according to whether they assess the degree of difficulty in performing a specific task or whether the activity can be completed with assistance. Some instruments classify a person as dependent only if human assistance is required, while others include mechanical assistance such as grab bars, special beds, or walkers as indicators of dependency. Again, the importance of this difference is more than just semantics, since the more inclusive definition will assess more elderly as frail. Moreover, measures which are limited to only two response categories, "can or cannot perform," will provide different estimates from those which inquire about the amount of assistance or supervision needed.

To further complicate the issue of measuring frailty, tools also differ with regard to how respondents are asked to define themselves. Some may ask the extent of difficulty encountered in completing a specific task while others phrase the response categories according to how much assistance is needed. In the former instance, an individual may respond that the activity is completed without any difficulty and fail to mention that this is due to receiving assistance. In the latter, the responses may reflect whether a person requires assistance but not whether such assistance is actually available. Moreover, response categories such as *a lot, some, not much*, or *none* offer much latitude for subjective interpretations.

Weiner et al. (1990) provide examples of the variation among instruments according to the types of information used to record disability. Among 11 national surveys collecting information on the ADL status of older persons, three recorded whether the disability had lasted for a minimum period of time, four recorded the level of difficulty in completing a task, and three recorded whether or not the person required assistance. All of the 11 instruments asked if the person received human assistance, while nine out of the 11 asked if the person used special equipment in completing the activity. This lack of consistency among instruments underscores their fallibility as measures of frailty.

An important and often overlooked aspect of impairment is that it is not a constant. It is estimated that at least 50 percent of the impaired elderly alter in their ADLs in a six-month period (Liu and Cornelius, 1989). Such intense change in status has important ramifications for services and needs for assistance. However, instruments do not necessarily measure the duration of the impairment or plan for reassessments. Many only record the older person as functionally impaired if, at the time of the interview, a difficulty in completing an activity is reported. Other instruments define a limitation in functioning only if the disability has lasted or can be expected to last for 90 days or longer.

## INSTRUMENTAL ACTIVITIES OF DAILY LIVING

The Instrumental Activities of Daily Living (IADLs) are also used as indicators of impairment and frailty. These activities are tasks commonly performed by individuals in the community as a normal part of daily living and are essential for adaptation in the environment. They include using the telephone, shopping, housekeeping, doing laundry, taking medications, using transportation, and managing finances. Unlike the ADLs, these activities measure cognitive as well as physical capacity and therefore can provide a more comprehensive assessment of the individual.

## Measuring the Instrumental Activities of Daily Living

A frequently used scale for measuring IADLs is one developed by Lawton and Brody (1969). Data are collected from the elderly individual or a caregiver on independence in using the telephone, shopping, food preparation, housekeeping, laundry, use of public transportation, taking medications, and handling finances. Scoring ranges from totally independent in each activity to totally dependent with item scores measured on an eight-point Guttman scale for women and a five-point Guttman scale for men. Higher scores reflect greater total dependence.

Instrumental activities of daily living are also measured with the Older Americans Research and Service Center (OARS) instrument (Duke University Center for the Study on Aging, 1978). This instrument includes seven items: telephone use, travel, shopping, meal preparation, housework, taking own medications, and handling personal finances. In contrast to the Lawton and Brody scale, all items are asked of both men and women and responses are recorded in only three categories: can be performed unaided, some help is needed, and cannot be performed at all. In order to overcome the bias that might accompany gender-related responses, the items may also be asked "Could you perform?"

Further refinement of this scale suggests that it may be accurately reduced to only five items and still identify elderly individuals in the community who are impaired (Fillenbaum, 1985). Accordingly, the ability to use the telephone and to take medications independently are not necessarily predictive of the ability to remain independent in the community. Instead, the items may be reduced to the ability to use transportation, shop, prepare food, do housework, and manage finances. These items facilitate the identification of those elderly requiring specific services and interventions.

The Assessment of Living Skills and Resources (ALSAR) is an example of another instrument used to measure IADLs (Williams et al., 1991). This tool builds on earlier measures by incorporating both the skill of the individual in completing each task as well as the resources available. It also combines the skill and resources scores to determine the ability of the individual to accomplish a task.

Skills and resources on the ALSAR are rated on scales of 0–2 with 0 being independent, or adequate resources available. Functioning is assessed on 11 items associated with independent living. A risk score for each task is obtained. The total risk score for the items can be used in planning for services, since it indicates specifically where more support is necessary.

As with the scales measuring the activities of daily living, important discrepancies exist among scales measuring IADLs. Scales may include as many as 16 activities which break larger functions into small tasks. Thus, dressing may be subdivided into activities such as combing hair, filing nails, and fastening buttons, while household chores may be subdivided into such distinct categories as turning a light switch on and off and turning a key in a lock (Kuriansky et al., 1976). Scales may also include much more strenuous activities such as the ability to shovel snow, mow the lawn, or climb stairs. With these additions, more individuals will be categorized as disabled.

Differences in the wording of the IADL instruments also have significant consequences on the measurement of frailty and the consequent assessment of the elderly. As an example, the noninstitutionalized elderly in Cleveland, who were measured using the OARS instrument, appear to be three times as disabled as elderly in other parts of the United States who were assessed by the National Health Interview Survey (Ford et. al, 1988). The discrepancy is due to the fact that the former asks about specific activities, such as, "Can you go shopping for groceries or clothes?" The National Health Interview Survey inquires only about shopping for personal items. The more discrete measure of the OARS elicits more negative responses and, therefore, classifies more individuals as impaired.

As with the ADL measures, there is no standardization regarding the categories of responses on the IADL instruments. Some record ability according to level of difficulty ranging from no difficulty to unable to perform with or without help. Others record the frequency of performing activities, while still others rate each item on the degree of "problem" encountered in the performance.

Data on the ability to perform the IADLs is generally collected through self-reports or from the caregiver. However, because of the complexity of the tasks and the many factors that can influence performance, these assessments are not necessarily accurate. A critical limitation is that standardized instruments do not generally make allowances for the many variables that can influence both responses and abilities.

Ethnicity is one factor which can significantly affect the scores on IADL instruments. Depending on the degree of assimilation into American culture, many older ethnic or minority people may not be competent in

IADL tasks. Those who are not fluent in English, who have remained within ethnic communities, and who have tended to rely on others to do shopping or manage their money are likely to score poorly on many measures while actually functioning perfectly adequately within their traditional environments.

Gender, with its accompanying socialization differences, may also affect the scoring on IADL measures. Elderly men are frequently less competent in performing routine household chores, while older women may be less accustomed to making decisions or managing finances. These factors, however, are frequently unaccounted for in measurements where one summary score records the amount of disability. Final scores may therefore not be reliable indicators of actual ability to function.

A lack of motivation or a memory impairment on the part of the elderly person can severely affect both reported ability and performance. Depression, which can strongly influence mood, may subsequently influence the validity of self-reported abilities. Thus, at any one time, the description of abilities may be more reflective of the current mental status of the individual than of his or her actual capacity for self-care. Moreover, measurements at one time do not necessarily reflect usual performance ability.

Obtaining reports from family members does not necessarily improve their validity. Relatives are not always knowledgeable about the individual's functioning. Moreover, those who are experiencing a great deal of stress in their caregiving activities may report greater degrees of impairment than those who provide assistance without such stress. Other motives, such as a desire to protect the older person or a desire to obtain more assistance, can also influence these proxy responses.

## Combined ADL and IADL Instruments

Instruments have sought to improve on the ADL/IADL scales by combining the measures as well as adding a measure of mental competence. The Hebrew Rehabilitation Center for Aged (HRCA) Vulnerability Index (Morris, Sherwood, and Mor, 1984) is composed of 11 items which can be completed through either self-report or by a proxy. Instrumental activities include meal preparation, taking out the garbage, and housework. ADLs consist of the ability to walk up and down stairs, the use of a walker or wheelchair, the ability to dress oneself, and the number of days in a month that the individual went outside. In addition, the Index asks to what extent bad health or pain prevents the person from engaging in activities.

A combined ADL and IADL scale which measures both sets of activities in a hierarchical relationship has also been developed (Spector et al., 1987). This scale builds on the concept that the elderly in the community are more likely to be impaired in certain IADL activities than ADL ones. The two IADL activities in the scale are shopping and transportation, while the ADL include bathing, transferring, dressing, and feeding.

The use of the scale with various elderly populations indicates that it accurately discriminates among levels of functional impairment, showing a hierarchical relationship among the different activities. In all age groups, older individuals were more likely to be dependent in only IADL than both IADL and ADL measures. The proportion of those dependent in either increased with age, and those dependent in only IADL functions were more likely at a later point to become dependent in their ADLs. This type of instrument, with its sensitivity to specific areas of functioning, can be valuable in determining appropriate interventions.

## IMPLEMENTATION OF THE ADL AND IADL CRITERIA

One of the largest programs to institute standard criteria for frailty was the nationwide Channeling Demonstration funded by the Health Care Financing Administration, the Administration on Aging, and the Office of the Assistant Secretary for Planning and Evaluation (Phillips et al., 1986). The demonstration was implemented at ten sites to test whether expanded home care services to the frail elderly in the community would reduce nursing home admissions and improve the well-being of the elderly and their caregivers. Services were to target the most frail as defined by their risk of nursing home placement.

Eligibility for services was based upon impairment in two ADLs, severe impairment in three IADLs, or severe impairment in one ADL and two IADLs. Cognitive or behavioral difficulties could be used in lieu of one IADL. Throughout the programs, the ADL-IADL criteria were used as standards for program eligibility.

The importance of ADLs and IADLs as criteria for program eligibility is highlighted in a review of the ten community-based demonstration projects (Kemper et al., 1987). The findings of this review reveal the inconsistency in eligibility determinations based on ADL and IADL measurements. As an example, most questions measuring ADL performance used at the ten sites inquired as to whether anyone helped the person with a specific activity such as bathing rather than assessing the ability of the older individual to do the activity independently. Consequently, those receiving help are identified as more dependent than those not receiving help, when, in fact, the response may be reflecting availability rather than need.

Most states use some measures of ADLs or IADLs in assessing eligibility for public service programs. A survey of criteria measures in 12 states reveals that all used the six traditional ADLs and the established set of eight IADLs (Luehrs and Ramthum, 1989). However, states also expand these measures and may even assess social and environmental supports.

Findings from the survey show that states also vary in the tasks used to determine dependency. For example, programs in Illinois inquire as to the ability to perform activities, the availability of assistance, and the frequency of its provision. The three scales are summed independently to provide a more sensitive measure of both functional need and service requirements.

The criteria for eligibilty for community services differ even within states. Programs under the Older Americans Act, Medicaid waiver programs, and state-funded services, as they vary in their targeting, will also use distinct assessment measures. Under the Older Americans Act, services are intended to benefit all persons over 60, but programs such as in-home services offered through Area Agencies on Aging may define their own eligibility criteria and target groups based upon local priorities and needs. However, given the emphasis placed on those with the greatest economic and social needs, services are charged with giving priority to elderly identified in those categories.

State-funded programs usually have no income provisions and provide services based on functional limitations and client needs in conjunction with cost-sharing (Hasler, 1991). These assessments tend to rate the number of limitations in ADLs and IADLs using the total score to estimate the need for service and what the client may have to pay. In many states, these scores are used in conjunction with the subjective assessment made by a case manager who has the final determination of eligibility.

Differences also exist with regard to the use of objective and subjective measures for assessing functioning. Systems may weigh and sum the scores across the individual functioning activities with eligibility decided by a specific numerical score. Others use this method in conjunction with the subjective evaluation of the person making the assessment, who provides a more impressionistic estimate of the degree of frailty and need.

Stone and Murtaugh's (1990) review of the implications of using differing criteria in the measurement of disability suggests how such criteria affect the elderly and the disposition of services. As an example, with a criterion of impairment in three or more ADLs, lasting for at least 12 months, they estimate that there are 411,000 older persons eligible for home care services. If a less restrictive criterion for eligibility is used—active or standby help required with any ADL or IADL lasting for at least three months—the estimate of those elderly eligible for home care increases to 4.1 million persons. Currently, under most federal programs, based on assistance needed in two or more ADLs, the number of eligible elderly is estimated to be 857,000, but this could be expanded to 1.35 million if standby help is counted.

## The Two-Plus Criterion

The usual criterion for eligibility for publicly sponsored services is a deficit in a minimum of two out of five ADLs—bathing, transferring, dressing, toileting, and eating. Those with a deficit in only one ADL are referred to as the moderately impaired and tend to be those able to function independently with the use of special equipment such as walkers or guard rails. Under the Pepper home care bill, many of the long-term care proposals, and most public benefit programs, limitations in at least two of the core ADLs listed above are required for eligibility. It is also important to note that in using these criteria, the most common limitation found in the elderly living in the community is in bathing, while feeding and toileting show the least impairment.

Based on data from the 1984 Supplement on Aging, Rowland et al. (1988) find that those with two or more functional impairments are most likely to be 85 years or older, twice as likely to be living with a relative or friend, more likely to be women, and more likely to be poor. It is not surprising that these individuals also report poor health status, are likely to have been hospitalized in the past 12 months, are likely to have chronic problems related to arthritis, hypertension, heart disease and diabetes, and are likely to have some impairment in the IADLs. The two-plus criterion for services thus appears to be targeting those most in need of support.

The two-plus criterion is a commendable effort to assist in focusing services on those who are the most impaired in the community. However, using only the five core ADLs may exclude many who continue to have problems functioning due to mobility problems or difficulties in getting outside of the house. Many who could benefit from supports under seven ADL measures are thus excluded from programs.

## COGNITIVE IMPAIRMENT

In addition to physical impairments which limit functioning, frailty may also result from cognitive impairments which diminishes the capacity for independent living. Problems with memory, intellectual impairment, learning ability, calculation, problem solving, judgment, comprehension, recognition, orientation, and attention can severely impact the ability to complete IADLs and may even affect the ADLs. Dementia, an illness whose prevalence increases with age, can particularly affect functioning capacity.

The number of persons with mild or moderate cognitive impairment in the community ranges from 3 million to 3.5 million (Lombardo, 1990). The extent to which these individuals may require assistance with functioning is indicated in estimates from the Commonwealth Fund Commission, which suggest that over half of the 1.6 million severely impaired elderly persons (those needing assistance with two or more ADLs) living at home are also cognitively impaired (Rowland, 1989). In fact, the likelihood of cognitive impairment rises with the number of ADL limitations. Whereas 22 percent of the elderly with two ADL impairments are cognitively impaired, the proportion increases to 44 percent of those with four or five ADL impairments.

Dementia can severely impede functioning because it may entail behavior disorders and an inability to complete tasks required for living in the community. These individuals frequently require constant supervision, support, or direction in completing the tasks of daily living. However, impairments may not show up on traditional ADL/IADL measures if questions are not worded to include "Is supervision needed?" Without more precise measuring and wording of ADLs, assessments of functional ability in elderly persons with dementia is likely to be inaccurate (Hawes, 1990).

### Scales of Cognitive Functioning

One of the most widely used instruments in the measurment of cognitive functioning is the Mini-Mental Status Examination (MMSE; Folstein et al., 1975). This scale assesses orientation to time and place, recall, short-term memory, and ability to perform serial subtractions or reverse spellings. The test also measures constructional capacities by asking the person to copy a design and the use of language by asking the subject to write a complete sentence. The items are scored and summed; the maximum possible score for the 11 items is 30 points. A score of 23 points or less for a person with more than eight years of education is evidence of cognitive impairment (Folstein, 1983). However, using the total score to judge capacity for independent living may be an inaccurate assessment in that the individual may still be able to function adequately in his or her home environment.

With regard to measuring actual ability to function in the community, other scales may be more relevant than the MMSE. The Dementia Rating Scale (Kay, 1977) focuses on the ability to perform tasks associated with daily activities while also measuring memory and orientation. The information is provided by an informant who rates a subject's ability to cope with money, remember a three-item list, find his or her way indoors and around familiar streets, grasp explanations, and recall events of the previous six months. The abilities to eat, dress, and toilet are scored separately.

The Brief Cognitive Rating Scale (BCRS; Reisberg and Ferris, 1983) measures the degree of cognitive impairment in concentration, recent memory, past memory, orientation, and functioning or self-care. The information is obtained from the subject but in the presence of a caretaker thus increasing the scale's validity. Since denial frequently accompanies memory loss, completing the scale with the caretaker present can improve the validity of the responses (Reisberg and Ferris, 1983). The instrument has seven categories for assessing self-care abilities, ranging from "No difficulty, either subjectively or objectively" to "Requires constant assistance in all activities of daily living."

## Limitations in Measures of Cognitive Impairment

The underlying issue of defining the cognitively impaired as frail is that cognitive impairment does not necessarily correlate with functional dependency as measured by the ADLs. Many individuals who score poorly on mental-status examinations may still be able to peform the ADLs without assistance. Thus, the inability to remember the date or to complete a sentence does not mean an inability to dress oneself or to bathe. On the basis of the ADLs alone, these individuals would not be identified as frail although they may be at risk of dependence with regard to the IADLs.

Another limitation with regard to the traditional instruments measuring cognitive capacity is that the items typically focus on attention, orientation, and memory and ignore the capacity for decision making. An elderly person might score reasonably high on the measures of recall and orientation but still be unable to make daily decisions essential for independent living. It is conceivable that one could accurately state the day and year but not be able to dress, take medications, or remember the name of the physician.

A further issue in the measuring of cognitive functioning is whether the elderly person or the caregiver should be interviewed or asked to provide the information. The two sources will not necessarily provide identical responses, and it is not always easy to determine which is the more accurate. As with instruments measuring the ADLs, it is possible that the proxy respondent will either underestimate or overestimate the capacities of the subject. Obtaining information from both sources as well as using the subjective evaluation of the interviewer, as in the Brief Cognitive Rating Scale, may be the optimal method for increasing validity.

The limitations of the present emphasis on physical functioning as a criterion for elgibility in long-term care programs have been addressed by those concerned with the special needs of Alzheimer's patients. One recommendation is to supplement ADL criteria with provisions that recognize the special needs of Alzheimer's patients for supervision and cueing or directions given by the caregiver that enable the patient to complete tasks of daily living (Advisory Panel on Alzheimer's Disease, 1989). This more comprehensive assessment will more sensitively address the needs of those with cognitive impairment.

Further recognition of the impact that cognitive impairment can have on functioning is shown in the Pepper Commission's recommendations for comprehensive long-term health care (U.S. Bipartisan Commission on Comprehensive Health Care, 1990). The Commission report recommended that eligibility for public services include the need for constant supervision because of dangerous, disruptive, or difficult-to-manage behavior (p. 121). These modifications to existing assessment scales would greatly increase their ability to detect many in the community who are presently at risk for being excluded from services.

Many with cognitive impairment have difficulty with routine tasks that are fundamental to community living but are typically not assessed. The ability to write checks, understand bills, and make appointments are types of activities in which individuals with mild impairment frequently require assistance. To meet the needs of these individuals, measures for assessing these capacities and the degree of assistance required need to be developed and routinely used.

## MENTAL ILLNESS

Although the mentally ill may exhibit many of the same behaviors as the cognitively impaired, memory loss and changes in intellectual functioning, the two conditions have distinct etiologies and prognoses. Mental illness can respond to treatment, so that symptoms dissipate and the individual is able to resume normal functioning. Cognitive impairment, particularly that associated with dementia, is progressive and increasingly debilitating. Unfortunately, the mentally ill elderly, just as the cognitively impaired, are at risk for not receiving the supports they require to remain independent in the community.

The significance of mental illness as a condition contributing to frailty is perhaps best illustrated by depression, the most common mental problem affecting older persons. Between 15 and 22 percent of community elderly report depressed moods and between 10 and 15 percent have depressions which require clinical interventions (Blazer and Williams, 1980). As with both physical and cognitive impairments, depression can range along a continuum from minimal impairment to extreme impairment.

Among the many manifestations of depression are functional symptoms such as loss of appetite, lethargy, psychosomatic complaints, and loss of energy. In addition, cognitive changes are also common—the depressed individual may have a memory loss or an inability to make decisions. Difficulties in concentration and concrete thinking are typical symptoms among the depressed elderly. Consequently, many depressed elderly are restricted in their daily functioning as they are unable to complete daily routine tasks.

However, as with the cognitively impaired, those with depression are unlikely to be identified as frail unless there are coexisting physical problems which limit the ability to perform concrete tasks. Instruments, even those measuring cognition, do not typically assess interest and motivation. These elderly are at risk for being excluded from needed services since they do not meet existing criteria for eligibility.

## MEASURES OF SOCIAL FUNCTIONING

Social functioning, the existence of social networks, and the ability to interact with important others who can provide emotional support as well as concrete assistance are fundamental to the independence of many elderly. Impairments in social functioning imply that the older individual is restricted in interactions with others in the community who can play pivotal supportive roles essential for independence. Without such interactions and the ability to maintain these relationships, many elderly are at risk for forfeiting their independence.

Social functioning is a complex concept composed of many facets. Consequently, scales used to assess it measure many different domains. Self-concept, self-esteem, life satisfaction, intergenerational relationships, social interactions, and the use of resources are all assumed under the rubric of social functioning. But, at the same time, the particular relevance of any one of these measures to frailty is difficult to determine.

The many existing instruments used to assess social functioning have important limitations which affect the interpretations of their results (Kane and Kane, 1981). These include attempts to measure abstract and un-quantified concepts, vague terms, a lack of norms against which to assess responses, and the absence of a continuum among attributes. These weaknesses seriously jeopardize the ability of the measures to accurately identify those needing assistance.

A weakness in many instruments measuring social functioning is their failure to assess the respondent's satisfaction with his or her level of social involvement. This subjective evaluation is critical in that isolation or limited social relationships may be consistent with earlier patterns and not indicative of poor functioning or predictive of frailty and support needs. Moreover, having infrequent visits with adult children does not imply that the elderly would not have their immediate support in case of illness or disability. This type of information is not uniformly reported on scales assessing social functioning, which raises further questions about the validity of the measures.

As in the ADL and IADL instruments discussed earlier, there may also be discrepancies between responses given by the older individual and by an informant. Family members may want to underreport undesirable social behavior or overreport their own involvement while the elderly subject may want to present a favorable impression to the interviewer and thus overreport family assistance and support. The validity and reliability of responses may therefore be seriously jeopardized.

The accuracy of measures of social functioning is questionable due to a lack of validity, reliability, and consistency in assessment. These weaknesses, as well as the continuing emphasis on physical ability as the main contributor to impairment, reinforce the neglect of social well-being in the assessment of frailty. Moreover, even when assessments of social functioning are made, they tend to not be given equal weight with either ADL or IADL measures in determining service eligibility.

Other areas which are significant to social functioning and the status of the older person are frequently not assessed. Measures of economic well-being remain difficult to assess or standardize since they vary with living situation, geographic area, and even with the perceived needs of the respondent. The suitability and safety of the living environment, accessibility of services, and even the ability to drive a car are generally excluded from traditional measures. Thus, living in a high-crime area may severely restrict the autonomy of the older individual, while being unable to drive a car may force many others into isolation. In both instances, the effects of these environmental factors on functioning can be reductions in competency, social interactions, and the ability for self-care.

## MULTIDIMENSIONAL ASSESSMENTS

These assessment tools combine within one comprehensive instrument measures of several areas of functioning that are associated with independence and well-being. They typically measure behavioral competence, psychological well-being, environmental quality, and perceived quality of life. Because aging and disabilities involve many spheres of life which are interactive, these instruments can provide a more accurate description of the ability to function in the community.

The Older Americans Research and Service Center instrument (OARS) is perhaps the most widely used multidimensional instrument. It involves a 40–60 minute interview by a trained administrator who rates the subject on responses made on a six-point scale in the areas of physical health, mental health, activities of daily living (both physical and instrumental), social well-being, and economic well-being. Scores are summed for each area and may be combined to represent an overall score representing the level of functioning.

The Multilevel Assessment Instrument (MAI) (Lawton et al., 1982) measures physical health, functional health, cognition, time use, social behavior, personal adjustment, and perceived environmental quality. It is administered by a trained evaluator and, like the OARS, provides scores in each area that can be combined into a composite index.

The Comprehensive Assessment Referral Evaluation (CARE; Gurland et al., 1978) contains 203 questions with greater detail than either of the other two instruments. Interviewers rate subjects in the areas of psychiatric, medical, nutritional, economic, and social problems. Information is obtained through self-reports, observations, and global ratings, thus providing both objective and subjective evaluations of functioning. The detailed information provides a comprehensive evaluation of many domains that are fundamental to independence.

These comprehensive instruments have the advantage of giving a more valid measurement of the functioning of the older person, but they are not routinely used. Programs and services responsible for providing supports to the frail seldom use these more extensive measures. A lack of resources, including funds and trained staff, and a lack of reimbursement procedures are major obstacles to their utilization. In addition, as services remain targeted on the very frail, there is little motivation for service providers to employ these very comprehensive assessments to determine frailty.

One further model for comprehensive assessments is provided by Tinker (1984). She suggests that frailty be considered through four categories: normative—based on a scale that measures actual functioning; felt—what people feel they need in order to function independently; expressed—what persons actually demand; and comparative—how people evaluate themselves with regard to others. With this type of broader interpretation, there is more freedom for the older individual to participate in defining himself or herself and his or her perceived needs.

## MEASURES OF FRAILTY IN OTHER COUNTRIES

As other countries seek to meet the needs of their elderly they too have had to make decisions regarding the ways in which these needs and frailty are to be defined. A study of home-care services for the elderly conducted in England, the Netherlands, Manitoba, Argentina, and Sweden found that, in general, support to the elderly in the community is not restricted to a definition of frailty dependent only upon medical or physical impairments (Monk and Cox, 1991).

Need in these countries is generally defined as requiring help with some functional activities, but the basis for such help is very broad. In assessment for services, social deprivations such as isolation can constitute and serve as a basis for providing support services. In contrast to the usual practice in this country, assessments for services do not rely on functioning in specific ADL and IADL tasks. Thus, an elderly individual may be considered dependent and qualify for assistance due to an absence of supports in the home or simply because of age. In fact, needs for health care and health services to enable elderly individuals to continue in the the community are separated from needs for social care.

With an emphasis on maintaining the elderly in the community, assessments for care tend to be broad and comprehensive. An example of such an assessment is that of the community care program in Manitoba, Canada. The province uses one assessment form to determine whether or not an individual should receive care in the community or in a nursing home. In addition to evaluating the physical functioning of the older person, the assessment also examines the specific types of involvement of family members, the adequacy of the home environment with regard to the functioning ability of the older person, social activities and changes that have occurred in the past year, and how the individual feels about these changes. Deficits in any of these areas that can jeopardize the individual's ability to remain in the community can provide a basis for services.

Britain, which also emphasizes community care for the elderly, authorizes each social service department to develop its own assessments with the objective being to determine the best available way of providing help (Caring for People, 1989). These assessments elucidate needs for social care and support, which can include assistance in personal care, domestic tasks, financial affairs, accommodations, leisure, and employment. The intervention may therefore range from assisting the individual to arrange for services to assisting with bathing or eating. Furthermore, in making the assessments, the wishes of the elderly individual as well as the caregiver are given precedence.

## SUMMARY

Frailty is a complex term and therefore requires complex tools in order to be measured accurately. Instruments for this purpose have been developed, but they are not routinely used. Most instruments continue to rely on measures of physical functioning that may be combined with measures of instrumental functioning. Weaknesses in both the validity and reliability of these measures compromise their effectiveness. With so many instruments being used and each claiming to measure the same type of functioning, it is difficult to ascribe any consistency to the term "frailty."

The theoretical concerns associated with this limitation in measurement have practical implications for the lives of many elderly people. Individuals in need of support are in danger of not receiving it because of the wording of a question or the absence of an item. It is conceivable that an individual could be judged frail in one state and receive services and move to another state and be assessed as functionally competent and thus ineligible for support.

Another weakness with many assessment instruments is their emphasis on objective criteria that fail to incorporate the subjective feelings of the older person. Objective criteria cannot assess the degree to which the individual feels vulnerable or at risk for dependency. Even though the individual may be able to function in terms of daily living skills, he or she may be very anxious about maintaining current levels of functioning or the extent to which assistance will remain available. These feelings can greatly affect well-being and continued independence but are generally not measured.

The more restrictive definition of frailty, common in the United States, as well as adhering to the accepted medical model, also reflects the politicization of the concept. It thus is more responsive to the needs, interests, and resources of policy makers than to those of the elderly. By restricting the definition of frailty to areas of physical functioning, services are provided to only a small proportion of those who might otherwise be eligible under the more comprehensive interpretation.

Frailty will be defined in a more conservative or liberal manner according to the philosophy of those controlling the resources. Moreover, the availability of resources may in itself affect the definition in that it may be more comprehensive and inclusive in periods of growth while it becomes more exclusive in periods of recession, when resources are scarce. Careful targeting, which attempts to conserve resources, can in itself have negative effects in that it frequently neglects preventive and remedial services that could slow the course of dependency.

The definition of frailty is fundamental to the design of policy and services while also being strongly influenced by them. Policies and programs tend to target the most impaired with little service available for those requiring only a small amount of assistance or supervision. Other countries that have a more comprehensive perspective of frailty are less targeted. They, therefore, give less emphasis to physical impairments as a basis for services. Consequently, in accordance with the many deficits which can imply frailty and dependence, even the most minimally impaired and their families may be eligible for support.

In order to provide the support required by many elderly if they are to remain in the community, frailty should best be viewed along a continuum. Thus, rather than waiting until impairments become so severe as to seriously impede functioning or exceed the resources of a caregiver, interventions may be warranted earlier than indicated by current ADL measures. Until these more comprehensive assessments are utilized, many elderly individuals are in danger of remaining unserved and vulnerable in the community.

*Chapter Three*

# Policies Towards the Frail Elderly

Policy reflects the values and prevailing ideologies of society while also providing the framework for services. One consequence of the aging of the population in this country has been an impetus to design new policies that address their concerns and needs. The United States is not alone in this effort. As the population has continued to age in many other developed countries, these countries too have wrestled with the formation of priorities and policies for the elderly. Responding to the needs of the frail in the community remains a particularly pressing challenge to social policy. This chapter discusses the attempts being made to meet this challenge.

In the 1970s, the Federal Council on Aging critiqued public policies towards the frail as being deficient in several ways, including: having a tendency to ignore the frail living in the community; requiring the use of a means test as a condition for receiving long-term care; having an inadequate commitment to home and ambulatory health and social supports; and neglecting the social needs of the frail elderly (U.S. Department of Health, Education, and Welfare, 1978). Subsequently, the Council made recommendations for policies that would attend to these shortcomings.

Years after this critique, it is questionable whether much real progress has been made in meeting the needs of the frail elderly in the community. Changes in policies have tended to be incremental and have not necessarily kept pace with the demands of this population. Moreover, the emphasis has remained concentrated on medical needs with a tendency to ignore the many other aspects of the older individual's life which can affect frailty and well-being.

Echoing the ambiguity in the definition of frailty, policies have wrestled with dilemmas over services, eligibility, and the roles of the private and public sectors in accepting responsibility for the frail. Concern with resources and the recognition that the needs of the elderly have far-reaching effects on society have generated debates and proposals, and even new legislation, at both federal and state levels.

## MAJOR POLICY ISSUES

A primary issue and dilemma confronting policy makers is whether services for the frail should be universal and comprehensive, serving all older persons based on need alone. If universal, then age, disability, or another criteria would make persons eligible for services regardless of income or other resources. Thus, all elderly, based on their impairments, would be entitled to services. A comprehensive policy would provide a basis for services able to meet all identified needs of the frail older person rather than only those related to physical health and disabilities. A ramification of this type of policy is that criteria for service eligibility would have to be broadened from the traditional ADL/IADL standards of assessment.

Whether to seek equity in the distribution of benefits or to concentrate on cost containment is a perpetual dilemma. Equity refers to the reasonable and adequate provision of services at a cost which does not constitute an excessive or impossible burden (Monk, 1990). However, such equity may be impossible if cost containment is a policy prerequisite. In fact, the two aims, equity and cost containment, are perceived as contending goals (Callahan and Walach, 1981). An overarching interest in reducing government expenditures conflicts with the equitable distribution of benefits. Consequently, efforts to provide such benefits as long-term care insurance are carefully scrutinized in terms of cost control.

The role of the public vis à vis the private sector in meeting the needs of the frail elderly is another policy issue which has yet to be resolved. Services through the private sector are generally beyond the means of the majority of elderly who consequently must rely on programs in the public sector. Concerns over costs and resources inhibit the expansion of public services to meet demands of this population. Without government support, the role of the private sector in community care, with the possible exception of the insurance industry, will remain negligible.

With the collapse of the Medicare Catastrophic Coverage Act in 1989, the private-insurance industry has become more involved in both medigap policies and long-term care insurance. As these policies may include community services, such as home care and case management, they do offer some resources that can enhance the functioning of the frail in the community. However, the impact of these benefits remains limited in that such insurance remains unaffordable to the majority of the older population (Rivlin and Weiner, 1988).

Another policy dilemma concerns the role of formal supports to the frail vis à vis the informal ones. At issue is whether the introduction of formal services in the care of the elderly will result in a decrease in the assistance offered by the informal support systems. An underlying fear is that formal services will replace the care provided by relatives, thereby increasing costs to the public sector.

This dilemma is intensified by traditional values that underscore the autonomy of the family and its independence from government control or interference. With these values shared by both policy makers and their constituents, it is not surprising that the elderly and their families bear the problems associated with frailty on their own without much formal intervention. In fact, interventions are likely to be used only when the burden of care becomes overwhelming and informal resources are exhausted.

The United States maintains a bias towards institutional rather than community care for those who are frail and dependent. Strong evidence for this bias is offered by the fact that 80 percent of long-term care dollars are allocated to nursing homes (U.S. Bipartisan Commission, 1990). Evolving from the values and traditions of the Elizabethan and Puritan societies, the locus of care for the frail has been in institutional settings. Reinforced by a medical bias, nursing homes, rather than the community, have been perceived as the most appropriate settings for the frail elderly. A major outcome of this lack of attention to community services has been a fragmented system of care replete with many gaps. The continuum of services required to provide frail elderly with choices has yet to be developed.

Consequently, as these policy issues remain unresolved, it is not surprising that the deficiencies elucidated in the 1970s continue to influence the care of the frail elderly. Noble and worthwhile aims, such as increasing individual potential for independence, maintaining or restoring the level of functioning, and maximizing individual potential, are commonly expressed. But in as much as these aims remain vague, their impact on the lives of the frail elderly is questionable. Without resolving the dilemmas in social policies, concrete aims and objectives and the programs necessary for obtaining them will remain inaccessible to the majority of the frail elderly.

The fragmentation of existing policies further complicates the development of any coherent system of services for meeting the needs of the older population. The present diversity in the governmental agencies responsible for policy development means that each may have its own distinct goals and target groups. One result is frequent confusion with regard to service eligibility and benefits on the part of both service providers and the intended consumers. Unfortunately, the frail, to whom these policies and services are directed, remain among the most vulnerable to this fragmentation.

A further weakness with existing policies towards the frail elderly is the difficulty in assessing their effectiveness in meeting the needs of the intended population. With goals remaining broad and undefined, it is difficult to determine the extent to which they are being reached or to evaluate the programs that they mandate. In fact, this vagueness makes assessing the appropriateness of the goals themselves difficult. In order for policies to have any impact on the problems they seek to address and in order to evaluate the policies themselves, they need to define who should receive assistance, where care should be provided, when care should be provided, how it should be provided, and the type of service most appropriate in any given circumstance (Tinker, 1980).

The frail elderly with their disabilities and dependencies personify the most negative aspects of aging. As individuals fear the aging process and have a predilection to avoid or shun the disabled and dependent, care for the frail in the community remains jeopardized. Moreover, in a society which stresses productivity as a measure of self-worth, the value of the frail is questionable. These factors contribute to a policy which would seclude these individuals and deny them their basic rights.

On the other hand, a humanitarian ethic supports the tenet of responsibility for care for those needing support. The primary provider of this care for the frail has been the family. But with major demographic changes occurring in society, the family is frequently unable to meet these demands and responsibilities. The limitations being encountered by this traditional support system accentuate the conflict of values associated with the care of the frail elderly. Policy in this country has both safeguarded the rights of the family and refrained from intruding into the families' domain.

An inherent conflict exists between public support of dependent persons and the belief in self-reliance, autonomy, and protection from government intrusion. Policy makers are therefore cautious about infringing on individual rights, while, at the same time, those in need may shun services which identify them as dependent. Unfortunately, this reluctance can further deter actions by policy makers whose tendencies are towards incremental rather than radical change.

## PATERNALISM

Paternalism is a value which has also pervaded policy towards the frail elderly. Due to their limitations and impairments, the frail are at risk of being identified as incapable of the same degree of self-fulfillment and self-realization as the dominant groups in society (Cohen, 1988). The result is that their options for self-determination are severely limited as others are permitted to encroach upon their decision-making capacity, a consequence of policies that are supposedly in their "best interest." An effect of this paternalistic perspective is that the goals for this population remain constricted with little aspirations for change, improvement, or empowerment. Identifying frailty with incompetence, resignation, passivity, and stagnation provides a framework for discrimination. Paternalistic policies also deter autonomy in that frail individuals are frequently unable to physically act on their decisions. It is this loss of executional autonomy which makes the frail elderly particularly vulnerable to coercion in long-term care (Collopy, 1988). The paternalistic framework of policies presents risks to human individuality and freedom that can further jeopardize the equality of the frail elderly.

## THE PROTECTION OF INDIVIDUAL AUTONOMY

Autonomy and self-determination, the freedoms to make decisions and to act on them, are two of the most sacrosanct values in our society. For the frail elderly, issues of autonomy center around interactions with formal services and with informal caregivers, relatives, and friends, who provide the support and assistance necessary for functioning in the community. This dependence can, however, pose a threat to their autonomy as agencies and others seek to provide what they perceive to be in the frail individual's best interest.

Issues of beneficence run concurrent with those of autonomy. The criterion "best interest" has its roots in the medical profession where beneficence directs the physician to promote and protect the best interests of the patient by seeking the greater balance of benefits over harm in treatment and care. Within the broader framework of social policy, the notion enables others to decide on services that they determine to be in the older person's best interests (Hofland, 1988). But these "best interests" are not necessarily congruent with the individual's own desires.

The potential for conflict between autonomy and beneficence in the care of the frail elderly is great. The inherent problem is that it is often difficult to substantiate that the need for security is more worthy than the need for autonomy or self-determination, particularly when the frail individual appears to be at some risk in the community. Within the area of health care, Gadow (1980) has argued in support of autonomy in that it offers more gains to patients through their exercising personal judgment according to their own "uniqueness and values." There is no reason to suppose that these gains would be any less in other areas of the individual's life.

The issue of autonomy pervades many of the informal relationships of the frail elderly. Out of concern and worry over the older person's welfare, family members may intervene in the lifestyle or desires of the frail relative. Though motivated by the best intentions, such interventions not only threaten autonomy but also may induce further dependency.

Losing control over one's life increases the vulnerability to learned helplessness, a state characterized by diminished mastery over the environment (Maier and Seligman, 1976). Feelings of passivity and a tendency towards withdrawal associated with this state lead to poor self-esteem and decreased well-being (Teitelman and Priddy, 1988). Learned helplessness can further impair an older person's interactions and coping abilities. Thus, the beneficence principle may, in fact, accentuate the problem that it is attempting to resolve.

## POLICY AND THE INDIVIDUAL

### Informed Consent

Policy to safeguard the rights and autonomy of the elderly is implemented through two legal procedures, informed consent and guardianship. Informed consent relates primarily to medical care and signifies that the individual has understood and agreed to a specific treatment or to participate in a given project. In order to obtain informed consent the patient must be competent to make a decision on his or her own behalf (Stanley, 1983). It is in this latter area, the determination of competency, that the rights of the frail elderly are most at risk.

Studies of the ability of older persons to make informed-consent decisions have found that such ability decreases with age and with educational level (Taub, 1980; Taub, Kline, and Baker, 1981). As these factors are often associated with frailty, many frail elderly are at increased risk of not making appropriate informed-consent decisions. Moreover, when older age and poor education interact with feelings of dependency, there is the risk that informed consent may be more reflective of the interests of others than of the elderly themselves.

The cognitively impaired elderly are particularly vulnerable to misunderstanding informed-consent procedures. Research findings indicate that these individuals have difficulty making treatment decisions, especially about the purpose of treatments or procedures, although they may be able to comprehend the risks and benefits (Stanley et al., 1988). In order to safeguard the rights of these frail individuals, cognitively impaired patients must be evaluated with regard to their ability to give informed consent. Without such an assessment, the validity of the consent is dubious.

## Guardianship

Individuals judged to be incompetent may be assigned, by the court, legal guardians, who have the right and authority to make decisions on their behalf. Based on the doctrine of *parens patriae*, "father of his country," states are given the right and duty to protect the persons who are unable to care for themselves and their property (Iris, 1988). As the proportion of frail elderly has expanded, the use of guardianship in surrogate decision making has concomitantly increased (Bulcroft, 1991).

Policy governing guardianship is designed and implemented at the state level and therefore many variations exist in its implementation. Basically, there are two forms of guardianship, guardianship of the person and guardianship of the estate. A guardian is appointed by the court to make decisions for a person whom the court has judged to be incompetent. These decisions may be restricted to specific areas, such as health care or property, or may encompass all aspects of the frail individual's life. The common underlying assumption is that the guardian will be acting in the "best interests" of the person. Once granted, guardianship is seldom revoked (Iris, 1988).

Concerns about guardianship and the rights of the frail elderly abound. First, the determination of competency is frequently based solely on medical testimony which focuses on the ability of the individual to consent to treatment. There is no requirement that these medical assessments involve a history of the individual's previous behavior, medications, or physical conditions, although each of these factors could influence the current status.

Second, the evaluation of competency in one area does not necessarily coincide with other aspects of decision making. An individual unable to make a medical decision may be perfectly capable of functioning adequately at home. However, the norm is to grant full guardianship rather than a limited guardianship, which would be restricted to only one aspect of decision making (Statement of Recommended Judicial Practices, 1986).

Next, guardianship rests on the assumption that the appointed guardian will act in the best interest of, and according to the perceived wishes of, the frail older person. The problem is that there are few guarantees to assure that these assumptions are upheld. Moreover, even with the best intentions, family members may not make decisions in accordance with the wishes of their relative. In addition, their own emotional and financial burdens may intervene in their treatment or care decisions. It remains debatable as to whether these relatives make decisions congruent with the preferences of the older person (Uhlmann, Pearlman, and Cain, 1988; Zweibel and Cassel, 1989).

One cannot overlook the relationship between the protection of the interests of the frail and their interactions with their families. According to Jecker (1990) any policy changes must also consider the resources of the family upon whom the elder person may be dependent. A more appropriate approach to the issues of rights and care may be the "best interests model," which examines the wishes and needs of both the older individual and the family in any decisions. This model recognizes the interrelationships of the two units and therefore is sensitive to the interests and needs of each partner in decisions of future care.

## POLICY AND SERVICES

The government's involvement with the frail elderly is directly expressed through policies that mandate and offer support to specific programs and services. These programs aim at enabling this frail population to function as independently as possible, with the maximum sense of well-being, in the community. Skinner (1990) classifies these programs into three basic categories: client assistance, which provides income or benefits to support older persons; system optimizing, which aims to ensure effective services; and service enhancement, which directly funds providers to provide services to those in need. Two of these categories of programs, service optimizing and service enhancement, fall under the purview of the Administration on Aging and are directly funded under the Older Americans Act.

## The Older Americans Act

The Older Americans Act, enacted in 1965, was the federal government's first comprehensive policy towards improving the lives of the elderly. Although its original objectives were broad, they provided a framework for a wide array of services to assist older persons to remain in the community. Since its enactment, the act has tended to give more attention to the frail elderly, those with the greatest needs.

With the 1973 amendments, the act gave priority to meeting the needs of the most vulnerable, those elderly defined as having the greatest social and economic needs, giving official recognition to needs' being determined by other than medical impairments. Greatest social need was attributed to noneconomic factors including physical and mental disabilities, language barriers, and cultural, social or geographical isolation caused by racial or ethnic status which restrict an individual's ability to perform normal daily tasks or threaten such individual's capacity to live independently. Economic need represents an income level at or below the poverty level set by the Office of Management and Budget.

With these amendments, specific grants for multipurpose senior centers, as well as funds for congregate meals, were authorized. Both were programs which could foster the independence of the elderly in the community. The 1973 amendments also created the Title III model projects program, giving priority to projects that involved special services to assist the physically and mentally impaired elderly.

The 1975 amendments mandated state and local agencies to develop programs in the areas of transportation and home services to assist the impaired elderly. System optimizing was to be accomplished through special funding allocated to ombudsman projects, services to meet the needs of those not being served adequately, and ambulatory day-care services. These areas were consolidated in 1978 into three categories: access services (transportation, outreach, information, and referral); in-home services (home health aid, homemaker, telephone reassurance, chore maintenance); and legal services. With the 1978 amendments, state and local offices also had to provide assurances that preference in the delivery of services would go to those with the greatest economic or social need.

The 1987 amendments authorized funds specifically for nonmedical in-home services for the frail elderly. This group includes those having a physical or mental disability, Alzheimer's Disease, or a related disorder with neurological or organic brain dysfunction that restricts the ability to perform daily tasks or to function independently (U.S. House Select Committee on Aging, 1990a). Further emphasis was also given to those with the greatest social and economic need by targeting the low-income minority elderly. In addition, additional provisions were made for the disabled elderly with the amendments requiring that state plans identify, coordinate planning, and assess the needs for services for older disabled individuals.

The Older Americans Act is the basis for policy dealing with the frail elderly in the community. However, its ability to adequately meet these needs is challenged due to funding limitations. As an example, funding for in-home services for the frail elderly was budgeted at $25 million in 1988, increasing to $28,941,000 in 1991 (U.S. Senate Special Committee on Aging, 1991). However, approximately seven million elderly in the community had demands for in-home assistance, suggesting that the budgeted amount could never adequately serve this population.

In actuality 1990 appropriations for social services and nutrition programs, Title III of the Older Americans Act, declined 20 percent from the 1981 allocations when adjusted for inflation (Kusserow, 1990). With these reductions, the ability of policy to have any real impact was sharply curtailed.

Cost sharing, means testing, sliding fee schedules for payments, and private partnerships have been proposed as measures to increase the resources of the Older Americans Act. Proponents of cost sharing view it as a means of obtaining additional revenue by having service recipients pay according to a sliding fee scale. Opponents see it as discouraging the participation of the low-income elderly, particularly minorities, the very groups that the services are striving to reach. At the same time, there is concern that cost sharing might be an incentive for local agencies to direct services to those who can share part of the costs. As the Older Americans Act (OAA) was intended to give comprehensive services to the elderly in need, any mechanism which begins to target and involve eligibility criteria may be a threat to its original universal goals.

A major weakness in the OAA affecting its effectiveness in addressing the needs of the frail elderly, is its inherent incremental approach to change. It seeks to build on existing programs rather than to attempt any serious restructuring of services. This slow transition means that policies and services have failed to keep pace with the changes which have occurred in society since 1965. Providing services that support caregivers as well as the frail elderly and that serve to strengthen the skills and rights of each are sorely needed.

Finally, the effectiveness of the OAA in meeting the needs of the frail may be compromised by its focusing on them as a priority group. Targeting those with the greatest need increases the risk that they will be excluded and discriminated against in other programs. Moreover, participants in the

OAA programs could become vulnerable to being identified as impaired and therefore "less worthy" than other elderly. They may face the stigma associated with welfare, and consequently both the frail and the more well elderly may withdraw from the programs.

In order to best meet its goals and aims, the Older Americans Act should be restructured into a more comprehensive platform that addresses the needs of the family caregiver as well as the frail. Sufficient resources to provide for all elderly, regardless of type of need or impairment, with a continuum of services are required.

## Title XX and the Omnibus Budget Reconciliation Act

Other major federal policies with an impact on the frail elderly are Title XX of the Social Security Act and the Omnibus Budget Reconciliation Act. Title XX, passed in 1974, designated the federal government to allocate funds to the states for supportive social services for low-income persons. The objectives of these services were to increase self-sufficiency, deinstitutionalization, and home-based care.

Although the elderly were not directly identified as a specific targeted group, the goals of the act addressed their needs by virtue of income status and the programs offered. Title XX became a major provider of services, such as home-delivered and congregate meals, to elderly recipients of Supplemental Security Income. In fact, under Title overall service to the elderly was as large as or larger than what was offered under the Older Americans Act (Nelson, 1982).

The Omnibus Budget Reconciliation Act (OBRA) of 1981 amended Title XX by creating a Social Services Block Grant to be given to states with funding based on a formula according to the size of their populations. The intention was to transfer authority for services to the states while also reducing federal spending. States were given the power to decide which programs to offer and to develop their own eligibility criteria. The act broadened the scope of Title XX by rescinding the requirement that 50 percent of the recipients had to be participants in Medicaid, Supplemental Security Income, or Aid for Dependent Children programs.

Unfortunately, the changes had little effect on services to the elderly, who now had to compete at the state level with other groups for funds. Most states attempted to maintain the previous levels of assistance, although services did not adequately meet demand (Gaberlavage, 1987). The types of services most frequently provided to older persons were homemaker, chore, home health, adult protective services, adult day-care, transportation, and nutrition—all programs which could potentially be of great benefit to the frail. However, a survey of state programs found that an average of 18 percent of the funds available through the Social Services Block Grant were spent on services for the elderly (Gaberlavage, 1987).

Social Services Block Grants provide another means of meeting the needs of the frail in the community. But, as with other federal programs, their ability to adequately do so is dependent upon resources. Furthermore, placing the elderly in a competitive position with other groups, such as families and children, may be detrimental to their interests. However, the block grant system does establish a policy framework for services which may complement those of the Older Americans Act. It also enables states to develop such services in accordance with the characteristics of their populations.

## HEALTH CARE POLICY AND THE FRAIL

As frailty is primarily defined according to physical disabilities that limit functioning, it may be anticipated that it is in the arena of health care policy that the clearest provisions for the care of the frail will be found. But, as with social policy, health policy towards the frail remains limited and, rather than being universal, targets those who also have the greatest economic need.

Fundamental in the development of health care policy is the continuing debate as to whether or not health care is a basic right to which all are entitled or whether it is a commodity to be purchased through private financing and expenditures. If it is the former, then the needs of the frail, as those of all Americans, will be met under a comprehensive program. If it remains a commodity, many of the frail, as well as others, will continue to find the costs of their health care prohibitive.

### Medicare

Current health care policy provides fairly comprehensive coverage for a limited period of time within designated cost constraints through the Medicare program. Medicare, Title XVIII of the Social Security Act, enacted in 1965, assists older persons with their health care expenditures. As a government-sponsored program, it also attempts to curtail the health care expenditures by reimbursing hospitals and physicians for reasonable costs only. As a national insurance program for the elderly, it offers universal coverage for the majority of elderly Americans requiring hospitalization for acute medical problems.

Medicare's applicability to the frail elderly is limited in that it does not provide for chronic care. Coverage for the types of services and items required by the frail to enable them to remain in the community is severely restricted. Home care, day treatment services, and reimbursements for items such as glasses, hearing aids, or dentures are generally not reimbursable. Other equipment such as wheelchairs and lifts are subject to strict payment schedules and may be unavailable in regions of the country where Medicare coverage does not meet the fee charged by the supplier. These factors imply that the independence and functioning of many of the frail, dependent upon Medicare for assistance, are in jeopardy.

Medicare underwent a significant programmatic change in 1983. Due to the failure of the program to restrain medical spending, the cost-based reimbursement was changed to a prospective payment system. The incentive for this change was to reduce costs to the health care system by encouraging hospitals to discharge patients earlier, avoiding prolonged stays. Prior to this change, patients were covered per day in hospital as ordered by the physician. Under the revised system, hospitals are paid according to the patient's diagnosis and are penalized by not being reimbursed for days exceeding the specified period. There are currently more than 470 diagnostically related groups (DRGs) into which health care problems are classified.

This revised reimbursement system, although it has managed to curtail medical expenditures, also presents particular risks to the health care of the frail elderly. The primary risk is that as these patients are discharged more quickly from hospitals, they may be less able to manage at home. The program operates under the assumption that once the acute need is attended to functioning will have been restored. But, as has been noted earlier, the frail elderly commonly have multiple chronic conditions. Accordingly, their ability to function adequately after discharge may be impeded. Without careful discharge planning and post-hospital care, the well-being of these individuals in the community is questionable.

There are several ramifications of this system for the frail. First, they are at risk of being discharged before they are able to manage adequately at home. Support systems, both formal and informal, may not be accessible or available to provide the amount of care required. Second, because hospitals are responsible for the discharge plans of their patients, these institutions may become increasingly reluctant to accept the frail older person as a patient. To do so can place them at risk of assuming the financial burden of non-reimbursed days of care. The system also places severe pressures on discharge planners to quickly arrange for services and discuss post-hospital care with the patient. Under these pressures, the potential for developing inappropriate plans is increased. Moreover, without visiting the home environment, it is difficult to assess the plan's feasibility.

Butler and Hyer (1989) discuss two other significant limitations of the present Medicare system which can be detrimental to the care of the frail patient. The complexity of the frail patient's medical conditions often requires an exceptional amount of time from the physician. If quality care is to be provided, additional time for counseling and education may also be required from a nurse or social worker. The time spent with these professionals is not accounted for in the present payment scheme. The comprehensive geriatric assessment which is particularly pertinent to the needs of the frail elderly and essential for an accurate care plan is also not covered. As it continues to concentrate on acute medical problems, Medicare's ability to meet the chronic care needs of the frail is sharply affected.

## Medicaid

Medicaid, Title XIX of the Social Security Act, is a joint federal and state assistance program for the poor and medically indigent. Because it covers chronic illnesses and has the option of providing for more services than commonly found under Medicare, it may be more relevant to the needs of the frail. But the fact that it is not a universal program (it is available only to those meeting strict income eligibility criteria) compromises its effectiveness. Moreover, the bulk of Medicaid funds are used on nursing home rather than community care.

Each state administers its own Medicaid program, determining eligibility and benefits, under federal guidelines. Services that are required by the federal government to be provided include hospital inpatient care, medical services, skilled nursing care, laboratory and x-ray services, home health, hospital outpatient care, family planning, and periodic screening. These services are more extensive than those offered under Medicare and meet more of the chronic needs of frail patients.

Since 1981, states have been permitted to offer services under a Medicaid waiver that allows them to provide community and home services to persons who would otherwise be institutionalized. Under this waiver, nonmedical problems that might result in institutionalization and dependency are acceptable criteria for assistance. Social and personal care as well as case management, day-care, homemaker, home health aide, personal care, and respite care are commonly offered. Personal care ordered by a physician but provided on an outpatient basis is also allowable under the waivers. A survey conducted by the American Association of Retired

Persons (AARP) in 1990 found that 39 states had waiver programs (Lipson and Laudicina, 1991).

The waiver programs also have specific restrictions that curtail their activities. Under the programs, the costs of services to a client must not exceed the cost of Medicaid care in an institution. The determination of the cost-effectiveness of the care may be difficult to make and may entail a cumbersome process. This restriction, along with federal and state concerns with cost containment, have limited the impact of the waiver programs in meeting the needs of the frail elderly.

The Omnibus Budget Reconciliation Act of 1990 broadened the scope of services that states could offer under Medicaid. Under a new entitlement option, Home and Community Based Waiver Program, states are able to provide home and community services without being budget neutral. That is, they no longer have to show that such services cost less than care in an institution. The states may also target these services to specific populations of the elderly.

Under the option, each client has an individual care plan designed by a case manager. Moreover, the array of potential services is expanded and includes homemaker/home health aide, chore services, personal care, nursing care, respite care, training for family members, adult day-care, and other services. Eligibility is restricted to those 65 and over who are unable to perform two out of three specified activities of daily living (toileting, transferring, and eating) or have Alzheimer's Disease.

With these changes the new waiver option is a realistic approach to dealing with many of the problems of the frail elderly. It is particularly significant in two areas. First, it gives consideration to functional limitations as criteria for eligibility. As individuals do not have to be nursing home eligible, the program may serve a population of frail who would otherwise be without benefits. Moreover, by extending services to this population, the program underscores the fact that individuals with limitations and impairments may be adequately cared for in the community.

The new option also recognizes the needs of the caregivers of this population. It therefore constitutes a major step forward in health care policy for the frail. As the option addresses the comprehensive needs of the frail and their families, it may serve as a framework for the development of future policies and programs supporting community care.

## POLICY TO SUPPORT THE FAMILY

The role of the family is critical to the support and well-being of the frail elderly, yet governmental policy, with the exception of the program described above, fails to recognize the role that the family plays or the stresses that caregivers may endure. Unlike other countries such as Britain, Sweden, and Norway, which offer financial as well as other supports to caregivers, policy in this country has remained reluctant to intervene or provide assistance. Self-reliance and freedom from government interference, as well as concerns about substituting for family care, partially account for the absence of any family policy. The result is that relatives are virtually alone in shouldering the care of the frail.

The burden on two groups of caregivers is particularly severe: those who are elderly themselves and those who are employed. For the former, policy that provides services that relieve and assist the older caregiver may enhance his or her coping abilities. For the latter, policy that enables these caregivers to continue working while being able to attend to caregiving responsibilities is essential. Without assistance for elder care, productivity—as measured by days lost from work and by the worries which can detract workers' attention and concentration—may be seriously affected.

In fact, many caregivers find the difficulties of maintaining two roles and sets of responsibilities too strenuous and, consequently, are forced to give up their employment. Surveys of female caregivers indicate that approximately 12 percent quit their jobs to provide assistance to a frail relative (Stone et al., 1987; Brody et al., 1987).

Government policies to support caregivers are noticeably absent. The responsibility for care is largely unshared, leaving these caregivers vulnerable to emotional and physical strains as well as financial burdens. Even among those who seek community services such as home care or respite, the shortage of trained workers, eligibility requirements for public programs, and the costs of private services mean that options for assistance in the community are limited. Consequently, many of these caregivers are forced to place their relative in a nursing home.

The United States remains one of the only industrialized countries without a policy in support of family caregivers. Federal family allowances to caregivers, stipends, and payments that are common in other countries have yet to be enacted here. The federal government's assistance to caregivers is primarily through the dependent care tax credit. This federal credit is available to caregivers who incur employment-related expenses that relate to the care of a dependent child, spouse, or other dependent person. Caregivers are able to deduct a percentage of those expenses, up to a scheduled maximum amount, from their federal income tax.

As a measure of financial support for caregivers, the tax credit provides only limited assistance. Moreover, for nonworking caregivers, the credit has little relevance. Consequently, the majority of caregivers do not receive any federal subsidies. Those receiving the most benefit from the credit are those with lower incomes in that the percentage of tax credits they receive is higher than for those with greater incomes. However, even these credits may not realistically approach the actual costs of care.

## Tax Incentives

To compensate for the absence of federal assistance, many states have become involved in offering reimbursement programs for caregivers. Isensee and Campbell (1987) report that 29 states have instituted dependent care provisions, 21 in the form of tax credits and eight in the form of tax deductions. The states vary with regard to specific provisions such as the coverage for out-of-home as well as in-home expenses. Contrary to the federal scheme, some state programs make the tax credits more valuable to higher income taxpayers by reducing the benefit to lower income families. Other states have targeted the assistance only to the lowest income families, leaving out those with more moderate incomes.

In a review of two tax incentive programs, those in Arizona and Idaho, Hendrickson (1988) found the objectives of both programs were to provide support to the family caregiver and therefore reduce the need for formal services, particularly nursing homes. With nursing homes consuming a large proportion of state Medicaid budgets, the programs were considered a means of providing alternative, less expensive care in the community. The Idaho program offered either a $1,000 tax deduction or a $100 tax credit to caregivers caring for an elderly relative in their home.

The tax incentive program in Arizona allows caregivers a $1,000 personal exemption if they paid 25 percent or more of the total yearly costs of an elderly person's stay in a nursing home or other facility, 25 percent of home health costs, or at least $800 in medical care. Deductions may also be made for any other payments made for the elderly person. Thus, in contrast to the Idaho program, this program relied more on financial incentives than credit for informal care.

Both programs served the most impaired in the community and had some impact on the amount of care being provided. Family caregivers in Idaho expanded their assistance to the elderly as measured by hours of informal services and financial contributions. The results of the Arizona program, which did not give credit for informal care, were that the incentives did stimulate caregivers to provide greater financial support for their frail relatives. These results suggest that the very frail may benefit from incentive programs that assist their caregivers and that such assistance may be less costly than that offered by formal services. Such incentives may actually relieve the burden on formal services and prolong the period of time of family caregiving.

## THE PEPPER COMMISSION

In response to the problems associated with long-term care and the health care system in the United States, the Pepper Commission, a bipartisan congressional body, was assigned the task of providing recommendations for legislation that would guarantee all Americans quality coverage for health and long-term care (U.S. Bipartisan Commission on Comprehensive Health Care, 1990). Many of the proposals of the Commission have direct benefits for the frail elderly.

Key recommendations of the Commission that have direct bearing on the frail include: (1) social insurance for home and community-based care and for the first three months of nursing home care, (2) protection against impoverishment for those in nursing homes and for their spouses, (3) standardized criteria for disability based on deficits in three out of five activities of daily living, cognitive impairment, or the need for supervision due to behavioral problems, (4) case managers with a wide array of services individualized to client needs and preferences, and (5) measures to ensure the quality of care.

The Commission also recommends specific supports to the family. Conscious of the role that family members play in caring for the frail and yet not wanting to replace the role, the case manager would be empowered to develop an individual care plan made in conjunction with the desires of the individual and the family that would include among its services respite, day-care, and training for family caregivers. In addition, the report underscores the role of choice for the consumer, thus addressing the issue of individual rights in decision making.

Although these recommendations have yet to be enacted in a national health care plan, they are being absorbed into various health care proposals and state programs. Case management, the standardized criteria for functional disability, and respite services are found in the majority of legislative proposals for long-term care reform. In addition, the new Medicaid waiver option has also included case management, respite, and training for the family as appropriate services. These actions are encouraging in that they suggest real interest in major reforms that can assist in meeting the needs of the frail in the community.

## PROPOSED FEDERAL LEGISLATION

The involvement of the family with the frail elderly is beginning to be recognized at the federal level. Most notable is the Family Caregiver Support Act of 1991 (S.972), introduced in the Senate in 1991, which proposes to establish a federally funded and state administered program of respite services for primary caregivers of functionally impaired persons under a new title of the Social Security Act. The intended purpose of the act is to provide varying types of respite services to caregivers and the impaired relative. These services include companion services, personal assistance, homemaker, home health, adult day-care, temporary care in a licensed facility, peer support and caregiver training.

Under the act, the functionally impaired are defined as those of any age needing hands-on or supervisory assistance daily with three out of five ADLs, or who need substantial supervision because of cognitive or other mental impairment that impedes the ability to function or causes behaviors that are dangerous, disruptive, or difficult to manage. The primary caregiver is defined as a spouse, child, relative, or other person who has major responsibility for the daily care of the individual, does not receive financial payment for the service, and has provided regular and continuous care for at least three months.

The Long Term Care Family Security Act of 1992, introduced in the Senate in April of that year, is a further indication that the role of the family is no longer being ignored. This act would amend the Social Security Act and assure universal access to long-term care benefits based on need. Senator Mitchell in his introduction of the bill emphasized its cost containment provisions in that individuals are required to share in the costs through copayments. The bill gives substantial roles to long-term care insurance, case management, and quality assurance of services.

## THE ROLE OF THE PRIVATE SECTOR

The role of the private sector in the care of the frail elderly has been small in comparison to that of the public sector. Existing policy has emphasized publicly funded programs. Most private-sector options that could assist the frail—home equity conversions, continuing care retirement communities, social/health maintenance organizations, and individual retirement accounts—are too expensive for the majority of older persons (Weiner et al., 1988). It is only in recent years, due to the pressure being placed on the government by the increasing older population and the continually escalating health care budget, that the role of the private sector has been seriously considered. Most of this attention has been given to the role of long-term care insurance.

Long-term care insurance is primarily a means for protecting the elderly against the devastating financial hardships that can result from a long chronic illness and the dependency which may accompany it. It is therefore a potential means of enabling the frail to maintain their social and economic independence. In 1987, 70 companies were selling long-term care policies and more than 400,000 elderly had purchased them (Task Force on Long-Term Health Care Policies, 1987).

However, the value of private long-term care insurance as a means of protection for the frail elderly is compromised as it remains beyond the means of most older Americans. Moreover, existing plans do not necessarily offer the elderly protection from financial burdens, cover mental and cognitive disorders, or provide coverage for home care. In addition, plans often have a long waiting period, which further jeopardizes their applicability. Although newer policies have begun to address these contingencies, many of the elderly continue to hold older policies which offer little protection.

Federal policy has not yet fully established the role of private insurance in protecting the elderly from the costs of long-term care. The number of companies offering policies has continued to increase to meet the demands of the older market; however, there is still some concern over the regulation of these policies since an absence of standards has meant that many elderly have been victims of consumer and policy misrepresentation. Inadequate coverage, restricted benefits, a lack of inflation protection, increasing premiums, and requirements for hospital stays before nursing home coverage are among the frequently reported problems (*Consumer Reports*, 1991).

Legislation has been introduced into Congress which would regulate the industry through standards for sales practices, prohibiting the sale to those who would be eligible for Medicaid, premiums, safeguards for inflation, prohibiting high-pressure sales tactics, requiring agents to meet specific training and certification requirements, and setting limits on commissions (White, 1992). Most proposed legislation also requires that the insured have refundable premiums and guaranteed renewability with adequate protection against inflation.

Long-term care insurance has the potential of playing a critical role in the health care of many frail elderly. As it becomes more affordable and comprehensive, it may enable many older persons further options with regard to their care and subsequent ability to remain in the community. Thus, as proposed plans include day-care, home health, personal care, respite care, counseling, and transportation, they begin to provide a truly viable framework for care for the frail elderly.

## SUMMARY

As reviewed in this chapter, policy is essential for the development of services appropriate to the needs of the frail elderly. Unfortunately, the trend in policy in the United States has been to provide care for the frail and dependent in institutions—a trend that is derived from earlier historical eras and reinforced by attitudes in society as well as the medicalization of frailty. Consequently, changes in policies have tended to be incremental without offering any sweeping alterations in existing services. However, many factors, notably the demographic changes in society as well as demands for cost savings, are beginning to have strong influences on policies that may be enacted into new reforms and programs.

As the country is being forced to deal with health care issues on a national scale, the problems associated with long-term care and the needs of the frail and their caregivers are beginning to be addressed. Proposals are being offered which broaden the scope of services as they recognize the concerns of families as well as those of the elderly themselves. These reforms can provide the framework for programs that can have significant impact on the ability of the frail elderly to remain as independent as possible in the community.

The Older Americans Act as well as the Omnibus Budget Reconciliation Act of 1990 provide the blueprints for comprehensive policies and services for the frail elderly. The effectiveness of the Older Americans Act, however, has been restricted due to a lack of adequate resources, which has forced consideration of targeting as a means of meeting the act's objectives. Given an appropriate level of funding, which would enable it to provide services to all elderly in the community according to their needs, the act could play a major role in the lives of the frail elderly.

The Omnibus Budget Reconciliation Act with its expanded Medicaid services has made major contributions to recognizing the needs not only of the frail but also of their caregivers. It highlights the fact that the problems of this group of elderly affect many others and that it is the support offered by these relatives that is crucial in community care. Although restricted to those with limited incomes, the policy provides a basis for services which can eventually affect all elderly regardless of income level.

Policy for the frail elderly is complex just as are the needs of the population it intends to service. However, change is occurring and, as we approach the twenty-first century, there is reason for cautious optimism that the needs of the frail will be better served in the community.

*Chapter Four*

# Community Responses

With policy as a framework, society has responded to the needs of the frail with services which theoretically should enable the elderly to live with maximum independence in the community. Ideally, programs and services should foster autonomy rather than dependence while compensating for the impairments that impede functioning. Striking this balance in the provision of services is critical, since providing too much or too little can reinforce vulnerability.

Services for the elderly have been classified in many ways. The Gerontological Society (1978) categorizes services based upon the degree of impairment of the intended population group—unimpaired, minimally impaired, moderately impaired, and severely impaired. Using this type of classification, services can be offered in terms of the status of the group— for example, preventive for the unimpaired, supportive for the moderately impaired, and protective for the severely impaired. Depending upon the level of services needed, decisions can also be made as to whether care is best provided in the community or in an institution (Monk, 1990).

Other classification schemes group services according to whether they are primarily client assisting, service enhancing, or system optimizing (Skinner, 1990). Those focused on assistance provide minimum financial support, service enhancement programs fund service providers, and system optimizing services aim to increase the effective use of programs by monitoring the rights of the frail elderly.

Programs are also grouped according to whether they are community-based, home-based, congregate-residential, or institution-based. Each group may serve the frail, although impairment levels between groups can overlap so that the more impaired may actually be cared for in less restrictive settings (Tobin and Toseland, 1990). Using this type of classification may be beneficial in that levels of dependency are not necessarily related to a specific setting.

The problems involved in the classification of services are reflected in the programs funded under Title III of the Older Americans Act, the title responsible for authorizing and funding community and nutritional services. Funding is allocated to states under Title III-B for supportive services and senior centers, access services, in-home services, and legal services; Title III C-1 for congregate meals; Title III C-2 for home delivered meals, and Title III-D for in-home services for the frail. For reporting purposes, states are required to present data in the appropriate categories.

Because categories are vaguely defined and there is much overlap between services, accurate reporting of data is a difficult task. States tend to define and classify services according to their own criteria. As an example, transportation may be classified as both an access and "in-home service," and respite care is reported as both an in-home and a community service (U.S. House Select Committee on Aging, 1990a). This absence of definitive criteria and guidelines is more than an academic or bureaucratic problem. Critical information essential to program planning and allocations may be misreported or underrepresented.

The confusion involved in classifying services for the frail reflects the problems related to the definition of frailty and the almost impossible task of isolating it to only one sphere of life. Because frailty has pervasive effects on many areas of functioning, there is a natural overlap in services. For example, support services may have both physical and social benefits while serving the individual as well as the family. Nutrition programs meet both physical and social needs, while senior centers offer socialization and access to other services. Thus, efforts to restrict services to only one category can impede their effectiveness, since such restrictions do not necessarily reflect their scope.

The arbitrariness of boundaries between services also contributes to the fragmentation of the system. Under the present scheme of services, there is little coordination and significant gaps between programs. Consequently, providers, the elderly, and their families are often unclear about eligibility, program goals, and even the existence of specific services. The result is that many in need of assistance may never obtain it.

## SERVICE UTILIZATION

The presence of services does not guarantee utilization. Just as gaps exist between types of programs, they commonly exist between the intended service clients, the frail elderly, and the services themselves. In fact, the frail, by virtue of their impairments, may be the most difficult population for services to reach.

Studies of service utilization have relied heavily on the model of health service utilization developed by Andersen and Newman (1973). According to this model, service use can be predicted using three groups of factors: predisposing, enabling, and need. Predisposing factors include sociodemographic characteristics, attitudes, and previous experiences. Enabling factors can include transportation, income, insurance, and informal supports. Need is the individual's perceived need for the service and perception that it will help. A review of research regarding the importance of these factors in predicting service use has found those associated with perceived need to be the most predictive of utilization (Mindel and Wright, 1982).

Another framework for understanding service use is one which identifies the factors affecting perceived need and service utilization (Yeatts et al., 1992). In this model the barriers to service are addressed according to three conditions considered basic to utilization: knowledge of services, of procedures, and of need; access; and intent as defined by service attractiveness, cultural differences, and attitudes towards service use. With this type of framework, service providers can develop strategies to overcome barriers in each area as experienced by specific groups.

Wallace (1990) presents a model of service utilization which focuses on service availability, accessibility, and acceptability. Obstacles in any of the three areas can severely jeopardize a program's effectiveness in reaching intended clients. Availability pertains to the presence of programs, accessibility is the ease with which services can be utilized, and acceptability is the degree to which services and staff are perceived by clients as being compatible with their needs and values.

Studies of actual utilization suggest that the frail elderly may be among the most difficult to reach. McCaslin (1989) examined differences in use between well-functioning and poorly functioning elderly by comparing "well services" with "preventive services." A general awareness of services and a positive orientation towards them was related to utilization for all elderly but was more important to the well than the frail. The latter used specific supportive services associated with need, using a smaller range of services that concentrated on assistance with functioning. Seeing the physician frequently and having specific functioning problems contributed to the frail elderly's use of preventive services. These factors were less important to the better functioning elderly.

Chapleski (1989) examined the role of social networks in service awareness by the elderly. Her results showed that awareness was related to having nonkin advisors, membership in clubs, contacts with community agencies, and moderate-sized family networks. Those elderly most likely to be unaware of services were less educated, without transportation, black, old, poor, female, and had few community ties. As discussed earlier in the book, these characteristics are associated with impairment and frailty among the elderly.

Understanding the utilization process is basic to meeting the needs of the frail elderly in the community. Effective planning requires a comprehensive and inclusive data base so that services can achieve their intended goals. The design of such programs is a formidable task, particularly under the current system with its multiple funding sources and eligibility criteria. Consequently, it is not surprising that existing services are frequently underutilized, as both providers and the intended target population are uninformed and confused regarding programs and their specific aims. Unfortunately, it is the most frail who are both most in need and most at risk for remaining outside of the service system.

Community services for the frail elderly population will be examined according to the classification of access, home-based, community, and supportive. As discussed earlier, the boundaries between these categories are not definitive since one program can encompass more than one role. The classification is also not based on a continuum of frailty, since home-based and community programs may each serve varying levels of impairment. Given these limitations, this classification does provide a means for describing services, their aims, and their scope.

## ACCESS SERVICES

Access services concentrate on linking individuals with the programs that can meet their needs. They are the entry points into the service system and are therefore critical to subsequent utilization.

Access services are generally considered as part of the publicly funded service network. However, an important means of access is offered through the media. Newspapers, television, and radio are major avenues of access to many elderly (Cox and Monk, 1990a). In fact, the media may play an even more critical role with regard to access for the more isolated in the community.

## Information and Referral

Information and referral programs have pivotal roles as access services. Under the Older Americans Act, access has continued to remain a priority area for funding. However, the programs do have limitations which can jeopardize their effectiveness in meeting the needs of the frail in the community.

The function of information and referral programs is to provide essential information to those requesting it and to link those in need with the appropriate services. The programs are typically offered through senior centers, nutrition sites, social service departments, and many private voluntary agencies. For many persons, these programs are the first contact with the service system. As such, their responsiveness and sensitivity to the needs of the elderly can be vital to the future utilization of services. Well-developed information and referral programs increase awareness of services, help individuals to formulate problems in the context of these services, and assist them in making contact with the appropriate service (Gelfand, 1984).

An inherent weakness in most information and referral programs is that they provide information but do not necessarily ensure that the person actually follows through with the referral. With the plethora of potential services, the elderly, and in particular the frail elderly, are susceptible to having problems in linking with the appropriate program. Moreover, as with many other services, the frail, who may be most in need of information and referral, are often the least likely to know of the service's existence.

Another limitation with regard to information and referral as an access service for the frail is that the service is most often provided over the telephone. Trained staff who are both knowledgeable about services and empathetic to the needs of the frail are fundamental to effectiveness. These characteristics are often more likely to be found in specialized information services dealing with only one specific illness than in those services offering information on a wide range of community programs.

## Transportation

Accessing services is difficult, if not impossible, without adequate transportation. However, the nature of the impairments of the elderly often precludes their use of either public or private transportation without supports and assistance. But without appropriate transportation, the frail elderly are at risk of not receiving assistance and of being isolated in the community. The ability to use programs and services as well as to engage in preventive care is dependent on transportation.

There is no place where the pivotal role of transportation is as noticeable as in the rural and suburban regions of the country. The majority of these areas lack the coordinated mass transit programs found in urban areas. Furthermore, with services dispersed over hundreds of miles, the rural elderly are at risk for being greatly underserved. It is not uncommon for the frail in rural areas to travel 50 to 60 miles for medical care (U.S. Senate Special Committee on Aging, 1990). Many problems go untreated due to both the lack of available services and accessible transportation.

But even the availability of public transit does not mean that it is accessible to the frail. Buses without special lifts for the handicapped, long walks, and crowded stations can deter utilization. In recognition of the need for accessibility, the Urban Mass Transit Act of 1964 was amended in 1970 to have funds allocated for the purpose of modifying transportation for the frail and disabled and ensuring that new transportation would be designed to be accessible. Subsequent legislation, the National Mass Transportation Assistance Act of 1974 and the 1978 Surface Transportation Assistance Act, provided reduced fares to the elderly and handicapped as well as federal support to programs in nonurban areas.

In 1986 the Department of Health and Human Services and the Department of Transportation, in an attempt to rectify some of the problems beseiging the transportation system, formed a Coordinating Council which would oversee transportation programs, support local specialized human services coordination, and develop demonstration programs. However, even with this integrated effort, the ability of existing transportation programs to keep pace with the needs of the frail elderly has remained limited due to funding restrictions.

Legislation presented in Congress in 1991, the Elderly and Handicapped Transportaton Improvement Act of 1991 (H.R. 2804), is another attempt to improve the situation for the "neediest citizens and the disabled." The aim of this proposed legislation is to increase funds provided under the Urban Mass Transportation Act to nonprofit transportation services for new services and operational costs. For the past five years, funds for these services have been capped at $35 million annually, severely curtailing any planned expansion. The intent of the legislation is to rectify this situation.

## Case Management

Due to the emphasis being placed on case management in proposed long-term care legislation as well as in existing programs, the topic warrants considerable discussion. Case management is an access service in that it seeks to optimize the elderly's utilization of programs. The service assists individuals to locate and receive appropriate services while also monitoring their appropriateness. By carefully assessing individual needs and designing individualized care plans, case management can play a major role in enabling the frail to live in the community.

The key services provided through case management are assessment, care planning, service arrangement, and monitoring. In addition, the case manager also acts as the client's advocate in the community.

Case management is offered by a variety of agencies including home nursing programs, social service agencies, and private agencies. The common goal of the programs is to prevent unnecessary institutionalization of the frail elderly through the provision of services and assistance in the community.

The process begins with a comprehensive assessment, which usually evaluates the physical, mental, social, and financial status of the applicant. In addition, it reviews the support network, assessing the extent of available informal care. However, eligibility is determined by criteria related to specific programs and thus may vary greatly depending upon the auspices of the agency. The absence of standards for case management contributes to this variation.

Critical to effective case management is the individualized care plan which should be made in conjunction with the older person and the family. Specifically, with regard to the needs of the frail elderly, the plan should serve to supplement existing skills and levels of assistance rather than supplant them. A sensitive care plan can be an important basis for enhancing independence and the functioning of the frail.

Coordinating and monitoring services are the next phases of case management. The risk in coordination is that the manager may assume responsibilities that either the client or the family should be assuming. By doing too much, the manager may actually undermine the capability of the client. The frequency of monitoring should be closely related to the impairment level of the client and the involvement of informal caregivers. Furthermore, regular monitoring is necessary if the care plan and its services are to be appropriate to the changing needs of the client.

Studies on case management have not confirmed the effectiveness of its role in the long-term care system. The most complete evaluation of the system was through the Channeling Demonstration, which sought to assess the extent to which case-managed care could substitute for nursing home placement.

The findings of the demonstration projects indicated that the case managed services reduced the level of unmet needs among the frail in the community, increased life satisfaction among users and their caregivers, increased a sense of confidence in the service system, and increased the use of needed home care services without reducing informal care, but the program did not reduce overall costs (Kemper, 1990). The primary reason for the failure to reduce costs was that although Channeling served the frail elderly, these were not individuals who were at actual risk of nursing home placement. As has been found with day-care programs, the service was meeting the needs of another group of frail elderly.

Case management has been criticized as adding another layer of service to an already fragmented long-term-care system rather than focusing attention on altering the system (Callahan, 1989). Moreover, most older persons and their families want information but do not want to be "managed cases." Case management, according to Callahan, is a response to the needs of the system rather than to the needs of the elderly.

Other concerns must also be raised about case management. Presently, there are no guidelines or standards for case management. The service is performed by nurses, social workers, and others who do not necessarily have any background or training in case management. The fact that it may also be performed by the agencies that are providing the direct services raises further questions about its objectivity.

In spite of these limitations and the fact that it has not been proven to be cost-effective, case management programs have been proliferating and have received federal government support. Under the changes in Medicaid made in the Omnibus Budget legislation of 1990, case managers will be responsible for all client care plans and monitoring. Moreover, virtually all pending long-term-care legislation gives a major role to case management.

There has also been a proliferation of case management in the private sector. These services are assuming substantial roles in caring for the frail when families are not available. In a study of these services in the Northeast, Dobrish (1987) found that the majority of managers visited their clients weekly and talked to the families on a weekly basis. Fees averaged $60 an hour. When families are not in the area, the manager takes on the familial caregiving role, checking regularly on the client and assisting where necessary. Only 50 percent of the managers provided counseling to the clients, although the majority did offer educative counseling to the families. Clients in need of counseling were referred to other professionals.

Case management can play a unique and essential role in the community care system through its flexibility, which enables it to remain congruent with the changing needs of the client. To be most effective, it requires that the services to be coordinated are available and accessible. Given these parameters, along with the careful training of the workers and their ability to advocate effectively, the program can assist many elderly who may otherwise be at the complete mercy of the system.

## HOME-BASED SERVICES

Home-based services concentrate on fostering the ability of the frail to remain in their own homes. These services assist the elderly with the activities of daily living as well as household management. Providing home-delivered meals to the frail is also becoming a major component of home-based services.

### Home Care

Many of the frail elderly benefit from home care services that help them to function independently and may actually be the key factor in enabling them to remain in their own homes. Home care covers a vast rubric of services ranging from highly skilled technological care to assistance with routine household chores such as cleaning and cooking. It may also include personal care, medical supervision, and emotional counseling.

In order to best meet the needs of the frail and to support functioning rather than contribute to dependency, home care services should be based on careful assessments of the abilities and needs of the elderly client. The assessment provides the basis for the care plan, which indicates the types of services, the amount and duration of each, and the type of assistance to be expected from both formal and informal supports.

The Home Care Quality Assurance Act of 1987 is an attempt to assure that care is being monitored and that it is compatible with patient needs. This act requires agencies to develop care plans that identify services, provide a means for identifying additional client needs, and include coordination mechanisms with other service agencies.

Because of the diverse services and levels of care that may be required, various professionals and nonprofessionals are involved as direct service providers in home care. Generally, a registered nurse is responsible for the assessments and the development of the care plan. Home health aides, under nursing supervision, assist with personal care such as bathing and grooming, exercising, and ambulation. Homemakers are responsible for domestic care, meal preparation, laundry, cooking, and other routine household tasks. Although home care can potentially play a critical role in the maintenance of the frail elderly in the community, current policy severely limits its effectiveness. Home care services are restricted under Medicare, which permits only a limited number of visits within very restrictive eligibility requirements. As a result of Medicare's focus on acute medical problems, the frail elderly with chronic conditions who require minimal but ongoing assistance in the home do not qualify for care.

Home care under Medicaid is also medically oriented, although there is more provision for homemaker assistance and for a wider range of home-based services. Under the Medicaid waiver program, states are able to offer many services to those who would otherwise be institutionalized, thus permitting more assistance with domestic care. However, eligibility for the program is confined to those in or near the poverty level.

## Home-Delivered Meals

Home-delivered meals, provided through private nonprofit organizations or nutrition programs under the Older Americans Act, can be a vital resource in maintaining the frail in the community. Additionally, the staff and volunteers of the programs can offer emotional support to the homebound as well as being links to other services.

Most of the 15,000 nutrition sites provide home-delivered meals to the elderly. Indicative of the need for this service, in many sites the number of meals delivered actually exceeds those served in the congregate setting (National Association of Nutrition and Aging Services, 1989).

There is little available data on the characteristics of those receiving home-delivered meals or their levels of impairment. Because eligibility criteria are unique to the independent programs, levels of frailty as well as the reasons for program use may vary considerably. But this variation and flexibility are particular program strengths. For as the service is offered on the basis of need alone, it assumes a truly universal character.

## COMMUNITY-BASED PROGRAMS

Community-based programs serve the frail elderly in congregate settings and may serve individuals who are mildly to extremely impaired. A major advantage to congregate programs is the opportunity for socialization and interaction with peers, which is usually lacking in home-based settings. Such activities can be particularly important to the frail, whose needs for mental and social stimulation can easily be overlooked.

## Nutrition Programs

A basic need of the frail elderly, as indeed is true for all age groups, is an adequate diet which meets nutritional requirements. In order to meet these needs, nutrition programs were formally authorized under the Older Americans Act of 1973 to provide at least one hot meal a day in a congregate setting to all persons over the age of 60 years. The original goals of the program were to improve the health of the elderly and to increase social interaction. At the same time, the programs were intended to foster independence through counseling and referrals to other social services. Thus, from the beginning the programs sought to serve the more frail in the community.

Nutrition sites exist in virtually every community of the country and remain one of the most utilized programs under the Older Americans Act. Moreover, as the elderly population has aged, the participants in these programs have similarly become older and more impaired. Descriptions of participants depict them as being poor, with considerable disability, isolated, and with an average age of 72 years (Harel, 1985).

In many areas of the country, nutrition sites provide information and referral, transportation, outreach, recreation, counseling, and education in additional to a meal. They may also have extended hours, thus becoming more like day-care programs. The expanded services in some centers enables them to meet many of the pressing needs of the frail participants.

Nutrition programs have the potential of serving many of the frail elderly in the community. Unfortunately, they remain hampered by restricted funding and resources. Usually sites do not permit special diets, offer more than one meal a day, or offer meals seven days a week (U.S. House Select Committee on Aging, 1990a).

## Senior Centers

Senior centers have continued to play a major role in the network of community-based services since their early beginnings in the 1940s. The first centers focused on socialization activities for seniors who were well-functioning but who might be experiencing the loneliness and isolation that frequently accompany the aging process. Centers continue to be one of the most utilized of all programs for the elderly with approximately 15 percent of those over 65 having frequented a center; use of senior centers is highest among those elderly living alone (Stone, 1986). The desire for social interaction is a primary motivating factor for center particpation (Krout, 1988).

The important role that centers can play in the lives of elderly individuals in the community is underscored in their being designated as focal points for comprehensive service delivery under the Older Americans Act of 1965. Centers offer a wide range of programs and activities ranging from information and referral, meals, and educational programs to exercise classes and trips. They can therefore potentially serve a diverse elderly population including the more impaired.

Early descriptions of senior center participants describe them as being older, active, and relatively healthy (Hansen et al., 1978; Trela and Simms, 1971; Ralston, 1984). Centers in general have been viewed as wanting to maintain their original focus on the well elderly and therefore have failed to target the minority, low-income, and frail populations (Krout et al., 1990). In fact, to focus on these groups may affect the ability of centers to attract and retain their current well participants (Ralston, 1991).

However, centers may be forced to change as their participants continue to age (Krout, 1989). Accordingly, centers may begin to reexamine their roles in light of a more frail group of participants. The extent to which they are doing so or actually serve the frail elderly will be examined later in this chapter.

## Day-Care

Adult day-care concentrates on serving the functionally impaired by offering a comprehensive program of health, social, and special support services in a protective setting (The National Institute on Adult Daycare, 1984). Day-care can therefore play a significant role in the lives of the frail elderly as it offers support and social interaction while providing caregivers with respite assistance.

In a survey of 60 day-care programs, three models of day-care were identified (Weissert et al., 1989). These models are those associated with a nursing home or rehabilitation hospital that serve the most dependent elderly; centers affiliated with a general hospital that serve a less physically frail but often more mentally impaired population; and centers which serve only one population, such as Alzheimer's patients or patients belonging to the Veterans Administration. Each model offers in varying amounts case management, health assessment, nutrition education, transportation, and counseling.

Weissert's survey also showed that although participants were functionally dependent, with almost one-third having some mental disorder, they were younger than most nursing home patients, more likely to be married, less dependent, and less frequently mentally impaired. In fact, most day-care participants appeared to be at low risk for nursing home placement. Thus, if cost-effectiveness with regard to being an alternative to institutionalization is a criterion for the development of day-care programs, there is some doubt that the service is caring for those who would otherwise be in nursing homes.

The distribution of day-care centers, as found in another survey, is not equal throughout the country (Conrad et al., 1990). The majority are located in urban areas. Centers in the Midwest offer the greatest number of hours but also have lower attendance, enrollment, and capacity. Moreover, centers in the South have the highest pecentage on waiting lists, while the Midwest has the lowest.

Data from the survey also indicate that for any particluar ADL, the majority of participants are unimpaired. Impairment was highest in needing help with bathing, grooming, and dressing. Impairment levels were greater in the IADLs as participants required assistance in handling money and shopping. However, according to program administrators, more than half (51 percent) of participants would require nursing home placement if day-care was not available.

In an effort to reduce the costs of day-care offered by the Veterans Administration so that its efficacy in comparison to nursing home and other types of care could be increased, a cost model for programs has been developed (Chapko et al., 1990). According to this model, the criteria for admission into a day-care program require that the participant be at risk for nursing home placement as indicated by dependence in specific ADLs and poor cognitive status. In a detailed evaluation of the program, it was estimated that costs could be reduced if the program were more aggressively marketed to increase referrals, if outreach were increased to enhance commitment to the program, and if the centers provided respite care to those about to enter a nursing home.

Day-care is apparently serving a different population of frail from that at risk for institutionalization. Therefore, rather than reducing overall costs, it has added a new service sector which requires resources and funds. If cost reduction remains the primary criterion for services, day-care may not be viewed positively. Conversely, if qualitative concerns are paramount, the high rates of satisfaction with the service given by participants and their families must be considered. Day-care can have an important role in extending the options of the frail elderly.

## SUPPORTIVE SERVICES

Supportive services are not confined to either the home or the community or to any particular level of impairment. They can be critical, however, in the lives of the frail, who depend upon support and assistance with functioning. This section will discuss only a few of the major types of support programs available to the frail.

### Respite Care

Respite care is a support program which seeks to foster the caregiving ability of the family by offering temporary relief. Services may be offered at home through a nursing home or hospital. Findings on the use of respite care show that it can improve the physical and mental well-being of caregivers, their social relationships, and their confidence in their caregiving abilities (Scharlach and Frenzel, 1986; Meltzer, 1982).

Respite care is classified as short-term (provided a few hours a day) or all-day care provided by a home care worker, senior center, or day-care program. The latter, although a formal community service, is frequently classified as a respite service through the relief it provides to the caregiver. Respite may also be longer, involving 24-hour care, weekend, or even weekly or monthly care. This is generally provided in the home, nursing homes, hospitals, or foster homes.

In-home respite is the format most desired by caregivers, since it causes little disruption to the frail older person. It is similar to home care in that the respite worker often assists the individual with functioning or performing household tasks. On the other hand, the respite worker may be employed to act only as a companion. In-home respite is provided by paid or volunteer workers who have been trained and are supervised with the cost dependent on the skill level and administrative costs of the program (New York State Office for the Aging, 1990).

Respite care out of the home can permit caregivers to have a longer period of relief. Placement in an institution such as a hospital or nursing home may also be more appropriate for those frail who require more intensive supervision. However, such services may also be a link to eventual institutional placement of the older patient. In one study of nursing home respite, many of the caregivers using the service used it as a trial program. Following the temporary placement, they felt less stress and guilt about permanently placing the relative in the home (Miller and Goldman, 1989).

Although respite would appear to be a much sought after service by families, like day-care it remains underutilized. In a study of respite services offered in-home, in a nursing home setting, and in day-care facilities, Montgomery (1988) found that caregivers were difficult to reach and resistant to using the service, even though they agreed to use it and even though the service was offered free of charge. Of those using the respite, the majority preferred short in-home respite, which was easier for them to use. Those receiving nursing home respite were more disabled than those using in-home or day-care respite. However, all caregivers were highly satisfied with the programs and interested in using other services such as seminars and support groups.

Specific factors associated with the use of respite have been identified, including older ages of the caregivers and the care recipients and greater functional impairments of the frail individual (Lawton et al., 1989). The nature of the disability is also associated with the type of respite used. Behavioral problems are related to more in-home and less day-care respite.

A concern of many policy makers is that respite service will encourage caregivers to reduce their assistance. However, there is no evidence that families using respite care decrease their amount of help. In fact, as shown by Lawton, they may actually increase their involvement.

The underutilization of the programs remains a barrier to their effectiveness. Apparently, not all caregivers perceive a need for formal respite programs, depending more on informal help. Caregivers may also feel hesitant about having strangers in their home or concerned about leaving their relative either in the care of a stranger or in a day-care program. Lack of knowledge about the program and its intentions can be a further obstacle to its utilization. On the other hand, people will use respite if they understand it, if it is provided in sufficient amounts, and if the aide is reliable and trained (Blume et al., 1990). Respite programs remain an important supportive service to families. The fear that their provision will undermine the traditional family support system is apparently unfounded. Instead, the services can enhance the competency and ability of caregivers and thus strengthen their support. Unfortunately, as with many other services, those most in need may have the greatest difficulties obtaining access.

## Telephone Reassurance/Friendly Visiting

Both of these support programs provide emotional and practical support to the frail elderly in the community. The services are commonly staffed by volunteers under the supervision of a professional. Social service agencies, senior centers, and churches are the primary providers of these services.

In telephone reassurance, the elderly participant is telephoned at least once daily. If there is no answer, the volunteer contacts the police or another specified individual who will then visit the home. Additionally, the volunteer can provide both advice and counseling while acting as an important link to other services.

One of the major barriers to program utilization is the attitude of the frail themselves. Suspiciousness regarding the nature of the service and an unfamiliarity with the particular volunteer can prevent its being used. Acceptability remains a major obstacle.

Friendly visiting to the homebound elderly is also done primarily by volunteers. Again, these individuals can be links to other services while also providing emotional support to those at risk of becoming isolated. These visitors are usually not trained in counseling and are thus expected to limit their services to conversation and leisure activities. However, in many instances they may be the only ones available to perceive marked changes in an elderly person's condition which could signify a need for more intense care. These volunteers can thus be important links in the fragmented and often anonymous service system.

## Mental Health Counseling

Counseling for the frail elderly to assist them in coping with their limitations as well as preserving and strengthening their existing capabilities can be vital to their functioning in the community. However, funding for counseling, as is true of most other programs, is limited. Under the Older Americans Act, few funds are available for psychosocial counseling, and funding for outpatient treatment under Medicare is also restricted.

Counseling is frequently offered by the staff of senior centers, day-care centers, or nutrition programs. These individuals do not necessarily have any formal training, but in their relationships with the participants they are often turned to for advice and support. However, there is a limit to the ability of these staff to provide counseling assistance. A lack of time as well as training can severely inhibit their involvement. Moreover, program staff often find it difficult to deal with elderly individuals who have problems such as depression that demand a great deal of time and skill.

Consequently, many elderly individuals in need of counseling have no service to which to turn. Only 4 percent of visits to private psychiatrists are made by older persons with even fewer visiting psychologists (Schurman, et al., 1985). Barriers to the use of services include a lack of coverage by insurance programs and Medicare, the stigma attached to mental problems, and service accessibility (Crook and Cohen, 1983).

Community mental health centers are also unlikely to serve the elderly. Centers focus on the younger populations with centers in one survey reporting a mean of only 8 percent elderly clients (Swan et al., 1986). Centers serving the largest proportions of the elderly are those which have specialized geriatric services, specially trained staff, services in various community sites, reduced access barriers, and have coordinated programs with Area Agencies on Aging (Light, et al., 1986; Lebowitz, et al., 1987). These findings suggest that accessibility may be a major factor affecting service utilization and that linkages and coordination between programs can greatly contribute to overcoming this barrier.

## PROTECTING THE FRAIL

The maze of services with varying eligibility criteria, compounded by a dependency on both informal and formal supports for assistance, means that measures to protect the rights and interests of the frail elderly are essential. These safeguards can be decisive in enabling them to remain in the community.

As a response to these needs, the Older Americans Act authorizes funds specifically for legal services for the elderly. Priority status to legal services was allotted under the 1975 amendments to the act, while the 1981 amendments required that Area Agencies on Aging spend a proportion of their service funding on legal services. Underscoring the importance of these services, the 1987 amendments specified a minimum proportion of state funds that must be given to legal assistance. Moreover, Area Agencies on Aging were required to contract with local providers, such as law schools, private attorneys, Legal Services Corporation grantees, and social service agencies, to provide legal assistance.

Several community programs are also committed to providing legal assistance to the frail elderly. The Legal Services Corporation (LSC), established by legislation in 1975, is authorized to serve the legal needs of the poor, including the elderly. Twelve percent of the LSC's caseload are persons over the age of 60 (U.S. Senate Special Committee on Aging, 1990). However, funding allocations severely inhibit its capacity to meet the needs of its elderly clients. As in many other community services, the elderly must compete with other groups for assistance.

The legal problems of the elderly have also been a concern in the private sector. The Commission on Legal Problems of the Elderly, established in

1979 by the American Bar Association, has attempted to stimulate the interest of private attorneys in providing legal services to the elderly. The Commission also gives assistance at the local level to associations and services interested in working with the aged. Many local bar associations have telephone advice lines to assist the elderly with legal problems. Other activities include free legal advice and education on legal services to seniors.

Adult protective services under the jurisdiction and support of the individual states are mandated to protect the elderly from exploitation, abuse, and neglect. The programs are placed within social service departments and offer preventive, supportive, and surrogate services to the vulnerable elderly.

The two primary functions of protective services are to offer assistance and to assume, when necessary, the legal authority to act on behalf of the client (Regan, 1990). Services are provided through Title XX and Older Americans Act funds and include meals, homemakers, and transportation. These are coordinated under a case manager, who is responsible for the client assessment, service arrangement, and monitoring. The case manager also has the legal authority to act on behalf of the client. This authority is granted when the client voluntarily gives it or when the manager invokes the power of the state to act in the client's best interests. In this latter situation, the manager assumes a role similar to that of guardian. In fact, the manager may actually become the guardian of the client through guardianship or special court proceedings.

Guardianship through protective services presents risks similar to those entailed in other forms of guardianship. The criteria for assuming guardianship are vague and lack consistency. Adult protective services can assume guardianship on the basis that the elderly client is unable to care for himself or herself or protect himself or herself from abuse and exploitation by others. Once protective services assumes this role, the agency is able to intercede in almost every area of the client's life unless specifically restricted by the court.

A major concern with regard to protective services is its ability to effectively carry out its role due to its funding allocations. The primary source of federal funding has been through the Social Services Block Grant monies, which have continued to be reduced. Furthermore, adult protective services at the state level uniformly receives a much smaller proportion of funds than child protective services. Data reveal that in 1989 states spent an average of $3.80 per elderly person for protective services as compared to an average of $45.03 per child (U.S. House Select Committee on Aging, 1990b). Moreover, the same data show that the share of the budgets going to adult protective services declined between 1980 and 1990. Thus, the effectiveness of the services in carrying out their roles of protecting the elderly should be seriously questioned.

## SERVICES FOR THE COGNITIVELY IMPAIRED

In recent years growing attention has been given to the special needs of the cognitively impaired elderly, particularly those with Alzheimer's disease. The progressive nature of the illness and its devastating effects on both the individual and the family intensify this population's needs for assistance.

Day-care and respite care are two services that have been developed to meet the needs of these individuals. Day-care programs serving the physically frail have generally been reluctant to admit the dementia patients. Staff resistance, staff expectations that the demented will negatively affect the programs, resistance by the physically frail, and a lack of knowledge about how to serve this population contribute to this reluctance (Cherry and Rafkin, 1988).

Consequently, there has been an increase in day-care programs that serve only dementia clients. A comparative study of Alzheimer's day-care programs as compared to other adult day-care programs found that the former provided more support for families, therapeutic recreation, personal care and training, and entertainment (Conrad and Guttman, 1991). The Alzheimer's centers offered fewer clinical services than other day-care programs. However, the attention given to the families by these centers can be particularly important as a caregiver support service.

Respite care is particularly important for caregivers who are unable to transport the dementia patient to a day-care program, who do not have access to a program, or who are caring for an elderly individual who resist going to any service, and for those who are in the later stages of the disease. As in other respite programs, the service can give significant relief to relatives.

In spite of their pressing needs, elderly individuals with dementia and their families use fewer services than the physically impaired. One of the primary causes of this underutilization is the difficulty that people have in identifying and locating appropriate services (Maslow, 1990). The fragmentation of the system, with many different agencies offering services with distinct eligibility criteria, accentuates these barriers. Moreover, poor coordination between programs means that linkages and referrals between agencies are often absent.

Data also indicate that caregivers have only limited knowledge of community services. Findings from a study in Cuyohoga County conducted for the Office of Technology Assessment showed that the majority of caregivers did not know about available services (U.S. Congress, Office of Technology Assessment, 1990). Cox (1991) found that a majority of caregivers of dementia patients were unaware of most community services, including referral programs, home help, transportation, and case management. These data suggest that one of the prime concerns in providing services to dementia patients and their caregivers must be the development of effective outreach and access programs.

A major barrier to accessing services is the lack of funding available for Alzheimer's patients and their caregivers. Home care for dementia patients is not covered under Medicare or under most private insurance programs. Expanded home care services are available under Medicaid, but these are only for those meeting poverty criteria. Thus, for the majority of elderly suffering from Alzheimer's disease, services must be paid for privately.

## INTEGRATING THE FRAIL AND WELL ELDERLY

In developing community programs to meet the needs of the frail elderly, the issue of integration of the frail into other programs for the elderly warrants particular attention. Services that target only the frail elderly risk further separating them from their well peers while fostering an image of disability and dependency. Programs that attempt to incorporate the frail into other services are at risk of not meeting their specific needs. The dilemma of integrating or providing special services to the frail elderly is comparable to that of mainstreaming or separating children with special needs.

As people age, they frequently become less tolerant of disabilities due to their own fears of becoming disabled (Gozali, 1971). Professionals and other service providers often display the same negative attitudes towards impairments due to their own fears and anxieties about aging and death (Greene, 1986). The most discrimination has been found against those with more visible impairments and those with communicative, cognitive, locomotive, and inter-relational difficulties (Safilios-Rothschild, 1970).

Few studies have focused on the integration of the frail and well elderly in the same program. In a study of congregate meal programs acceptance of the more impaired was difficult without a strong educational effort by the program managers (Prosper, 1987). Because senior centers continue

to serve a large proportion of elderly, and with the aging of their participants, research has focused on their ability to serve both the well and frail
in integrated programs (Cox and Monk, 1990b).

## The Frail Elderly in Senior Centers

Data collected from senior centers in New York State found that almost
half of the center directors (48 percent) felt that they could successfully
serve a population of no more than 10 percent frail while only 27 percent
believed they could possibly incorporate as many as 27 percent frail into
the programs (Cox and Monk, 1990b). Moreover, these directors felt better
able to integrate those with physical impairments than those with behavioral or emotional ones.

Participants were described as being more accepting of established
members who become frail than of those who are frail when they join.
Analysis of data from the centers also revealed that the proportion of well
participants significantly decreased as the proportion of frail increased.

Overall, the findings showed a reluctance to integrate the frail on the
part of both staff and participants. Thus, although the majority of center
directors stated that they had formal guidelines for serving the frail, few
had actually developed programs specific to their needs. Consequently,
even when the frail are in centers, the extent to which they are integrated
with other participants is not known. Few centers actually made their own
assessments of the impairment levels; most were based on referrals from
other agencies, and very few were based on medical screenings. Consequently, the extent to which a supposedly frail individual could actually
participate was not evaluated on-site.

The centers with the highest proportions of frail participants were those
with specially trained staff and those with programs coordinated with other
agencies. The expertise of these staff and the links with other services
promoted integration, although it is not clear whether the training and
coordination preceded or followed the increase in frail participants. As in
the nutrition programs, education appears to be a critical factor for
integrating the frail elderly into established programs.

The study's findings raise many questions about services for the frail
elderly. Primary obstacles to integration are staff training, education, and
coordination of programs. Without these factors, a two-tiered system
of services, one for the well and one for the frail elderly, with each
competing for funds and resources is likely to develop, increasing the
fragmentation in community services. Furthermore, a danger in this frag-

mentation is that it can subject the frail elderly to further segregation and discrimination in the community.

## SUMMARY

As frailty is difficult to confine to only one dimension of a person's life, so are the services that he or she needs. Recognizing this necessitates that a responsive system of care be comprehensive and coordinated. Without this approach, fragmentation and service duplication will remain with large gaps between services as planners, providers, and the intended clients are unclear about program aims or functions. Future cohorts of the frail elderly will place new demands upon the service system, underscoring the need for a creative, dynamic, comprehensive, and flexible system of care.

Unfortunately, the needs of the frail are among those likely to be overlooked, since the very impairments which necessitate assistance are those which may most hinder efforts to obtain it. Utilization of community services is dependent upon many factors, and providers must play active roles in assuring that services are appropriate to their intended populations. Awareness and understanding of specific needs and the barriers that may affect service use are fundamental to the development of responsive programs.

Many services are in place that can have a significant impact on the lives and functioning of the frail in the community. However, limited funding continues to restrict their scope and effectiveness. Moreover, overriding concerns with costs in evaluating services in comparison to more qualitative measures of satisfaction and an improved sense of well-being may seriously hamper program development. Overall, services for the frail must be comprehensive in accordance with this population's needs, and they must be offered in a manner that fosters integration rather than discrimination.

*Chapter Five*

---

# Housing Needs and Options

Independence in the community is predicated upon living in an environment that is compatible with the individual's functional status. For the frail elderly who require some degree of assistance and support, this compatibility may be difficult to achieve. The home must be managed either through special adaptations or support services. When adaptations are not possible and support services are not available, the individual usually has no choice but to move to a more appropriate environment.

Moving is often not based on the level of impairment of functioning or frailty. Instead, individual and community resources are frequently the main factors influencing the decision to move. Individual interests and preferences as well as actual needs for assistance are frequently overruled by a scarcity of funds, resources, and services. Thus many individuals could remain in their homes if adaptations could be made or if services were accessible. The availability of these options, however, remains limited, particularly for those with reduced incomes.

Within these limitations, there has been increasing recognition of the housing needs of the older population. Alternative types of housing programs as well as support services and technological devices that can make existing housing more compatible with the needs of the frail are being developed. Although most of these programs remain limited in scope and fragmented under our existing system, they represent varying responses that can affect the ability of the frail to live in the community.

## PROVISIONS FOR STAYING IN THE HOME

### Home Repair and Home Adaptation Programs

The elderly tend to live in the oldest housing and in housing that is of less value than that of younger age groups (U.S. Department of Housing and Urban Development, 1988). Moreover, it is important to note that this poor housing is not equally distributed throughout the older population and that minority elderly are likely to suffer the most from inadequate housing. Twenty-three percent of elderly African-American home owners live in inadequate housing as compared to 13 percent of elderly Hispanic home owners and 4 percent of elderly white home owners (Mikelsons and Turner, 1991).

Older housing frequently is in need of minor if not major repairs. These repairs are often beyond the capacity of the frail householder. In addition, attending to the routine maintenance of a home, repairing a gutter or broken windows, mowing the lawn, and unclogging a toilet are chores which can be impossible for the frail to complete. Although such repairs are generally inexpensive and require little expertise, the inability to complete these tasks or obtain assistance means that they have no option but to move.

Funds for home repairs are available from various federal, state, and local sources. In addition, many communities have developed cadres of volunteers who routinely assist the elderly with these tasks. However, as noted by Pynoos (1992) the absence of any national program means that many elderly in need of assistance are unable to obtain it under the gaps in the current system.

The Farmer's Home Administration provides loans to low-income elderly in rural areas who need assistance in removing health or safety hazards or in bringing their home up to established standards. Loans for home repairs are also available to low-income elderly through the Department of Housing and Urban Development. As with all government programs, the availability of such funds fluctuates, compromising the real impact that they can have on the housing needs of the frail elderly.

Assistance with minor repairs and routine maintenance is also offered through many local Area Agencies on Aging with funding from the Older Americans Act and through block grants. However, services under the Older Americans Act are not mandated and are therefore not uniformly available throughout the country. Block grant funding is likely to go to specific neighborhoods and is not necessarily allocated to the elderly. As a result, home repair and home maintenance may remain among the greatest unmet needs of the frail in the community.

Since the preference of most elderly people is to remain in their own homes, it is also important to examine what accommodations may be necessary in order to make these homes adaptable to their needs. Assistance with household and personal care is only one type of intervention that may be required. In addition, changes may be necessary in the actual structure of the house. Lowering sinks, widening hallways for accessibility to wheelchairs, having bathrooms on the first floor, and installing ramps are some of the adaptations that can permit many frail to remain in their homes.

The frail elderly are those most likely to be affected by inadequate housing in need of adaptations. Approximately half of the severely frail elderly living alone reside in houses with no adaptations to support them (Soldo and Longino, 1988). Special features such as grab bars and handrails are found in the homes of only 6.6 percent of those elderly with health or mobility impairments (Struyk, 1987). It is important to also note that in some instances adaptations are actually resisted. Many elderly individuals reject devices that would identify them as "disabled" (Christenson, 1990). These attitudes, in conjunction with sparse availability of adaptation programs, suggest that many of the frail are in jeopardy in their own homes.

Programs and services to adapt homes to the needs of the frail are very limited. In most instances, elderly home owners must pay privately for the adaptation, although some loans are offered through government programs. The scarcity of government funds means that adaptations are not routinely made. The majority of the frail must cope with less than adequate homes or move to more sheltered environments. Unfortunately, in many instances this may mean moving to a nursing home.

## Technological Adaptations

Home adaptations are not limited to structural improvements and installation of assistive devices such as handrails. The growing application of technology to the needs of the aged has produced many new devices that can make the home more accommodating to the frail individual. Telephones with memories that allow numbers to be dialed by pushing only one button, lifelines which contact a central number in case of an emergency, and telephone services which phone each day to check on the older person and also provide reminders regarding tasks such as taking medications are examples of the ways in which technology may be applied to the needs of the frail elderly.

Personal Emergency Response Systems (PERS) are important devices which can attend to emergencies that might occur in the home. They may be particularly critical to the well-being of the frail elderly living alone. The system consists of a small radio transmitter, worn as a bracelet or necklace, which can send a telephone signal to a 24-hour emergency center when help is needed. The person does not need to be at home to make the transmission. Systems are also available that automatically call the person if no activity has been noted in a particular period of time. The response centers may be in hospitals or in private companies. The center operator contacts local persons identified by the user (such as friends or relatives or a formal agency) as soon as an emergency signal is received.

Stafford and Dibner (1984) in their study of 335 Lifeline programs in the United States describe subscribers as being mainly women in their late 70s and early 80s, living alone and with multiple disabilities, mainly cardiovascular, musculoskeletal, and rheumatoid disorders. Other research indicates that although these individuals are very frail and likely to become even more physically impaired, with the installation of the reponse systems, their self-ratings of health significantly increase (Gatz and Pearson, 1988). They report less symptoms and felt less vulnerable about themselves and their safety.

In addition the systems appear to have broader effects on the lives of these elderly. Relatives feel less burdened and less worried about the older individual with the system. These feelings also are mirrored in their interactions in that they report less anger as the person becomes less dependent and more secure.

There is some evidence that users of the system are able to use it as a substitute for home care. As such, it can significantly reduce costs for the frail elderly. An evaluation of PERS' ability to replace home attendants was made by giving the device to 54 clients in a Medicaid-funded home health care program matched with a control group who did not receive the device (Coordinated Care Management Corporation, 1989). Both groups had impaired functioning with the majority of each eligible for residence in a health-related facility. The results of the 25-month study showed that the PERS users used fewer hours of home care, resulting in a large cost savings to the program. The majority of clients also felt much more secure with the system and felt that it increased their independence.

These systems thus are a potential source of significant support to the frail, but relatively few of those who could benefit actually have them. According to Dibner (1990), only 1 percent of persons over the age of 65 in the United States and Canada have a personal response system. However, the technology continues to be developed. New devices include answering machines that can be used from any room in the house, smaller systems such as wristwatches, transmissions of electrocardiograms over the phone lines, and immediate two-way voice communication.

Making these techonological devices available to a larger proportion of the frail elderly would be a major step in enabling them to remain in the commmunity. However, as with many new devices, there does exist a potential for fraud. As noted by a report from AARP (American Association of Retired Persons, 1992), buyers must be aware of high-pressure sales tactics, warranties, and the need to periodically test batteries and equipment. Given these precautions, PERS can be an important aid to many frail elderly.

## THE DECISION TO MOVE

The restrictions placed on housing adaptations and housing assistance means that many frail elderly have little alternative but to move to another, often more restrictive environment. Moving is the last choice for most elderly, even those who may be considered frail. People prefer to stay in their homes and do so until their impairments severely affect their ability to function and remain independent.

The motivating factors leading to a move are generally impairments in IADLs such as shopping, cleaning, routine household chores, and cooking, and the absence of either a spouse or close relative to provide assistance (Longino et al., 1991; Reschovsky and Newman, 1990). Informal supports play a dominant role in the ability of these elderly to remain in the community. Thus, the motivation to move is compounded when the individual is impaired and alone.

It is important to also note that assistance, even from informal supports, is more readily available for the sporadic tasks associated with home maintenance and home repair than for the daily ones essential for maintaining independence. The frail elderly are more likely to find someone to fix a roof than to do cooking or laundry. But it is the absence of assistance with these routine tasks that can be the major influence on the decision to move.

It is not surprising that in a comparison of housing preferences and satisfaction between well and impaired elderly, the impaired were more dissatisfied with the amount of physical labor the house required (Gonyea et al., 1990). Moreover, those who were socially isolated from friends and family were more likely to anticipate a future move, although their strong preference was to remain in their homes with paid help for household and personal care.

Differences in the impetus to move exist between home owners and renters. Frail elderly who rent are more likely than frail home owners to move when their household needs exceed their capacity. Nevertheless, renters also prefer to remain in their established homes. When supports are introduced, they frequently are able to do so.

A survey of housing managers in San Francisco, found that landlords and managers of rental housing offered a wide variety of both formal and informal services to frail long-term tenants which enabled them to remain in their apartments. Such assistance included grocery shopping, errands, housekeeping chores, and transportation (Barker, et al., 1988).

In addition to offering practical assistance to frail tenants, there is evidence that landlords and managers serve as an important source of social support. In a study of apartment managers of HUD-subsidized buildings in San Francisco, the managers were relied upon for help in a medical emergency. Moreover, the relationships between the elderly and these managers were strongly personalized, with managers describing the relationship as one of trust and dependability (Wolfson, et al., 1990).

The housing managers studied were better able to deal with physical than mental impairments among the tenants. They found it difficult to cope with confusion and behaviors that may be disruptive and even harmful to the tenant or others. Thus, these individuals were more likely to be evicted than those requiring only physical assistance or special housing adaptations.


## RETIREMENT HOUSING

### Naturally Occurring Retirement Communities

In the last few years, throughout the country, the naturally occurring retirement community (NORC) has become increasingly common. NORCs are buildings or housing complexes where at least half the residents are over the age of 65. The buildings were not designed for the elderly and do not offer any services but have residents who have aged in place. As the buildings begin to house large numbers of elderly, other older people become attracted to them.

A study of three NORCs in Madison, Wisconsin, found that 80 percent of the residents were widows living alone and 50 percent had moved to the building between the ages of 60 and 75. Sixty percent of the residents had lived in the buildings for more than ten years. Residents would consider moving only if large rent increases occurred or health necessitated it (Hunt and Gunter-Hunt, 1985).

The presence of NORCs throughout the country further documents the desire of most elderly to remain in their own homes and also suggests that building special units adapted to the elderly may not be necessary. The elderly, similar to other age groups, enjoy living near others with whom they can share a common lifestyle and develop relationships. Improving these buildings by offering accessible services such as home help or meal programs within the complex or neighborhood may be sufficient to enable these persons to remain independent.

## Planned Housing

Planned retirement housing is designed for and marketed towards the elderly. It is age segregated and usually has activities and offer meals and some security. Elderly moving to retirement housing usually do so due to difficulties in maintaining a house and a desire to remain independent and not be a burden to the family (Malozemoff et al., 1978).

Various types of retirement housing exist. Depending on the location and region of the country, the housing may be retirement villages, mobile home parks, retirement hotels, single-room occupanicies (SROs), and independent apartments. The villages are frequently large and composed of independent apartments and detached houses which are purchased. They may also include shopping malls, transportation, and even golf courses for the residents. The advantages of villages are the services, recreation, maintenance, security, and large social network that they offer. Retirement villages are beyond the means of most of the elderly. Moreover, because the villages generally do not provide supportive assistance, if the individual becomes too impaired, another move will be necessary.

Mobile home parks are often developed only for the elderly. The individual generally rents space for the mobile home. These sites offer social interaction but generally lack any services. Frequently, they are in isolated areas which require that the older person have transportation. The advantage of these homes is their low cost and the relative ease with which they can be maintained. This low maintenance is particularly important to those with impairments, and therefore, as long as transportation is not a problem, mobile homes may be a housing alternative for many frail elderly.

Retirement hotels are appropriate for many elderly individuals accustomed to urban environments. These hotels are usually located in cities rather than rural areas. Many have been adapted for the elderly, and all provide housekeeping. Hotels may also serve meals as well as have social activities. There is a wide range of retirement hotels from luxurious to very inexpensive ones offering only basic facilities. These latter are the SROs frequently occupied by the low-income elderly and those at risk of being homeless. Unlike the more expensive hotels, the SROs usually do not offer meals or any other services.

Both types of hotels offer advantages to the frail elderly. Being located in urban settings, they tend to be accessible to services. They also offer security and housekeeping, and for the wealthier elderly, meals and activities. Hotels also offer flexibility in that long-term commitments are not necessary. Thus, for many of the elderly the autonomy and independence that these environments permit is extremely attractive.

Retirement apartment buildings are another type of housing alternative for the frail elderly. Unlike the NORCs, these buildings are designed specifically for the elderly population. The apartments do not necessarily provide meals or services, although most do have recreation programs. Buildings that receive government funding generally have an on-site nutrition program. More expensive private buildings often have a dining room where meals can be purchased. The buildings offer privacy while providing the opportunity to engage in social interactions. They may also offer a greater sense of permanency than is found in retirement hotels.

However, there is some question about the appropriateness of these buildings for the more frail. Individuals may be attracted to the housing because of the opportunity for independence that they offer, but they often soon need more assistance than the housing can provide (Merrill and Hunt, 1990). According to tenants, services particularly needed within these buildings are housekeeping, security, and an assurance that additional care will be available when needed.

Administrators of retirement housing constantly face the dilemma that if the buildings are to be attractive to the elderly, they must stress wellness and independence but if they are to maintain the residents they must also provide support. Not surprisingly, as in other settings, well residents disapprove of seeing the supportive services and devices required by the frail. Administrators similarly prefer the well and independent elderly but remain aware of the needs for support of many tenants. Findings from the survey by Merrill and Hunt showed that the housing managers accommodated the needs of tenants on a case-by-case basis; however, as discussed earlier, mental problems generally cannot be dealt with.

## Continuing Care Retirement Communities

In recent years, continuing care retirement communities (CCRCs) have become increasingly popular as residential environments for the elderly. For the middle-income and wealthier elderly, these residences, often called life care communities, offer a housing option which can be adjusted to their needs for assistance. The communities typically provide personal care, social and recreational services, congregate meals, and nursing home care. This continuum of on-site services related to the functional status of the elderly means that as impairment levels shift, the residents are not at risk of eviction. Instead their needs for assistance can be met within the community.

There are approximately 700–800 continuing care retirement communities in the country with an estimated 230,000 residents (U.S. Senate Special Committee on Aging, 1990). These facilities are geared toward the middle-income elderly with entrance fees in 1988 ranging from median prices of $32,800 for a studio to $68,250 for a two-bedroom apartment and with monthly fees ranging from $695 to $938. The differing rates are due to variations in the services provided, the type of units, and the amount of health care.

Increasingly, the CCRCs have begun offering rental units with fees for services. This system allows residents more choice with regard to care, although it may also mean less assurance against future expenses, less pooling of individual risks, and thus an added level of economic insecurity (Stearns et al., 1990).

Residents of CCRCs have a contractual agreement with the facility that includes an entrance fee and monthly fees but for which they are guaranteed health and nursing home care as required. With health and supportive services such as nursing and personal care a part of the contract, the communities offer protection against the risks encountered by frail elderly in independent housing. In fact, access to medical care and long-term care services are often cited as main reasons for moving into a CCRC (Cohen et al., 1988).

The number of CCRCs has continued to increase as corporations have become involved in their development. Regulation of the facilities is primarily left to the states with little federal involvement. One of the primary risks to residents is the financial solvency of the communities. This risk may be greatest for those tenants most in need of care—that is, the frail. In a study of 109 CCRCs, those providing full nursing care had the most precarious financial status, although it is not clear whether this is due to characteristics of residents, low charges for services, or excessive resident demand (Ruchin, 1988).

There is some question, however, as to the extent to which these communities actually provide the full continuum of care. Data on CCRCs in Florida indicate that the three most commonly supplied services are emergency call, skilled nursing care, and at least one meal daily (Alperin and Richie, 1990). The least provided service was sheltered care, which is often the balancing point between independent living and nursing homes. Only 52 percent of the facilities provided home health care, another service which can assist to maintain elderly in the community. Without these core supportive services, the viability of these communities with regard to maintaining the independence of their residents remains uncertain.

Continuing care retirement communities can offer an important option to the elderly through an array of services congruent with residents' changing needs. Health care and supportive services are guaranteed, and access is not a problem. With more regulations to assure that prospective tenants receive prospective services, these communities can act as an important housing alternative for those elderly with the resources to afford them.

## FEDERALLY SPONSORED PROGRAMS

As the 600,000 elderly residents of federally subsidized housing continue to grow older and more frail, increasing attention is being paid to "aging in place." In order to remain in their homes, these residents require more and more supportive services and assistance. Without interventions many are at risk of institutional placement. Based upon needs for personal assistance in one or more activities of daily living, 150,000 elderly individuals in this subsidized housing are estimated to be vulnerable to institutionalization (U.S. House Select Committee on Aging, 1990c).

The decision as to whether a frail individual can continue to live in public housing is left primarily to local housing administrators. Due to inadequate funds there has been little guidance to local authorities regarding policies or coordination of services for frail tenants. In addition, efforts to deregulate federal programs have left the decision of who should remain in public housing and who should be discharged to local housing authorities (Sheehan, 1986). Thus many frail elderly remain in federally subsidized buildings until their inability to function reaches crisis proportions.

In a study of subsidized senior housing in Connecticut, Sheehan and Wisensale (1991) found managers to be most concerned with senility,

Alzheimer's Disease, deterioration of health, arthritis, and feelings of alienation among the tenants. However, very few administrators had any discharge policies from which to make decisions. Those frail most likely to be able to remain in the apartments had family and/or community support to assist them with functioning. Without such supports, eviction was more likely.

## Section 202 Housing

A primary source of housing for the elderly has been through Section 202 of the Department of Housing and Urban Development (HUD). Federal housing designed specifically for the elderly with services was first established in 1959 under the Section 202 program. Through the program, loans are given to private, nonprofit organizations for the building of rental units for the elderly. Although the program has been extremely successful, units are in short supply. Turnover in the buildings is extremely low, with few persons choosing to move. In fact, the success of the buildings is attested to by the fact that transfers to a nursing home or death are the primary causes of vacancies.

The construction of new units for the elderly under the Section 202 program has fallen far short of meeting the need for housing. Even though construction of new units has continued, the demand by the elderly for apartments far exceeds their availability. Buildings have long waiting lists for apartments with an average of six units for every 1,000 elderly persons. In 1987 there were 11 applicants for every vacant apartment in cities with more than 1 million and 25 applicants for the newer buildings (U.S. Senate, Special Committee on Aging, 1991).

Although Section 202 buildings are required to provide services, only meals programs are actually mandated. Administrators are free to select which other services are offered. Case management, personal care, and housekeeping are among the types of other services frequently offered. The need for assistance is underscored by a report by the Urban Institute which estimates that 7 percent of the over 65 population of this housing require help in at least one activity of daily living (Struyk et al., 1989). The need for this assistance increases with age, and thus the residents can be expected to require more supports.

## Congregate Housing Services Program

In order to meet the support needs of the frail elderly in these subsidized units, the Congregate Housing Services Program (CHSP), the only part of

HUD to provide social services, was initiated in 1978. The program was designed to serve all eligible residents of Section 202 housing identified as vulnerable by local assessment committees. The goal was to prevent these individuals from having to enter institutions.

The primary service offered to tenants is meals with HUD requiring that two meals a day be provided seven days a week. Nonmedical services offered through the CHSP include housekeeping, personal assistance, transportation, escort, and social services. Fees are based on the older individual's ability to pay.

Although the aims of CHSP could have direct bearing on the ability of the frail to remain in the community, the effectiveness of the program was immediately hampered due to budget restrictions. Between the years 1979 and 1985 only $28 million was spent on services for approximately 3,500 people (U.S. Senate Special Committee on Aging, 1991). The program has never truly been able to become anything other than a demonstration program.

Accordingly, although funding has gradually increased, it is far short of the amount needed to make the program truly viable. The amount appropriated for this program for fiscal year 1989 was $5.4 million, for fiscal year 1990 it was $5.8 million, and for fiscal year 1991 it was $9.5 million. However, it is important to note that Congress requested $25 million in 1991 for the services program. This request suggests that the role that CHSP can play in preventing premature institutionalization is being recognized.

This recognition may be at least partially due to an evaluation of CHSP's impact on the lives of frail residents. A detailed evaluation and report by the U.S. House Select Committee on Aging's, Subcommittee on Housing and Consumer Interests (1988a) found that the program prevented institutionalization when targeted to the most vulnerable and was a cost-effective means for delivering services to the frail elderly and handicapped. Moreover, the local administrators and assessment committees were effective as they provided support to family caregivers, provided important support to those without family, and had positive effects on the life satisfaction of the participants.

## National Affordable Housing Act

The needs of the frail elderly are also addressed under the National Affordable Housing Act of 1990. Title VII of NAHA, Housing for Persons with Special Needs, was created to address the special needs of the elderly, those with disabilities, and others requiring supportive services. Under this title, federal congregate housing services must be coordinated on site and must include meals, personal care, transportation, case management, counseling, and medication assistance. Services must also reflect the desires of the residents as well as recommendations from community agencies.

In revising the 202 program, housing designed and built under NAHA must accommodate the physical needs of the elderly. To administer the program, a new position, Assistant Secretary for Supportive Housing, has been created. In addition, housing projects must employ, as much as possible, the elderly and disabled as service providers. This is a further attempt to promote the independence of these individuals.

Issues of autonomy of the frail in federally assisted housing are also being addressed through HOPE (Homeowernship and Opportunities for People Everywhere), a new demonstration voucher system in which vouchers can be used to pay for supportive services such as transportation, housekeeping, personal care, case management, and medication assistance. The elderly would be required to pay 10 percent of the cost of the supportive services but would never be required to pay more than 20 percent of their income for assistance. Funding for services will also come from the public housing agency and the federal government. The vouchers can be used to assist with the rent as well as services.

The thrust and intent of these programs are laudable in that they aim to meet the needs of the frail elderly while also fostering these elderly individuals' independence and rights of decision making regarding the use of services. Yet the effectiveness of the programs in reaching their goals remains dubious due to inadequate funding. In fact, in fiscal year 1991, HOPE received no appropriations. A further concern is that Section 202 housing is also being used to house the younger disabled and those with chronic mental illness. These populations are placed in competition with the frail elderly for the scarce accommodations. Moreover, the different needs of the groups for supportive services raise questions about the practicality of combined buildings.

## DEMONSTRATION PROJECTS

Supportive services in senior housing have also been provided under a national initiative (Supportive Services Program in Senior Housing) sponsored by the Robert Wood Johnson Foundation. The program has integrated housing and service programs in over 240 federally assisted housing developments since 1988. The goal of the program is to demonstrate that state housing financing associations can work with local housing developments and services to respond to the needs of elderly residents in subsidized senior housing (Callahan and Lansprey, 1991).

Services offered to the residents include housekeeping, transportation, shopping assistance, and meals. Most developments also offer routine health screening and assistance with Medicaid, Supplemental Security Insurance, Medicare, and food stamps. Most of the services are available to all residents regardless of income or impairment level. Residents are required to pay at least a portion of the cost of services, with the housing sponsors also contributing.

Both housing managers and residents appear satisfied with the program. By promoting tenant independence, resident turnover can be reduced. Concomitantly, the programs alleviate the stress placed on managers by the problems of the frailer resident. Moreover, having choices within a coordinated service system increases residents' sense of control over their lives and environment and promotes a feeling of independence.

The findings on the program also suggest that it represents a cost-effective means of meeting service needs and providing support to the elderly. By not attempting to target specific groups and by using co-payments, costs can be contained. Moreover, services can be designed to meet residents' needs and interests.

## Board and Care Homes

Board and care homes play an important role in the continuum of care for the frail elderly in the community. The homes, through the provision of services in a small facility, occupy an intermediate position between independent residences and nursing homes. In 1989 there were 41,000 licensed board and care homes in the United States and at least an equal number of unlicensed ones serving the elderly, a majority of whom are considered to be frail (U.S House Select Committee on Aging, 1989a).

Although the homes vary in size and type of ownership, they usually provide, in addition to rooms and meals, assistance with bathing, dressing, and the taking of medications. They tend not to provide the extensive medical services found in nursing homes. However, because many board and care facilities care for very frail elderly and also offer assistance with medications, distinguishing them from nursing homes can be difficult.

Homes are usually in urban areas, have an average of 23 beds, and are privately operated (U.S. General Accounting Office, 1989). The majority of residents are physically impaired, requiring "protective oversight," have limited incomes, and have frequently been hospitalized in a mental institution. They are also likely to be isolated with few relatives or friends.

Problems exist in the definition of board and care homes that are relevant to the establishment of policy and the collection of adequate data (McCoy and Conley, 1990). The distinction between board and care homes and other institutions for the elderly is not clear in that there is frequently overlap between the two with regard to community involvement of residents and protective 24-hour care. However, small board and care homes are more restrictive with residents than many nursing homes which encourage participation in community programs.

Critical to the definition of board and care is the home's responsibility for "protective oversight." This term connotes that the home is given some degree of control over the activities of those with ADL or IADL limitations. To date, this term has not been clearly defined and can thus be interpreted in many ways. As long as it remains ambiguous, establishing standards and quality assurance procedures for facilities will remain difficult.

The responsibility for licensure of homes is mainly at the state and local levels of government, and therefore there are vast variations in rules and regulations. Most states do not have any licensing regulations for home administrators, although they do license the facilities. Moreover, inspections tend to focus on the physical aspects of the facility rather than on the degree of assistance offered or the quality of life of the residents. Consequently, training and staff requirements have not been established.

The Keys Amendments, amendments to the Social Security Act enacted in 1976, require states to identify group homes in which the majority of residents receive Supplemental Security Income (SSI) and to ensure that appropriate standards of care are set. However, the effectiveness of the Keys Amendments has been seriously compromised in that they do not penalize substandard homes. Instead, the SSI payment to the resident is reduced. Many states have yet to establish standards, develop sanctions with regard to compliance, or to be involved in regular inspections. Furthermore, these requirements do not apply to unlicensed homes or those not serving SSI recipients.

Board and care homes can provide an important alternative to institutionalization for the frail elderly as they occupy an important place in the continuum of housing options. The small settings and the greater informality of the residence can address many of these older individuals' needs for support. Unfortunately, these homes have many shortcomings that need to be rectified in order for them to truly satisfy the requirements of this population.

As noted by the U.S. House Select Committee on Aging (1989a) the homes suffer from inadequate federal protection, no standard definition, no data to accurately identify homes, a need for training for staff and administrators, no uniform regulatory standards, and massive red tape for administrators trying to license facilities. Consequently, many residents, particularly the frail and most vulnerable, are at risk for abuse and neglect in substandard homes. Conversely, with only marginal profits, placing too many restrictions on the facilities may force them to discontinue operation (Ekert and Lyons, 1992).

## OTHER HOUSING OPTIONS

### Shared Housing

Shared housing programs are increasing across the United States and offer a potential means for the frail elderly to remain in their own homes. The programs involve sharing an existing house with at least one other in exchange for either rent or services or both. Shared housing can therefore be particularly important in meeting the needs of the frail home owner.

A study of home sharing participants in Wisconsin found that the functional status of the home provider offered the framework for understanding the type of assistance required and the kind and amount of resources to be exchanged (Jaffe and Howe, 1988). Healthy elderly home owners were interested in having someone in the house at night and to assist with some home maintenance in exchange for reduced rent. A second group of elderly were those with some functional limitations who needed assistance with basic household tasks such as cooking and shopping. These home owners were willing to offer free room and board in exchange for these services. The third group were those who were so physically or mentally frail that they required almost constant supervision. This group offered free room and board in exchange for this supervision and also a small stipend for services.

In a study of home sharing in one of the oldest programs, Operation Match in San Jose, California, the primary reasons for sharing given by both providers and seekers were financial need and companionship (Pynoos et al., 1990). Elderly providers were most likely to share because of a need for help or security rather than companionship. Meal preparation, housework, and laundry were the tasks commonly required by the home owner. Assistance with heavier chores was generally not given. Contrary to the findings discussed above, levels of dependency were not necessarily correlated with assistance and services were not necessarily rendered by the sharer.

Home sharing enables many elderly to exchange an important resource, the home, for needed services. The program can impact on both the instrumental and affective states of the older person. It can offer real assistance and support in the home while also strengthening the sense of control by the older person who has something of value which can be exchanged for services (Danigelis and Fengler, 1990). Home sharing can also reduce the demands for care placed on the family and on formal services.

There are varying types of home sharing programs. In its simplest form, an agency, often an office within the local department of aging, acts as an agent between the home owner and the would-be sharer, screening the two to determine compatibility. Once the arrangement between the two is made, the agency has no further role. In other programs, the agency continues in a case management role to assist with the relationship. This case management role is particularly important when the home owners seeking to share are very frail and dependent. In these instances, the home seeker is expected to provide needed assistance to the owner. These expectations and requirements may not always be clear and thus the intervention by a case manager is warranted.

In a study of the case management function in shared housing, Jaffe and Howe (1989) find that it is relatively unnecessary when the home owner is well and independent. For elderly in a more transitional state, who, due to chronic problems, require some assistance which the sharer is expected to provide, case management can play a meaningful role. In situations in which the home owner is dependent due to mental or physical impairments and the person sharing is expected to provide care, case management is most important and needs to play an active role in the relationship.

Shared housing programs continue to expand across the country. With correct management and agency involvement, the program can be a responsive option in meeting the needs of the frail elderly. By offering financial assistance as well as services, social interaction, and a renewed sense of self-worth, the program can enable many frail elderly to continue to live in their own homes.

## Echo Housing

Echo, or "elder cottage housing opportunity," began in the United States in the late 1970s but has had only limited popularity due to zoning restrictions and the cautious involvement of both government and potential consumers. Originally known as "granny flats," the program is modeled after one originating in Australia.

Echo housing consists of special units that are constructed, usually on the property of relatives, for the elderly. They offer the elderly independence but close proximity to those who can offer support and assistance. The units may also be built in clusters with many units in one small area of land.

Several benefits are associated with Echo housing that may make it very attractive to the elderly (Hare, 1991). The housing fosters independence by allowing the elderly easy access to support systems but not making them completely dependent on these systems. The housing cost is low, thus providing the elderly with a means of obtaining needed funds. By selling larger homes and moving into less expensive Echo housing, elderly home owners can realize considerable profits that can be used to meet living expenses.

At the same time there are many barriers to the development of this housing. Zoning restrictions, which require long waits for approval, can significantly deter many elderly who need to move quickly due to deteriorating environmental or health conditions. Furthermore, some localities prohibit multiple dwellings on any tract of land, although they may make amendments for individual cases in which the resident applies for a permit to care for an elderly parent (Hare, 1991).

Although this type of housing has yet to become widespread in this country, its success in Australia, New Zealand, and Britain (Lazarowich, 1991) suggests that it might be adaptable to the United States. Involving the government in the funding of the program, regulation of its development, and increasing publicity about its advantages are measures that may increase its popularity. For many elderly individuals and their families, Echo housing can be an important measure for maintaining independence.

## Foster Care

Adult foster care for the elderly is another measure that may assist the frail to remain in the community. Although foster care is usually assumed to be a program focused on children who cannot remain with their families, it also has a long tradition of being used with dependent adults. This history can be traced to the Elizabethan Poor Laws of 1603 (Sherman and Newman, 1988). Under these laws, the aged and the dependent poor were to be assured food, shelter, and care often by unrelated families who would be paid from public funds.

Presently, foster care programs for adults are offered by states and by the Veterans Administration. The first program for the elderly began in 1967 as a demonstration program funded by the Department of Health,

Education and Welfare in the state of Washington. It is currently provided by several states, each of which establishes its own eligibility criteria. However, the programs tend to serve those elderly who require only custodial care and not constant medical services (Oktay and Palley, 1988).

Foster homes differ from board and care homes in that they generally house no more than six elderly residents and frequently have only one resident. Moreover, unlike board and care homes, they provide supportive services and have close linkages with rehabilitation programs and social services. The foster care home is also a family setting with care provided by nonprofessionals. The thrust is to integrate the older person into the family as well as to provide links with community programs.

A foster care program for the frail elderly established by Johns Hopkins Hospital focused specifically on elderly individuals without any supports who due to their functional impairments would have been placed in a nursing home. The evaluation of the program showed that those in the foster care program had lower mortality rates than did a comparative group entering a nursing home and were more likely to remain independent in the community one year after hospital discharge (Volland, 1988). Additionally, the patient and caregivers frequently developed warm personal relationships, with the patient being perceived as a part of the family.

However, the success of such programs depends upon the careful recruitment of caregivers, close case management, respite care for caregivers, and good financial management. As viewed by Volland, the expansion of the program for the frail necessitates a coalition between health and social services with one principal agent responsible for assuring resources for recruitment and training of caregivers, matching patients and caregivers, and providing case management services.

Foster care programs offer another alternative in living arrangements for the frail elderly. But, as with other programs, they remain fragmented, being offered through varying systems with differing eligibility. They also suffer from a lack of resources. Funding of caregivers comes from the resident's resources, SSI benefits, VA pensions, and in some cases Medicaid. In order to be truly effective as a housing option for the frail, such programs need to be more highly coordinated, administered, and supported.

## SUMMARY

The overriding desire of most older persons, including the frail, is to remain in their own homes. However, the ability of these individuals to do so is often restricted due to few housing options or alternatives.

Programs, services, and even technological devices that can enable them to remain in their homes are often not available or accessible to those in need. Without adequate resources many elderly are forced to move to more restricted shelters or even nursing homes in order to receive needed support and assistance. As this chapter has discussed, alternatives are available that can promote independence, but the elderly often cannot afford these alternatives.

The government is well aware of the needs of the frail in the community and is even cognizant of the impact that support services can have on helping the elderly stay out of institutions. However, although sensitive policies and programs have been established, their effectiveness is diminished by inadequate funding and by programs that place the frail elderly in competition with the younger disabled and the chronically mentally ill. These populations do not share the same service requirements, and thus the focus should be on creating more housing appropriate to the needs of each.

As discussed, there are many types of housing programs in existence that can provide a continuum of options for independent living. Standards and regulations for many of these programs are needed, but at the same time efforts should be made to encourage program growth. As the frail elderly continue to have diverse backgrounds and needs, diversity in housing options is also necessary. Perhaps most fundamental to the housing needs of the frail are programs and services that can help them to remain as long as possible, with dignity, in their own homes. In the long run, such programs can be far more cost-effective than building more housing or moving individuals to more sheltered environments.

*Chapter Six*

# Families and the Frail Elderly

The frail elderly, by virtue of their impairments, are dependent upon others for assistance. This assistance comes primarily from informal sources, such as family and friends, whose interventions are frequently the critical factors in preventing institutionalization. In discussing the extensive help offered by these caregivers, it is helpful to begin with an examination of some of the motives and theories that attempt to explain the nature of family support.

## MOTIVES FOR CAREGIVING

Reciprocity is often given as a motive for helping. According to the norm of reciprocity, people feel obligated to assist those who have cared for them at various points in their lives. To not reciprocate such care is to recant on a normative responsibility. As such, reciprocity provides a basis for social relationships in that each person in the dyad is expected to both give and receive assistance. The spouse and children are the ones most likely to be bound by these norms, but other relatives and even close friends may also perceive caregiving as a means of repaying a long-standing debt to the frail individual.

Family and friends are also motivated to aid the frail due to feelings of commitment and ties of affection. These sentiments appear to underlie many of the helping relationships and to remain strong without regard to distance or social class (Litwak, 1985). In fact, there is some evidence that it is the affection transmitted through the relationship which may be most important to the well-being of the frail older person (Antonnucci and Depner, 1982). The support provided by family and friends can reinforce the frail elderly's sense of self-esteem and involvement in society. These sentiments can diminish the perceived impact of the specific impairment.

However, the demands engendered in the caregiving relationship can also have negative effects on both the caregiver and the receiver. A failure to respond to the needs of the frail individual can result in feelings of guilt in many family members. Often, these feelings and the need to compensate for them may influence the caregiver's involvement. In many instances, regardless of the amount of assistance the caregiver is offering, the guilt remains, particularly since there is often no improvement in the condition of the frail relative.

According to Brody (1985) the persistent myth underlying this sense of guilt is that one should be doing more to meet the dependency needs in order to fully reciprocate for earlier care. The inability to alleviate the needs of the frail relative places the caregiver at particular risk, since in most instances no effort will reduce the impairment or increase the functioning capacity of the elderly.

Specific cultural norms can greatly influence the caring relationship. Values associated with filial piety, which demands respect for the elders and holds the family responsible for the care of elderly relatives, remain strong among many ethnic groups. Relatives who do not adhere to such behaviors are in danger or being treated as deviants within their immediate cultural groups. Moreover, to the extent that they themselves maintain these traditional values, they are susceptible to feeling guilty for not completely fulfilling them.

These normative behaviors are frequently reinforced by the frail elderly who continue to both expect and demand assistance from their children and other relatives (Cox and Gelfand, 1987). For these families, using any type of formal service may be interpreted as failing to fulfill one's responsibility. Consequently, in attempting to understand caregiving act-ivities, it is essential to examine the ethnic characteristics of the elderly and their caregivers.


## THEORETICAL PERSPECTIVES

Social exchange theory and continuity theory offer useful frameworks for examining the family's involvement in caring for the frail elderly. These theories provide a context in which the relationships can be under-stood and thus offer a basis for more effective interventions.

## Social Exchange Theory and Caregiving

Exchange theory views all social interaction as an exchange between two actors in which each seeks to maximize rewards and minimize costs (Dowd, 1980). Individuals will continue in the exchange only as long as it is perceived as more rewarding than costly.

The theory views the elderly as having diminished resources in relationships in that they possess little which is valuable to others. To the extent that they are unable to develop their resources, they are at risk of withdrawing from interactions as a means of protecting themselves from dependence. As discussed by Lee (1985) this lack of power in the exchange may account for findings which suggest that the elderly receive more gratification in their relationships with their friends than with their relatives. The former are more likely to be based on mutual interests and rewards while the latter may be more influenced by duty and obligation, which intensify the feelings of dependency. Elderly individuals who are unable to reciprocate in relationships with their children are likely to have a devalued sense of well-being and lower morale than elderly individuals who are able to reciprocate (Stoller, 1985).

However, the complexity of the caregiving relationship is underscored by contrasting findings which imply that receiving assistance from adult children can also be associated with increased morale. In a study of elderly widows, Mutran and Reitzes (1984) found that those who received more assistance than they gave had higher morale than those who gave more assistance. The receipt of assistance was perceived as the reward and thus made the exchange gratifying.

Other research suggests that giving more in the relationship is not necessarily essential for well-being in the exchange as noted in a study of elderly mothers and their adult daughters (Talbott, 1990). The mothers offered services such as financial assistance as a means of feeling less dependent and reducing the power imbalance in the relationship. But offering services did not necessarily restructure the balance, and these women continued to feel devalued. In fact, many of the mothers complained that the children did not offer sufficient help and that they continued to feel that they were a burden to their children.

It is conceivable that the caregiving relationship, while providing for the physical needs of the frail individual, may be deleterious to self-esteem and well-being. However, such negative effects do not always result. Research has shown no relationship between receiving assistance and morale (Arling, 1976; Lee and Ellithorpe, 1982). McCulloch (1990) speculates that this lack of relationship may be due to the fact that these older persons have additional systems or exchange dimensions that are not being measured and are based on previous exchanges. Thus, in most cases, well-being is sustained even when the older person is dependent and is the recipient of assistance.

The conflicting results of these studies are important in that they underscore the complexity involved in attempting to understand the caregiving relationship and its effects on the frail older person. In some instances the effects may be deleterious to well-being as they increase the sense of dependency, while in others they may reaffirm social ties and relationships. Consequently, the uniqueness of the relationship, the characteristics of both the caregiver and the older person receiving assistance, and their own personal histories must be considered when interpreting the effects on the well-being of the frail individual.

## Continuity Theory and Caregiving

From the perspective of continuity theory, dependency in a relationship can be particularly demoralizing to the individual who previously was used to being the authority and in control. Having to accept a new dependent role is tangible evidence that the accustomed ways of behaving are no longer possible, making role continuity difficult to maintain. Accordingly, the most deleterious effects on morale may occur in those for whom dependency poses the sharpest contrast to previous roles and thus the most discontinuity.

At the same time, as continuity assumes that individuals seek to maintain valued roles to which they are accustomed and which they find rewarding, it may be anticipated that any discontinuity may be just as problematic for the caregiver. Thus, the spouse or adult child accustomed to being dependent on the now-frail older individual may find it difficult to accept the new role of caregiver. This altered dyadic relationship will require a major shift in behaviors as traditional roles are no longer appropriate. On the other hand, to the extent that the caregiving role is a continuation of earlier patterns of interaction in that the frail individual was always dependent, both spousal and child caregivers should have an easier time of accommodating the demands associated with the impairments.

## MODELS OF CAREGIVING

Models are used to describe relationships between variables and their outcomes. With regard to the caregiving situation, these models suggest which factors may affect the well-being of both the caregiver and the care receiver. In general, these models have concentrated on the factors contributing to burden among the caregivers. The stress of caregiving, the outcome measure, is viewed as resulting from competing roles, the caregiver's perceptions of the stressors, and caregiver resources in dealing with patient behaviors. Models of the caregiving relationship which seek to explain both the positive and negative interactions as well as the effects on the care recipient are those offered by Young and Kahana (1989) and Roberts and Bengston (1990).

The model of caregiving presented by Young and Kahana views several patient and caregiver variables as influencing the outcome of the caregiving relationship. Attitudinal, behavioral, sociodemographic, and health characteristics of both the caregiver and the patient, as well as the extent of care and the home environment, contribute to the well-being of both. Thus gender, relationship, and living situation are important factors to consider when attempting to understand the outcome of a caregiving situation.

In a test of this model among a sample of elderly heart patients discharged from a hospital, gender and the relationship of the caregiver to the patient were significantly related to caregiver strain (Young and Kahana, 1989). A particularly important finding was that gender and relationship of the caregiver need to be analyzed independently in that wives and daughters experience varying reactions to the caregiver role. Furthermore, husbands and wives as caregivers also differ from each other in their reactions as well as differing from their daughters.

Roberts and Bengston's (1990) model of intergenerational family relations identifies familial norms regarding closeness, affection, intergenerational contacts, and the exchange of resources as being a basis for interactions and assistance to the frail relative. Within this framework, a balanced exchange of resources contributes to positive feelings and affection as well as the provision of more assistance.

In an empirical test of the model, helping behavior by adult children was a predictor of their affection and of their ties with their parents. Such behavior is based upon the adult child's endorsement of norms of filial responsibility, the dependency needs of the older individual, and the proximity of the child to the parent. Consequently, the stronger the feelings of affection and the more the child feels responsible to the parent and is able to offer help, the greater should be the involvement. On the other hand, the theory also suggests that children who are not in a position to act on their feelings, such as those separated by distance, may be particularly susceptible to stress.

## WHO PROVIDES THE CARE?

Families continue to accept the caregiving responsibility and respond to it with little assistance from formal agencies. Data from the National Long Term Care Survey (Stone and Kemper, 1990) reveal that spouses and children compose almost three-quarters of the primary caregivers to disabled adults. In addition, it is estimated that 7 percent of the U.S. population has a disabled elderly spouse or parent with the potential for caregiving responsibility most prevalent between the ages 45 and 54. The majority of these caregivers, 2.6 million, have primary responsibility for the older person, while another 1.6 million act as secondary caregivers. Spouses are more likely to be primary caregivers than are children, and among adult children, daughters outnumber sons by more than three to one. It is important to note that these figures do not include those providing assistance to the frail with cognitive impairments.

One-third of the caregivers of the frail are themselves over 65. As might be anticipated, husbands are the oldest group, and half of these male caregivers receive no informal or formal assistance in their caregiving tasks. Twenty percent of caregivers have children at home, and almost half of the adult daughters providing care are employed full time. With the needs that these families and their frail relatives are likely to have, it is startling to note that less than 10 percent receive assistance from any formal services.

The important role that these caregivers play in assisting the frail to remain in the community is highlighted by the fact that in their absence, the elderly are most vulnerable to nursing home placement. The functional disability of many nursing home residents is comparable to that of the frail elderly in the community. The main factor distinguishing the two groups is the absence or inability of the family to provide the needed care (National Center for Health Statistics, 1989).

In the hierarchical pattern of informal care, the frail elderly turn first to spouses, then to adult children, other relatives, friends, and, if necessary, neighbors for assistance. However, studies of caregiving also indicate that the primary responsibility for caregiving usually falls on one person (Fengler and Goodrich, 1979; Cox and Monk, 1990a). The others, or "secondary caregivers," provide supplementary or additional assistance. Having this network of potential caregivers assumes that the large reservoir of helpers will mean less demands on each as the amount of assistance can be more evenly distributed (Dowd, 1975).

The dependency needs of the frail, whether spouse or parent, alter established relationships and interactions, necessitating new patterns of behavior. Fundamental to this process is the acceptance by both the older person and the caregiver of the impairment and its ensuing limitations. Moreover, in order to maintain the highest level of functioning of the elderly, it is essential that these needs for support and assistance not diminish their sense of self-esteem.

## Spousal Caregivers

When available, the primary caregiver for a frail older person will be the spouse, with wives constituting 23 percent and husbands 13 percent of all caregivers (Stone et al., 1987). This group is likely to be older than other caregivers and to report poorer health. Frequently, they themselves suffer from chronic illnesses and could in fact be defined as frail. Although the needs of this group of caregivers may warrant the interventions of others to assist them, they actually receive less assistance from family and friends and from formal services than others providing care (George and Gwyther, 1986; Tennstedt et al., 1989). Thus, it is not surprising that they report higher levels of physical, emotional, and financial strain than do adult child caregivers (Cantor, 1983; Noelker and Wallace, 1985).

Spouses care for the frailest elderly, and as they share the same household, they provide extensive levels of assistance (Montgomery and Borgatta, 1989). Moreover, they are likely to have gradually been increasing the amount of assistance they provide and to have been providing some help for long periods of time. As the frail individual's needs evolve, it is the spouse who is most readily available to attend to them. In fact, it is not uncommon for these needs to be hidden from other members of the family as the couple continue to assert their independence. The help provided by other family members is generally supplemental to the basic care provided by the spouse (Johnson, 1983). Furthermore, spouses are the least likely of any group of caregivers to use formal services, regardless of the degree of frailty.

Obviously, the degree to which the spouse will be committed to the caregiving role will vary. One factor that appears to be essential are the affectionate bonds between the couple. The spousal caregiver who perceives such assistance as "reciprocity" for past affection and care will experience a higher degree of gratification from caregiving than the spouse who bases it only on responsibility (Motenko, 1989).

Gender also affects the nature of the caregiving role among husbands and wives. Higher levels of burden, depression, and negative feelings towards the spouse have been recorded more among wives than husbands (Zarit et al., 1980; Fitting et al., 1986). These findings have been attrib-

uted to the relatively younger ages of wives and the restrictions that
caregiving places on their activities. The burden experienced by wives has
also been associated with their poorer health, less emotional investment,
the greater spousal impairment of husbands, and the need for more hours
of assistance that husbands appear to require (Pruchno and Resch, 1989).

Behavioral problems are perhaps the most difficult for caregivers to
manage and the most significant predictors of burden for both husbands
and wives. Barush and Spaid (1989) attribute the increased strain that
wives encounter as resulting from the constant supervision and assistance
that these behaviors require. As wives are generally younger than husbands
and more involved in informal social networks, these caregiving demands
may be particularly stressful.

The negative reactions of wives to the caregiving role are seemingly
incongruent with the theoretical assumptions of continuity theory. Most
of these older women are a part of the cohort in which caregiving was an
expected and normative female activity. Therefore, providing care to a frail
husband might be perceived as role continuity.

The fact that women find this continuity stressful may be partially
explained by role reversal, a phenomenon believed to often occur in later
life. Accordingly, older men are perceived as becoming more nurturant
and affiliative, while older women become more egocentric and assertive
(Neugarten and Gutman, 1968). From this perspective, women would
have more difficulty accepting the role of caregiver at a time when they
are seeking to expand their own lives and develop other identities. Conversely, the caregiving role may afford husbands the opportunity to
express affection and repay wives for years of nurturing.


## Adult Children

Adult children provide the majority of assistance to the frail elderly. In
most instances this is provided by a daughter or daughter-in-law who often
combines this care with responsibilities to her own family. But, although
women dominate in the caregiving role, sons are not entirely absent.

The involvement of sons, however, is limited, and mainly occurs when
there is no female sibling to provide assistance. In general, their support
tends to be less extensive than the support provided by daughters (Horowitz, 1985). Men more frequently provide occasional household help,
transportation, and assistance with finances, while women are involved
with the daily household chores, personal care, meal preparation, shopping, and errands (Montgomery and Kamo, 1987; Stoller, 1990).

Daughters are more likely than sons to live with frail mothers and to act as their primary caregivers. A striking comparison between sons and daughters as sources of assistance is found in the fact that the availability of sons increases the likelihood of the older person's using formal services but does not increase the likelihood of having informal help. Conversely, the availability of even one daughter increases the likelihood of informal assistance and decreases the likelihood of the use of formal services (Soldo et al., 1990).

Although the major responsibility for caring for the frail elderly is assumed by adult daughters and daughters-in-law, assuming this responsibility is not without some stress. At the time of life when women begin providing this care they are frequently meeting caregiving responsibilities in their own families or are anticipating a period of growth as their caregiving comes to an end. Instead, their own desires are frequently overshadowed by the dependency needs of parents or parents-in-law.

That women continue to accept the caregiving role has been attributed to feelings of reciprocity for past caregiving, affection, norms, and values. Whether wives or daughters, they have been socialized to be expressive, nurturing, and responsive to the needs of others, defining themselves according to relationships (Chodorow, 1978). These characteristic feminine traits make it difficult for women to ignore the needs of frail and dependent parents. Concomitantly, as they have been raised to feel responsible for and sensitive to the well-being of others, it is not unusual that they should be stressed and guilty when their increasing efforts fail to compensate for the often deteriorating conditions of the frail relative. These factors may substantially contribute to the greater sense of strain that they experience as caregivers.

## Primary and Secondary Caregivers

Research studies have continued to examine the roles and tasks performed by the primary and secondary caregivers. Although the primary caregivers offer the majority of assistance, secondary caregivers are critical for the provision of additional help. Thirty percent of the caregivers providing help to the frail elderly are classified as secondary caregivers with, sons more likely than daughters to be in this role (Stone et al., 1987). In fact, it is in this secondary role that men are most likely to be found (Tennstedt et al., 1989).

In many instances these secondary caregivers are the children or spouses of the primary caregiver who offer more intermittent help such as shopping, transportation, and home repairs. However, these activities do not significantly alter the extensiveness of total assistance and likewise do not appear to reduce the likelihood of using formal services.

In examining the role played by secondary caregivers, it is important to consider its qualitative as well as quantitative aspects. The reactions of both the primary caregiver and the frail older person to the assistance offered by the secondary caregiver can help to describe the extent to which it meets support needs. If both the primary caregiver and the frail recipient are satisfied with the help, the relationships should be rewarding and supportive. On the other hand, if the assistance that the secondary caregiver provides is viewed as only minimal or as offered with resentment, it may be deleterious to the relationships.

Research also shows that among siblings tension can develop when the principal caregiver feels that the others are not doing enough, especially as the need for care increases (Brody et al., 1989). Unfortunately, such tensions are not uncommon and may also be partially accounted for by the commitment that the primary caregiver has to the role. The more involved the caregiver is in the role, even if stressed and needing assistance, the more difficult it may be to relinquish or share the responsibilities even temporarily.

A further point with regard to the role of the secondary caregiver is the extent to which this individual is available to assume caregiving responsibilities in the event that the primary caregiver is unable to continue. Studies suggest that although this person may be involved in assisting with routine tasks, he or she may not be available to assume the primary caregiving role (Cox and Monk, 1990a). This can place additional pressure on the primary caregiver in that he or she is aware of the limitations of other helpers.

## EMPLOYMENT AND CAREGIVING

The stress of caring for a frail relative is often compounded when the caregiver is employed. In the last few decades the percentage of women in the labor force has dramatically increased from 11 percent in 1940 to 56 percent in 1980 with 62 percent of the women between the ages of 45 and 65 employed (U.S. Department of Labor, 1986).

The extent to which such employment affects caregivers is apparent in the results of a survey conducted by the AARP. Findings reveal that 55 percent of the women caring for frail relatives were simultaneously employed outside of the home (American Association of Retired Persons and The Travelers Foundation, 1989). These caregivers spent approximately ten hours per week on caregiving tasks with more than one quarter, 27 percent, spending 21 or more hours per week caring for a frail relative.

The effects of attempting to combine caregiving and employment can be deleterious to both the employee and the employer. A survey of employees at 33 companies in Portland, Oregon (Neal et al., 1987), showed those with elder-care responsibilities likely to be stressed with regard to health, finances, relationships, and work. Emotional and physical strain can be the outcomes of efforts to fulfill both demanding roles. The juggling of both roles also results in lost time from work due to both absences and lateness associated with caregiving tasks. Having to take time off to provide home care, take the relative to the physician, or deal with a specific crisis are frequent occurrences. In a study made by Transamerica Life Companies (Scharlach and Boyd, 1989) it was found that one-and-a-half times as many caregivers as individuals who were not caregivers reported missing work or having to take time off due to family responsibilities. Moreover, employees frequently reduce the number of hours that they work or forego overtime due to their caregiving responsibilities (U.S. House Select Committee on Aging, 1990d).

The impact of caregiving responsibilities and the precedence that it may assume in women's lives is underscored by the fact that many caregivers actually give up employment in order to provide care. Surveys have found that between 12 and 15 percent of female caregivers stop work in order to care for their frail relative (Brody et al., 1987; American Association of Retired Persons and The Travelers Foundation, 1989). Consequently, caregiving can seriously affect the economic well-being and solvency of these women.

These findings suggest that women continue to be committed to the care of the frail but that this sense of responsibility may have to be balanced with other demands and responsibilities. In their efforts to fulfill dual sets of expectations, they risk jeopardizing their own mental, physical, and financial well-being.

## SUPPORT NEEDS OF THE CAREGIVER

Because caregiving can be an unrelenting task, caregivers are themselves in need of emotional and social support. Such support provides a buffer from the strains they may encounter. In fact, there is evidence to indicate that support may assist caregivers to continue longer in the caregiving role and actually delay nursing home placement (Morycz, 1985).

The support needs of caregivers cannot be restricted to just direct interventions through instrumental assistance. Knowing that individuals are available who will listen to worries and concerns and understand the problems that they face provides caregivers with needed reassurance. Having these types of bonds may protect caregivers from the associated burdens of their roles, while a lack of such relationships has been found to be associated with depression (Cox, 1992b). Supportive relationships also serve to reinforce caregiver self-image and the belief that the stressful situation is manageable (Clipp and George, 1990). Unfortunately, caregivers often feel that others do not truly understand their concerns or problems.

Professionals, particularly those in the health care professions and the clergy, can also be important sources of support for caregivers. However, this requires that these professionals be sensitive to the specific needs of caregivers. Often, in fact, caregivers are reticent to discuss their problems because they feel ashamed of them and fear that acknowledging these problems could suggest a lack of responsibility or caring. In order for these professionals to be most helpful, they must be aware of the problems and needs of these individuals as well as resources that can assist them.

## Caregiver Support Groups

The last decade has seen a rapid increase in the development of caregiver support groups aimed at helping caregivers to cope with the stresses associated with their roles through the sharing of both emotional support and information. These groups provide settings in which caregivers can discuss their concerns and problems with others in the same situation. Simultaneously, members can learn new ways of coping from each other. The groups are an important means for counteracting the isolation which caregivers frequently experience. In fact, many groups encourage members to exchange telephone numbers and to meet outside of the group, often sharing caregiving tasks.

Many support groups focus on specific medical problems or illnesses such as strokes, heart attacks, or dementia. The advantage of this is that the caregivers are better able to identify with the problems faced by the group members and thus assist each other with coping. Being able to ventilate frustrations with those dealing with similar illnesses can assist in creating a sense of solidarity that is fundamental to meeting support needs.

Evidence indicating the significant role that support groups can play with regard to the care of the frail elderly is shown by the fact that participation in such groups can deter the use of nursing homes. Greene and Monahan (1987) found that family caregivers participating in support and education groups had significantly lower rates of placement in nursing homes of their frail relatives than comparable caregivers not participating in such groups. The groups permitted participants to deal with negative feelings, overcome their sense of emotional isolation, and share difficult experiences. At the same time, successful problem-solving techniques were also discussed. Each meeting involved education; particular skills such as moving, bathing, and lifting were taught. Finally, the sessions also included relaxation training, which showed caregivers how to use many stress-reducing techniques.

However, in a thorough review of family support groups Toseland et al. (1989) find that their outcomes may actually be more limited. Many studies have not really measured the effectiveness of such groups in reducing caregivers' sense of burden and level of stress. Although most participants evaluate the group experience positively, reporting such gains as new insight and the development of a sense of community, there is no link between such programs and the development of new coping skills or the alleviation of psychological problems. Most of the outcome measures rely on member satisfaction as a criterion. On the other hand, satisfaction is not necessarily an invalid measure of effectiveness.

Perhaps a key limitation to the effectiveness of such groups is that family members often do not attend them until the stress is already quite severe. In fact, the very families who may benefit the most from such programs are also the most difficult to reach. Caregiving responsibilities that contribute to the need for support may also act as barriers to participation.

In reality, support groups should not be viewed as a universal answer for caregivers. In some instances, caregivers whose relatives are not as impaired as those of other members can find the sharing of experiences frightening and depressing as they begin to consider what the future holds. Unless groups are composed of those caring for relatives in the same stages of an illness, they may provoke further stress in those seeking assistance.

## THE INFORMAL AND THE FORMAL NETWORKS

Although informal support provided by relatives is the usual pattern of care, relying solely on such help is not always in the best interests of either the elderly frail individual or the caregiver. Needs of the frail elderly are not stable, and with increased impairment they may require more assistance than the informal caregiver can provide. At the same time, these increased demands can place greater levels of stress on the caregiving system. In order for the informal system to operate effectively, it must be flexible—that is, it must be able to expand and contract as needed (Sauer and Coward, 1985). Without this ability, it is fragile and vulnerable to collapse.

From this perspective, caregivers must be open and receptive to varying forms of interventions in order to adequately function in meeting the needs of the frail. Caregivers should therefore be both willing and able to use formal services. These services may be classified as competitive in relation to the family in that they may discourage family involvement, complementary in that they seek to augment the family supports, or substitutive in that they replace family assistance (Nelson, 1980).

Although policy makers fear that formal services will substitute for the care provided by the family and the informal system, there is little evidence to substantiate that this actually occurs. Instead, caregivers appear to use the assistance as additional to that which they routinely supply. Even employed women with home care attendants for their frail relatives have been found to remain responsible for the majority of care and its monitoring, delegating specific tasks to the formal providers (Archbold, 1982).

Findings also suggest that there is a strong correlation between the use of formal and informal help. In a study of the relationship of informal to formal supports, the proportion of the frail receiving formal assistance decreased with decreases in informal help, indicating that without these necessary supports, individuals are likely to do without any help (Penning, 1990).

Other research (Edelman, 1986) further documents the supplementary rather than substitutive role of the formal services. Caregivers commonly only turn to agencies for assistance with bathing, lifting, and transferring the frail individual. Help with these routine tasks does not require any specific skills but can be crucial to maintaining the frail elderly in the community. Until help is needed in these specific areas, caregivers tend to not use the formal system.

Litwak (1985) stresses the complementary nature of the formal–informal relationships in that the informal is best suited for the unpredictable, nontechnical tasks associated with care, while the formal system can better deal with the specialized tasks. Accordingly, caregivers are unable to substitute for each other. Thus, the informal system is best able to provide emotional support or assistance during a crisis, while the formal system may be best able to cope with the highly skilled or arduous aspects of caregiving.

Evidence that formal services may play both a supplementary and complementary role, depending on the characteristics of the caregiver, is presented by Noelker and Bass (1989). Formal services to supplement assistance are likely to be the reason for use by female caregivers, while males and those caring for the very impaired are more likely to use formal services for specialized care. Furthermore, caregiver needs, rather than the needs of the relative, appear to be the main determinants of service use for all caregivers. Thus, caregivers who are themselves frail or have had changes in their own health are more likely to use formal services regardless of the condition of the frail relative.

Caregivers apparently do not turn to formal services until they are no longer able to meet the caregiving demands. It is thus not surprising that both their physical and mental health may suffer and actually deteriorate as a result of the caregiving tasks. Rather than using interventions as preventive and support measures, they are used as remedial ones when the primary caregiver finds coping difficult. Even in these instances, such services do not appear to substitute for informal care.

## IMPAIRMENT AND CAREGIVING

It remains debatable whether the type of disability, physical or cognitive, has a greater impact on the caregiver than other relevant factors. Indeed, there is evidence to suggest that it is not the type of impairment alone but the care demands, the characteristics of the older person and the caregiver, the relationship of the frail individual to the caregiver, the types of supports available, and relationships with other family members that most influence the effects of providing care on the caregiver.

Among the many factors that have been isolated as impacting on the status of the caregiver are time demands associated with the functioning of the relative, the prognosis for care, the duration of caregiving, caregiving expectations, and the patient's response to care (Sillman and Strasberg, 1988). Family conflicts and relationships, as discussed earlier, may also be a source of stress. In a study of daughters and daughters-in-law caring for both physically and cognitively impaired parents, family relationships, rather than the nature of the elder's impairment, were the primary sources of strain for the caregivers (Cattanach and Tebes, 1991).

Caregivers have many problems that need to be met but that often are not addressed or even clearly understood by caregivers themselves. Information on the illness, proper procedures for care, legal information, psychological problems, and health problems are typical of these concerns. In a study of female caregivers of frail elderly parents and parents-in-law, Smith et al. (1991) identified seven major categories of pressing problems that these individuals brought to counseling sessions: improving coping skills; family issues; responding to elder's care needs;

quality of relationship with elder; eliciting formal and informal support; guilt and feelings of inadequacy; and long-term planning. The broad scope of these issues underscores the many areas in which interventions are needed.

Problems associated with "family issues" warrant particular attention. In describing this problem, the issue was not the frail older person but relationships with siblings. Caregivers cited feeling "angry, abandoned, unappreciated, and abused" by their siblings who were not providing sufficient assistance (Smith et al., p.19). These sentiments further highlight the importance of relationships and how conflicts and disappointments in these relationships can undermine caregiver well-being.

## Caring for the Physically Frail

Caregiving is a dyadic relationship, and therefore the more that the care recipient is able to participate or acknowledge the assistance, the more rewarding the relationship should be to the giver. Accordingly, providing care to a physically frail individual should be less stressful than to one who is cognitively frail in that the former will be able to respond to the assistance and even cooperate with the caregiver.

Many factors affect the ability of the family to care for the physically frail older person. These includes the size and composition (relatives and friends) of the social network, the dynamics and strengths in the relationships, the values and attitudes of those in the networks, and the capacity of those in the social network to actually provide assistance (Kaufman, 1990). However, as in all aspects of caregiving, many unique and undefined variables can be influential in determining the nature of the caring relationship.

One of the leading causes of disability in the elderly is stroke. The incidence of stroke ranges from 600,000 to 750,000 annually with approximately 50 percent of these patients discharged home, the majority to be cared for by a relative. Often faced with chronic speech and physical disabilities, the family remains the main source of support for these individuals and is critical in the rehabilitative process.

In a study of the recovery process of stroke victims, Norris et al. (1990) found that the family could be a source of both support and problems to the frail older person. Patients who felt they had problems with the assistance that their families provided actually showed a decline in their physical functioning after hospital discharge. Those who had more problems communicating with family members had poorer personal adjustment. The results suggest that the greater the dependency in the physical functioning the more problems patients are likely to have in receiving appropriate support from the families.

In some instances, families offer too little assistance, while in others they intervene too extensively. Finally, supportive interactions with friends appear to help in the recovery process, while problematic interactions with families may delay it. These findings further document the critical role played by supportive others in the rehabilitation process and in the functioning of the frail elderly.

Hip fracture is another leading cause of frailty among the aged. It can lead to complete dysfunction if not correctly diagnosed and treated. Patients discharged from hospital after surgery for the fracture typically require assistance with personal care, meal preparation, and housekeeping, as well as medical assistance and emotional support. Relatives play major roles in meeting these needs. A study of the support offered by families found that extended family members tended to meet the emotional needs of the patient while the immediate family met the personal and domestic needs (Kashner et al., 1990). The coordination of these support systems can be essential in the development of the discharge plan.

Osteoporosis, as discussed earlier, is a major contributor to frailty in the elderly, affecting primarily elderly women. As women are also the traditional caregivers, the effects of their disability can have further ramifications for the family. In fact, it might be anticipated that the caregivers to these women, particularly if the spouse, would use more formal services since they are less likely to have had experience in caregiving. However, these frail patients use few community services, depending most upon their families for support (Roberto, 1988).

In her study of older women afflicted with osteoporosis, Roberto found that the majority felt their husbands were most supportive when they took over household tasks and provided emotional support. Children were also perceived as supportive, although the frequency of actual help depended on the number of problems that the women had. In most instances the women claimed that they were satisfied with the support they received from their families.

Finally, in examining the role played by the family in providing care for the frail elderly, it must be recognized that needs for care fluctuate and gradually increase over time. As the demands for assistance become more taxing, they may surpass the emotional, physical, or financial resources of the family. Gonyea (1987) found that caregiver resources became ultimately strained when the caregivers had to provide personal care assistance. Such intimate care may violate established familial norms while also being more difficult to predict and schedule. Thus, even with the best intentions, family caregivers may reach a point when the demands of care exhaust their resources.

## Caring for the Cognitively Frail

Providing care to a cognitively impaired patient can be more demanding than providing care to a physically impaired relative. Although the cognitively impaired may not require direct physical interventions, they typically need constant supervision and direction, which is often more time consuming and mentally exhausting than providing physical assistance. At the same time, the prognosis for these individuals is usually poor, as both mental and physical deterioration are expected. Adding to the stress created by the nature of the impairment is the fact that the cognitively impaired are frequently nonresponsive to assistance or actually resist it. In some instances they may even accuse the caregiver of intentional harm.

Studies on the effects of providing care to a dementia patient continue to document its overwhelming nature—that is, its effects on the mental, social, and physical aspects of the caregiver's life. Chronic fatigue, anger, depression, and mental problems have all been associated with the caregiving role (Rabins et al., 1982; George and Gwyther, 1986). Frustration and isolation along with changes in physical health, increases in stress-related medical conditions, and financial strains are frequently observed (Chenoweth and Spencer, 1986; Aronson and Gaston, 1986; Motenko, 1989). In fact, it is the factors associated with the needs of the caregiver, rather than those of the patient or the degree of impairment, which may be most important in the decision to institutionalize the patient.

All aspects of the dementia patient's impairment do not contribute equally to stress in the caregiver. The greatest problems are related to difficulties in coping with behavioral changes. Agitation, embarrassing acts, wandering, and dangerous behaviors are unpredictable, require consistent attention, and are difficult to manage (Haley, Brown, and Levine, 1987). Disruptive acts are particularly stressful in that they demand constant supervision while also affecting other family relationships (Poulshock and Diemling, 1984; Diemling and Bass, 1986). Although frustrating, coping with memory loss and confusion is more predictable and generally easier for caregivers to manage.

In spite of their needs for assistance, family caretakers of dementia patients use fewer outside supports than those caring for the physically frail elderly (Birkel and Jones, 1989). Possible explanations for this underutilization include a lack of reimbursement for services such as home care under Medicare and most private insurance programs, the difficulties involved in providing care, resistance by the frail relative, and the unavailability of trained help. However, participation in support groups has been found to significantly increase the use of other supports (Gonyea and Silverstein, 1991). For these caregivers, these groups can be important links to the service system. In fact, the decision to use the groups, may reflect the need for more formal services.

## ELDER ABUSE

Unfortunately, not all family caregivers of the frail provide caring and humane assistance. The issue of elder abuse by family members first achieved national attention in 1981 with the publication of a congressional report documenting the occurrence of physical, financial, and emotional abuse of over 1,000,000 elderly by their families annually. The report recommended that states enact statutes designating agencies to identify and assist victims. A subsequent congressional meeting on elder abuse in 1990 revealed that in spite of the new statutes it continued to be a major problem with estimates of abused elderly reaching 1.5 million annually (U.S. House Select Committee on Aging, 1990b). Contributing to this increase in the problem is a lack of meaningful state or federal programs, inadequate funding, and the growth of the elderly population.

There appear to be a multitude of causes for elder abuse, but a major underlying factor is family stress resulting from attempts to meet the continual demands of the frail and dependent elderly. Many reasons have been given which attempt to explain the phenomenon. It has been attributed to retaliation for the way the parent had treated the child, the acceptance of violence in this society, unresolved conflicts in the relationship, a lack of close bonds in the family, financial demands which exacerbate the stress of caregiving, resentment of the dependency of the frail adult which increases the caregiver's anger and frustration, unemployment, psychological problems, a history of alcohol and drug abuse, and poor environmental conditions which precipitate stress.

But even with these profiles describing those caregivers most vulnerable to being abusers, there are many others who do not fit any of these categories. In a study of 104 adult children and their families, all of whom appeared to be model caregivers, 23 percent were found to engage in potentially very harmful acts to the elders (Steinmetz, 1988). In addition, these children frequently committed varying degrees of psychological, verbal, and physical abuse. Because of the many variables that can influence abuse, it remains difficult to accurately identify or predict those at risk.

Descriptions of the victims identify them as being primarily women, dependent, in conflict with the adult child, self-deprecating, isolated, and often provoking (U.S. House Select Committee on Aging, 1990b). In addition, similar to many of the adult children, the victims are frequently problem drinkers.

Elder abuse, rather than being a problem which is viewed as diminishing, continues to be widespread. A lack of funding of federal and state programs, a lack of reporting of suspected cases, difficulties in identifying abuse and neglect, and a reluctance of the elderly to accuse their families contribute to the problem. With the expansion of the elderly population and the dependency needs of the frail, compounded by the stresses that often develop in caregivers, the problem is likely to become worse rather than decline.

## SUMMARY

The family remains the main source of care for the frail in the community. Family members do not avoid these responsibilities. Affection, reciprocity, and proximity are among the many factors that underlie the caring relationship. These relatives continue to provide for even the most impaired, frequently struggling to do this when attending to other demands. However, the ability of families to provide ongoing assistance can be sorely taxed in the absence of additional support and interventions. The effects are particularly noticeable in the case of employed caregivers, who may suffer economic hardships as well as emotional and physical strains in their efforts to provide care to their relatives.

Families are generally reluctant to use formal services, utilizing them only when the caregiving demands become most oppressive. As has been discussed, many factors contribute to this reluctance. However, even when utilized, these formal services do not undermine the support and assistance provided by the families. In most instances, formal services are used only for the specialized types of help that the caregivers find difficult.

Families caring for the cognitively impaired face particular problems that may even exceed those of the physically impaired. The demands for constant attention and supervision coupled with the inability of the relative to express gratitude can be extremely stressful. This stress can be exacerbated when the relative actually feels that the caregiver is causing him or her harm.

The demands associated with caregiving can contribute to much stress as the tasks become overwhelming. Most families manage to cope with this stress, but often it is at the expense of their own health and well-being. In particular, research attests to the role that family conflicts can have in the development of strain. Concern must be given to the effects of ongoing dependency on many of these caregivers. Elder abuse represents the extreme negative impact that caregiving can have.

In order to prevent the stress that can in some instances lead to abuse as well as to maintain the well-being of these caregivers, it is necessary to conceptualize their needs in conjunction with those of their relatives. It is only through this perspective that a comprehensive framework of interventions pertinent to the well-being of each can be designed. The family remains the cornerstone of support to the frail elderly. However, without additional support the availability of these caregivers and their ability to meet the multitude of caregiving demands is in jeopardy.

*Chapter Seven*

---

# Ethnicity and Frailty

The definition and interpretation of frailty is influenced by many factors beyond the immediate physical impairments or limitations. Among the critical factors that can influence the perception and development of frailty is ethnicity. In fact, ethnicity, as it relates to the individual's role in society and interactions, provides the context in which the other factors such as gender, family, and the use of services are organized.

Ethnicity encompasses a distinct way of viewing and reacting to the world. Ethnic race, religion, or national origin distinguish ethnic groups with individual members classified according to the degree to which they identify with the group. Ethnic identity also involves a subjective perception in that individuals who perceive of themselves as belonging to a specific group or are so treated by others may also be considered "ethnic" (Shibutani and Kwan, 1965).

Ethnic groups commonly hold distinct cultural beliefs, values, and norms. These can influence the aging process, determining the ways in which individuals are expected to age, their status, and their interactions with other ethnic group members and society as a whole. Furthermore, they can influence the perception of frailty as well as the ways in which individuals and society respond to the frail.

However, the importance of ethnicity as a determinant of roles and behaviors should not be readily assumed. Ethnicity may play a stronger role at different points in the life course as well as among individuals of differing acculturation and socioeconomic status (Markides et al., 1990). In fact, as ethnic individuals live outside of traditional environments, the saliency of ethnicity in their lives may weaken (Gelfand and Barresi, 1987).

Ethnicity is not a constant, and therefore its power as a determinant of behaviors will alter with generation, residence, socioeconomic status, language, and involvement in traditional ethnic organizations and churches (Gelfand and Fandetti, 1986). Consequently, the nature of frailty among the elderly as well as responses to it may also be expected to change.

## PERCEPTION OF FRAILTY

Inasmuch as ethnicity influences one's view of the world, it may also influence the perception of frailty. Illnesses or disabilities that may be labeled as frailty in one population may not be in another. Thus, as impairments are perceived as part of the normal course of aging, they may not be associated with many of the negative perceptions that are associated with aging and dependency. The elderly themselves may be less likely to perceive themselves as "frail" within the context of a supportive traditional network which provides assistance along a continuum on the basis of need. Moreover, to the extent that relatives and caregivers remain influenced by traditional values and beliefs that permeate their roles, they may be expected to meet the needs of their older relative. On the other hand, as younger members diverge from traditional culture, their perceptions of frailty and needs for assistance are likely to differ from those of their older relatives.

Responses to impairment and frailty by ethnic group members cannot be solely attributed to traditional values and beliefs. Such responses may also reflect the realities of a lifetime of interactions with programs and service providers. A history of discrimination, poor services, and indifference can contribute to what is interpreted as "traditional ethnic behaviors." Thus, a reluctance to use medical care may be due to many years of long waits in clinics or hospital emergency rooms, while assistance from social workers or other professionals may be viewed with suspicion by elderly whose past experiences with these professionals included many forms, regulations, and probing questions.

Responses of ethnic groups to cognitive impairments in the elderly warrants specific attention. According to data from a survey of ethnic minority communities, dementia is frequently not recognized in these populations due to a tendency of families to regard the elderly's cognitive deficits and behavioral problems as being a normal part of aging (U.S. Congress Office of Technology Assessment, 1990). Frequently, relatives are ashamed of the patient's symptoms and thus do not seek care. Language barriers, customs, beliefs, and attitudes towards the formal services can further deter these individuals from seeking help.

If frailty is expected to accompany the aging process and aging is viewed as being the result of a natural decline in abilities, individuals may be more accepting and less likely to seek aggressive medical care or assistance. Understanding how need is perceived and the factors which contribute to it as well as the use of medical care can assist in understanding how ethnicity may affect the perception of frailty.

## UTILIZATION OF HEALTH CARE

For many years sociologists have examined the ways in which ethnicity affects the use of health services and the perception that individuals have illness. Zborowski (1952) observed ethnic variations in reactions to pain among Jewish, Italian, Irish, and "Old American" patients in a New York City hospital. Both Jewish and Italian patients responded to pain emotionally and tended to exaggerate it while the "Old Americans" were stoical and objective and the Irish tended to deny it. The Italians primarily sought relief, while the Jewish patients were more concerned with the meaning, significance, and consequences of the pain for their future welfare and health.

Suchman (1965) studied 5,340 persons in different ethnic groups in New York and their responses to medical care. Those individuals who were members of more cohesive and ethnocentric populations characterized by close friendship and family ties knew less about disease and were more skeptical of professional health care. These persons also relied upon their own group members for support during illness.

Groups also differ in their reasons for seeking medical care. Zola (1973) found that Italians went to the physician when symptoms began to interfere with their social relations or when some type of interpersonal crisis called attention to the symptoms. Irish and Anglo-Saxon patients were more likely to seek medical attention when the symptoms threatened to interfere with work or physical functioning.

Other research suggests that self-perceived health status and need for care are major predictors of physician utilization regardless of ethnicity (Coulton and Frost, 1983). However, need must be linked to the older individual's belief that the problem is serious enough to warrant attention in order for the person to seek physician care (Sharp et al., 1983). In this way cultural attitudes and expectations can critically affect the use of services as they determine perceived needs.

In investigating factors associated with physician utilization among elderly Hispanics, Portuguese, and Vietnamese, the perception of need was found to be a major predictor of care, but need was defined differently by the three groups (Cox, 1986). Thus, arthritis was a predictor of physician care for the Portuguese but not for the other two groups. Hypertension contributed to physician utilization for the Vietnamese but had no effect on the care of the Hispanics or Portuguese. An equally important finding was that a poor self-perceived health status influenced the use of physicians by the Hispanics and Portuguese but not by the Vietnamese.

A study of physician and hospital utilization by five groups of ethnic elderly found needs to be the primary determinants of care and to be more important in predicting the demand for physician services than is the case among nonethnic elderly (Wolinsky et al., 1989). However, it is the inaccessibility of services which presents the barrier to utilization. Thus, although minority individuals may desire care, the health care system itself can seriously restrict their utilization. But this notwithstanding, the findings also recognize ethnic differences in health beliefs and behaviors must be considered in efforts to understand the use of health services.

Data on the medical care of the African-American elderly indicate that they make as many or even more physician visits than white elderly but that they also have more health problems which can be limiting (U.S. Department of Health and Human Services, 1985). In ratio to these medical problems, they actually underutilize services. These elderly are also less likely to have a regular physician and more likely to rely on emergency rooms for treatment, meaning that preventive care is generally absent. When they do seek treatment, elderly African-Americans are likely to be in more of a crisis state with more complicated problems necessitating longer stays in hospitals.

As these findings imply, attitudes and cultural beliefs can provide a framework for health care utilization. But these factors must be considered in conjunction with the access that elderly have to services. Either set of variables independently or through their interactions can seriously impede the functioning of the elderly in the community.

## MINORITIES AND FRAILTY

Ethnic minority group members confront particular issues with regard to disabilities that contribute to frailty. In addition to their ethnic identity, these individuals are members of groups that have suffered some particular discrimination from the dominant society, being prohibited or restricted due to their ethnic trait (whether it be religion, race, or national origin) from integration. However, even among minority groups, the degree to which ethnicity is a significant factor influencing aging, vulnerability, and frailty varies.

Generally, in ethnic minority populations that have been subjected to discrimination, the role of the family has remained strong. Discrimination reinforces reliance on the family as a primary source of aid and support. The elderly in these populations, as well as their caregivers, are likely to be suspicious of the dominant culture and its services, relying primarily on internal sources of support.

Nevertheless, the availability of family members to provide this assistance to their frail relatives should not be overestimated. Acculturation, the number of children, the degree of contact between the generations, and finances can affect the caregiving relationship (Lockery, 1991). Even when desiring to assist, family members may lack the resources needed to support the frail relative. Moreover, with adult children frequently torn between meeting traditional expectations and their own needs, it is not unusual for tension to develop in intergenerational relationships (Stanford et al., 1990). As a result, the frail elderly may be at risk for being unattended to by either the formal or informal network.

The complexity of the factors involved in discrimination, the problems associated with distinguishing cultural traits from acquired responses, and the difficulties in data collection and in designing culturally relevant and comparative measures may partially account for the fact that research on the issue of frailty and ethnicity is extremely limited. However, several factors including the socio-economic status of minority elderly, their use of health services, and the prevalence of chronic illness suggest that frailty may indeed be a major problem.

## Status of Minority Elderly

African-American, Hispanic, and Native American elderly have incomes substantially lower than those of other Americans. In 1986 the median annual income for those 65 and older was $11,780 for white non-Hispanics, $6,570 for Hispanics, and $5,950 for African-Americans (U.S. Department of Health and Human Services, 1988).

Comparing the rates of poverty among minority groups in 1987 shows that 10 percent of elderly whites, 34 percent of elderly African-Americans, and 27 percent of elderly Hispanics lived in poverty (American Association of Retired Persons, 1989). Fourteen percent of Pacific Asian elderly lived below the poverty level, with the median annual income for men less than $6,000 and for women less than $4,000 (Gould, 1989).

Poverty is associated with poorer nutrition, poorer health care, less preventive measures, and more deteriorated housing. The elderly poor also have higher rates of arthritis, hypertension, hearing problems, vision problems, diabetes, more functional limitations, and poorer perceived health status than those with higher incomes (Rowland and Lyons, 1987). Moreover, impairments associated with frailty tend to occur at an earlier age among minority populations.

However, services to assist these elderly are not readily available. The minority elderly suffer from a lack of access to services, a lack of preventive medical care, and the absence of primary-care physicians. The inner cities, in which many of these elderly live, are particularly unattractive to office-based physicians, contributing to the excessive use by these individuals of hospital emergency rooms for care (U.S. Bipartisan Commission on Comprehensive Health Care, 1990). Community health care centers designed to meet the needs of these populations remain underfinanced and are thus frequently unable to provide the care that the frail require. Consequently, the treatments that may assist these individuals in coping with chronic problems are generally not available.

Medicaid remains the primary means of medical coverage for the poor elderly, and those under the Medicaid program are entitled to a vast range of services. However, the burden of poor health and functional limitations may be most severe among those minority elderly who are poor but above state Medicaid criteria. Data from the Commonwealth Fund Commission (1987) show that only one-half of minority elderly in poverty have Medicaid coverage. Thus, many in need of care do not receive it. For these individuals, functioning adequately in the community can be extremely difficult. In particular, hearing aids, prostheses, and adaptive appliances, which are not covered by Medicare, can enhance the ability to remain independent but may not be obtainable.

## African-American Elderly

Findings from the Task Force on Black and Minority Health (U.S. Department of Health and Human Services, 1985) show that the incidence of heart disease and stroke, cancer, cirrhosis, and diabetes is 80 percent higher in the African-American population than in the white. The African-American elderly are also more likely to have arthritis, an illness which is not life threatening but can be seriously incapacitating. With these illnesses, it is not surprising to learn that the health status of this population is poor and that they have excessive deaths in comparison to whites due to heart disease, malignant neoplasms, and cardiovascular disease.

African-American elderly rate their health more poorly and spend more days in bed due to an illness than other groups (National Center for Health Statistics, 1990). They are more likely to be ill, to be disabled earlier, to be more physically limited and more dependent than their non-minority peers (Johnson et al., 1990).

Other data from the U.S. Bureau of the Census (1990) underscore the extent of impairment among the African-American elderly and their needs for assistance in order to function in the community. In 1986, 22.7 percent of African-American elderly needed help with one or more of their ADLs in comparison to 15.4 percent of white elderly and 19.1 percent of Hispanic elderly. The African-American population exceeded the needs of the other two groups in assistance required with personal care, meal preparation, getting around outside, housework, and money management.

Furthermore, there is some question as to the extent to which these needs for assistance are actually being met. In a study of African-American elderly and their caregivers, Randolph (1990) found that the most prominent unmet needs for assistance were with bathing, housework, meal preparation, and transportation. It is particularly noteworthy that the majority of caregivers provided assistance without help from either relatives or formal agencies. These findings must raise concerns regarding the functioning of the frail in the community.

Although data on the prevalence of Alzheimer's Disease and other dementias in the African-American elderly population are lacking, the high rates of hypertension and cardiovascular disease in this population means that many elderly may be at risk for associated vascular dementia (Folstein et al., 1985). However, as noted by Harper and Alexander (1990), there are relatively few African-American elderly with dementia in the long-term health care system.

Apart from cognitive disability, there is some evidence to suggest that the mental health status of elderly African-Americans improves as they age. Gibson (1983) found that these individuals were more likely to have serious personal problems affecting their well-being and morale at mid-life than at 80 years of age and over. It would appear that the oldest group had learned to adjust to life's stresses and to have some sense of accomplishment and personal efficacy which contributes to their having reached the advanced age. This does not negate the fact that those elderly who are not yet 80 may still be battling with the problems which the oldest of the elderly have managed to resolve.

## Hispanic Elderly

Findings on the health status of older Hispanics indicate that they too are at increased risk of chronic disability and frailty. In a study on the health status of Hispanics, one-third of the elderly reported having at least one functional disability while 25 percent reported problems with their nerves and 11 percent stated they were depressed (Lacayo, 1982).

Data from the Commonwealth Fund (1989), which examined illness among several Hispanic populations, show a poor health status with 40 percent of elderly Hispanics reporting difficulties with one or more ADLs compared to only 23 percent of those in the general population. The Hispanics also reported extensive difficulty with their IADLs including money management, using the telephone, preparing meals, housework, and shopping.

It is therefore not surprising that elderly Hispanics rate their health as poor. Data from the House Select Committee on Aging (1989) found that 41.2 percent of elderly Hispanics perceived themselves to be in fair or poor health. A greater proportion of these elderly, 31.5 percent, had been bedridden in the previous 12 months as compared to 21.9 percent of elderly whites and 26.9 percent of elderly African-Americans. The Hispanics also were more limited in their activities than the white population, averaging 37 days of restricted activities compared to 31 days for the whites.

These findings are further replicated in a study of older Hispanics, primarily Cuban and Central Americans, in Washington D.C. (Ailinger, 1989). Sixty-three percent of the sample had mild to moderate impairments, although in this group, the majority reported no functional limitations that would impede their independence. Those over 75 years were significantly more impaired than younger persons. Particularly noteworthy is the fact that nearly half of the sample stated they had poor mental health, with one in five taking medications for depression or for their nerves.

Data on Puerto Rican elderly further underscore the level of functional disability present in the population. Using established criteria such as the ability to climb stairs, days of activity limitation, and days in bed due to illness, O'Donnell (1989) found the Puerto Ricans in New York to be more impaired than either white or African-American elderly. The level of disability remained constant when income and education were controlled, suggesting that factors other than social class may be a cause. However, the levels of disability increased with the elderly individual's inability to speak English. Those who were more fluent in English had the lowest levels of impairment. Thus, cultural assimilation may be negatively associated with frailty in these elderly.

## Pacific Asian Elderly

Health data on Pacific Asian elderly are very limited due in part to the fact that, nationally, health statistics do not collect separate statistics on Asian American groups. Thus, data that do exist are dependent on specific surveys or studies in select areas. In aggregate, the Pacific Asians are healthier than all racial/ethnic groups in the United States, including whites (U.S. Department of Health and Human Services, 1985). However, the group does have higher rates of hepatitis, anemia, tuberculosis, and hypertension, conditions that are major contributors to frailty. Consequently, these elderly face the same risk of encountering debilitating impairments as is experienced by the general population.

The mental health needs of these populations must also be considered. The Chinese elderly living in Chinatowns are susceptible to feeling isolated, to having inadequate housing, and to using few services. Mental health problems and depression afflict a high proportion of these elderly, who are also often limited in their activities (Lum et al., 1980). In fact, the suicide rate among the Chinese elderly is three times that of their white peers (Lyman, 1976).

There is little available information on the health status or impairments of Southeast Asians, the newest immigrants. Because of the trauma associated with their immigration, their lack of acculturation, and relatively poor socioeconomic status, they may be expected to have poor health and a greater susceptibility to impairment and frailty. In particular, these individuals, as they are isolated in the community, are likely to suffer from depression or withdrawal resulting from perceived neglect by other members of the family (Matsuoka, 1990).

## American Indian Elderly

The American Indian elderly are, according to many indices, the most impaired and potentially frail of any ethnic group. Moreover, this frailty begins at a much earlier age than in other population groups. Data, in fact, indicate that at the age of 45 American Indians experience the same limitations in their ability to perform ADLs as non-Indians at age 65 (Cook, 1989). Estimates have been made that 73 percent of the elderly Indian population is mildly to totally impaired in daily functioning (National Indian Council on Aging, 1981).

Although the elderly compose a small proportion of the Indian population, the population is aging at a fast rate with an expected doubling of the population over 75 years by the year 2000 (Manson and Callaway, 1990a). Concomitant with this aging will be increases in chronic diseases such as heart disease, cancer, and diabetes. Pneumonia, diabetes, alcoholism, arthritis, and dental health are presently major problems in the elderly population (Manson and Callaway, 1990b). In addition, Indians have glaucoma and hearing impairments at twice the national rate with few having the use of glasses or bifocals (Curley, 1990). Not surprisingly, elderly Indians also have high rates of depression, which can further limit their functioning (National Indian Council on Aging, 1981).

But the frailty experienced by American Indians can only be partially attributed to their immediate chronic health problems. Poverty is a pressing problem for the elderly. Among the rural population, nearly half of the American Indian elderly live below the poverty line with rural elderly living in families being eight times more likely to be in poverty than urban whites (Manson and Callaway, 1990b). Housing for the elderly is characteristically old and dilapidated and "replete with health and safety factors" with nearly half having no indoor plumbing (Cook,1989; Curley, 1990). The physical impairments of the population further hinder their ability to maintain the home.

Families play important supportive roles in relation to these elderly, with one report indicating that 46 percent of older tribal members are assisted by relatives in the tasks of daily living (National Indian Council on Aging, 1981). But there must be concerns about the ability of these families, who face poverty themselves, to care for their frail elders. Even though traditional values may compel them to assist the frail, the reality of their own situations may limit their support. Moreover, attempting to meet the demands of the frail relative can be an additional source of strain.

This discussion indicates how both ethnicity and minority group membership in particular can contribute to frailty in the elderly. As each ethnic culture maintains its own unique view of the world, its members will share a particular perspective on aging, the status of the aged, and the illness and disabilities that frequently affect the elderly. At the same time, society has contributed to these perspectives through years of discrimination which result in negative views of services, low expectations, and little opportunity for access by ethnic minority individuals. Underlying these factors is the poverty encountered by minority elderly, which contributes to poorer health and reduced access to services. As a result, frailty is likely to be a major risk for many in these populations.

## COMMUNITY SERVICES

Many of the factors which cause ethnic elderly to underutilize health care services act as barriers to their use of other services. Programs more likely to be used are those located in ethnic areas having staff members of the same ethnic background who speak the language from the country of origin (Gelfand, 1982). However, although these factors may facilitate utilization, they do not guarantee that it will occur. Attitudes and expectations, as well as knowledge of programs and their purposes and the perception that one's needs are appropriate to the services, also influence service use.

The model of health services utilization of Andersen and Newman (1973) has frequently been adapted to provide a framework for examining the utilization of other services. Predisposing factors in the model are demographics and socioeconomic characteristics. Enabling factors can be expanded to include economic resources, living environment, social resources, and personal resources such as life perspective and coping skills, and needs include physical health, mental health, and functional status (Harel et al., 1985).

In order for services to be used by ethnic elderly, they must be compatible with the older person's attitudes and preferences towards services, ethnic characteristics of the informal caregiver, and the perception that the elderly have of the services (Harel, et al., 1987). Thus, services offered by members of the same ethnic group who share the same background and culture as the elderly strengthen the enabling characteristics as the service becomes more attractive to the intended population. Perhaps most important is that the older individual must perceive the services as being able to assist with specific needs and problems.

Wallace's model of utilization (1990) structures use around the availability, accessibility, and acceptability of services. Ethnic elderly are at risk for finding barriers in each of these areas as services may not exist in their communities, may have restricted access due to eligibility criteria or problems associated with language or due to an inability of the elderly to understand the programs, and may be perceived as unacceptable due to cultural attitudes and values.

On Lok in San Francisco is an example of how availability, accessibility, and acceptability can be operationalized in both health and social services. On Lok Senior Health Services was established in 1971 in response to the health care needs of the frail elderly in San Francisco's Chinatown and surrounding areas. It began as a day-care center for the elderly and then served as a Medicare demonstration model of consolidated services providing all medical and social services. Beginning in just one location, On Lok has now expanded into community sites in the San Francisco area.

The population served by On Lok is primarily Chinese (75%), poor, and with multiple medical problems and disabilities (Zawadski and Ansak, 1983). Due to language barriers as well as cultural traditions, the population is one that is difficult to reach with either Western medicine or services. The success of the program with this strong ethnic population may be at least partially attributed to the way in which services were made available, accessible within the community, and acceptable to the intended elderly clients. Using ethnic professionals, and with services and outreach sensitive to the distinct culture of the population, the program has been able to overcome preexisting barriers to service utilization.

## Reaching Minority Elderly

Various efforts have been made by service providers seeking to reach minority elderly. Although these efforts have had varying levels of success, these do demonstrate that the needs of these populations are being recognized by both policy makers and programs. Success in these efforts remains an important challenge as they provide a continuum of services which can benefit the frail in the community.

Reaching Asian elderly is difficult for service providers. Pacific Asian Americans have been viewed as preferring informal assistance from their own ethnic community and family to formal services (Fujii, 1976; Salcido et al., 1980). Conversely, the lack of utilization has also been attributed to culturally insensitive providers, language barriers, and the shame of seeking help outside of the family (Timberlake and Cook, 1984). Lee (1987) further attributes poor utilization to organizational barriers that make services inaccessible, lack of knowledge, discriminatory treatment, and social alienation. The achievements of On Lok, described above, indicates how these traditional obstacles may be overcome.

The low participation rates by Hispanic elderly in both public and private programs has been attributed to ineffective outreach and the inability of the programs to meet the sociocultural needs of the population (Lopez and Aguilera, 1991). The result is that these elderly do not benefit from many existing services which could assist them in the community. Lack of knowledge about programs, a lack of information in Spanish, and few bilingual staff further impede utilization.

Hispanic participation in nutrition programs under the Older Americans Act declined by nearly 15 percent from 1981 to 1986 and in supportive services by more than 35 percent between 1980 and 1988 (Lopez and Aguilera, 1991). The decline is attributed to a lack of bilingual/bicultural staff, location of programs outside of the Hispanic communities, a lack of transportation, and a perception by the Hispanic elderly that they are not welcome in the programs. Traditional outreach methods which rely on written announcements are of limited benefit to the Hispanic elderly, whose educational levels are low and whose English proficiency is generally limited. Thus, many in the community who could benefit from these programs remain unserved.

But the frail may be served by projects designed specifically for their needs. An example is the Amigos del Valle program in the Rio Grande Valley of Texas (National Council of La Raza, 1990). Like On Lok, this program was designed to meet the needs of a specific group of elderly, the economically disadvantaged Hispanics, generally neglected by other programs. Amigos del Valle offers a comprehensive program of social, supportive, nutritional, and housing services but does not include medical care. It provides meals to the homebound elderly as well as transportation to senior centers and other services. The growth of the program further illustrates the needs of minority elderly which can be addressed through sensitive and appropriate services.

The use of targeting services as a means of increasing minority elderly participation in community programs has been suggested as an important means to serving this population. In a study of the use of services under the Older Americans Act homebound category, Harel (1987) found the African-American aged to be more disadvantaged than whites. The African-American elderly were more economically deprived, were more socially impaired, and had less knowledge and access to services. They also had greater fears for personal security and poorer housing. Contrary to findings from other studies, white elderly receiving the Older Americans Act services had slightly more children living nearby and higher levels of social support. Based on these findings, Harel suggests that it may be necessary to target services toward minority elderly if they are to achieve access equal to that of nonminority elderly.

Since 1987 the Older Americans Act has targeted services to the frail elderly and those with the greatest social and economic need, specifically minorities. But, as reviewed by Skinner (1990), there is some question as to the effectiveness of the services in reaching their objectives. Although the federal government allocates funds to the states with requirements for targeting specific populations, the actual service plans specifying which groups to target are made at the state and area agency levels. In fact, aggregate data at the state level may mask the real level of need in local areas. Consequently, targeting has not assured that services are available to those with the greatest need.

Nevertheless, even with its limitations, targeting has meant that services have reached many minority elderly who would otherwise have been without home- or community-based care and who might therefore have been forced to relocate to an institution. Improved assessment, planning, and evaluation with more accurate data are essential to ensure that targeting is effective. At the same time, care must also be taken to ensure that an emphasis on targeting does not ignore many other elderly who could also benefit from services.

## FAMILIES AND THE FRAIL

It is generally believed that family support networks among ethnic groups are strong and that they provide all of the assistance that a frail elderly individual may require. The fact that minority elderly are underrepresented in the formal service network is continually used as evidence of their lack of need. But, just as demographic changes are occurring within the majority population, parallel changes are occurring within the minority and traditional ethnic groups.

Younger cohorts are moving from ethnic areas in inner cities, often leaving the elderly to cope on their own, providing only minimal amounts of assistance. This lack of involvement can also increase mental problems among these frail elderly as they feel neglected and isolated by children who are perceived as no longer respecting or caring for them. In some instances, these older individuals suffer even more problems as the shame they feel in this rejection prohibits them from using formal services. These feelings are compounded when language presents another barrier to services.

With the increasing number of employed women, there are fewer caregivers available to provide for the needs of many of the frail older individuals. Ethnicity does not provide immunity from the stresses of society and may in fact cause even more intense stress as individuals are torn between adhering to traditional values of support and broader social values of self-enhancement and growth.

Evidence for the stress experienced by these ethnic caregivers is provided in studies of families caring for dementia patients. In a study of burden in Hispanic caregivers, Cox and Monk (1992a) found that although cultural values and norms continued to govern familial relationships and the care of the elderly, adherence to these values had consequences on the well-being of the caregivers. In fact, the greater their sense of adherence to feelings of obligation to their relatives, the greater their depression.

These caregivers felt very burdened by the patient's dependency and in their attempts to meet the continual demands.

There is evidence which suggests that assistance to the elderly may be strongly influenced by socioeconomic class (Cantor, 1979), years since immigration (Rosenthal, 1986), and socioeconomic mobility (Gelfand and Fandetti, 1980). Because of their efforts to assimilate into society and the demands which this assimilation places on them, adult children may not be able to meet the expectations of their parents who more strongly adhere to traditional expectations for assistance.

Cox and Gelfand (1987) found variations in expectations for assistance among elderly Hispanic, Portuguese, and Vietnamese. The Vietnamese, who had the poorest functional health status, had strong expectations for assistance from their children and were the least satisfied with the degree to which these expectations were being met. The Portuguese, who had the highest expectations of assistance, were the most satisfied with the amount of help being provided. The Hispanics were least likely to expect assistance and tended to be satisfied with the care that the children gave. An equally important finding was that expectations were greatest among those individuals born outside of the United States. Assimilation as well as impairments must therefore be considered in efforts to understand caregiving activities.

In a study of first- and second-generation Japanese-Americans living in Chicago, Osako and Liu (1986) found that the idea of filial piety, support to the older generation, remained strong among both parents and their adult children. In particular, this tradition actually assisted in the older individual's transition from an independent to a dependent status. Adult children, with more personal resources than their parents, continued to accept the norms of responsibility and to incorporate them into the pattern of American values.

The findings are important in that they illustrate the varying types of interactions that may exist between the elderly and their relatives. If expectations remain strong among the elderly that are not shared by their children, dissatisfaction can ensue regardless of the efforts that the children make. Furthermore, as both parents and children become acculturated, demands for familial assistance become weakened. Thus, as ties to the traditional ethnic culture become weaker, both the frail ethnic elderly and their caregivers may turn more to the formal system for help.

Data from the Long Term Care and National Survey of Informal Caregivers were examined by White-Means and Thorton (1990) to determine how ethnicity may affect informal care to the elderly among German,

Irish, English, and African-American populations. The results indicated that the African-American caregivers spent more time caregiving but that the English and Irish were significantly more likely to limit their leisure time in order to provide care. Of particular interest is that the factors determining caregiving hours differed among the four groups. For Germans, IADLs and an available substitute determined hours. The number of hours spent by Irish caregivers was determined by ADLs, an available substitute, and education, while hours for the English were determined by the caregiver's health status, IADLs, and available substitutes.

The hours spent by African-American caregivers were determined most by substitute availability and ADLs. Furthermore, the only factor constraining caregiving hours for the African-American caregivers was full-time employment. The findings illustrate the continuing saliency of ethnicity in the relationships of the frail elderly and in the support they receive from their families. However, they also indicate how other factors, such as employment, can impact on the support provided by informal caregivers.

Much research has been done on the informal support systems of the African-American elderly and the extent to which these systems are available to them. Older African-Americans have been found to draw on a varied pool of informal helpers, not restricted to immediate family, and one in which there is some degree of substitution (Gibson and Jackson, 1988). Thus, when children are unavailable to assist the elderly, other relatives, particularly siblings, will provide care (Taylor, 1985). In addition, elderly African-Americans have also been found to have more support from a wider network including church members and neighbors (George, 1988; Ralston, 1984).

The extended kin network of elderly African-Americans has been associated with low levels of education, income, occupational status, living in the South, and willingness to take care of children (Mitchell and Register, 1984). This extended system increases the possibility of others to provide support. But kin and nonkin appear to play varying roles in meeting the needs of the elderly. Kin are found to provide long-term, instrumental assistance based on an obligatory relationship, while nonkin are more likely to provide socioemotional support and care for short-term needs (Taylor and Chatters, 1986).

The type, amount, and frequency of help is on a sliding scale, with increases in disability contributing to increases in the number of available helpers and increased contacts depending on the proximity of the family (Johnson et al., 1990). However, the extent to which informal help is available to the African-American elderly should not be overestimated.

The African-American elderly are less likely to have spouses and adult children able to provide help and financial assistance.

In a study of the support systems of inner-city African-Americans, Johnson and Baher (1990) found that adult children, even when close to the elderly, did not tend to offer instrumental support because of strains and distractions in their own lives. Moreover, the elderly resisted being dependent on their children, preferring instead to use formal services such as home help and chore workers. However, a disturbing finding in the study was that 18 percent had no weekly contact with either relatives or friends and that these individuals were more likely to have serious physical and mental impairments. Thus, the most frail and those most in need of support may be those most at risk for being isolated due to their inability to maintain social networks.

The limitations of these informal supports was also noted in research by Cox (1992a). Data from a study of African-American and white caregivers who had contacted Alzheimer's associations for assistance, revealed that the African-American caregivers were not immune to the depression and strains experienced by their nonminority peers, but their well-being was more strongly affected by the support they received from others than by the actual status of the patient. These caregivers maintained very strong expectations for assistance, and a failure of others to meet these expectations was a strong contributor to their depression. Thus, as others in the family network are unable to provide the amount of assistance needed, the caregivers, and consequently the elderly that they care for, remain at risk in the community.

## THE USE OF SERVICES BY CAREGIVERS

Although the ethnic elderly may be reluctant to use formal services themselves, there is some evidence that their caregivers may be willing to utilize such programs to assist them with their caregiving tasks. In a study of African-American and Hispanic caregivers of Alzheimer's patients in New York, family caregivers, primarily adult daughters of the patients, were willing to use formal home care services to assist with their relatives (Cox and Monk, 1992b). For the African-American caregivers, this use was associated with the presence of other informal helpers, while for the Hispanics, the utilization of formal services occurred when there was an absence of informal help. Thus, for the former the informal network may provide an important link with formal services.

Both groups of caregivers adhered to norms of filial responsibility in that they each felt that children should provide care for their parents and both preferred familial to formal assistance. However, they also felt that using formal services could be justified and did not mean that the caregiver was relinquishing her role. Nevertheless, the use of such services can affect the well-being of the caregivers themselves.

Among the African-American caregivers, those who were reluctant to use professional help or give up employment to provide care experienced the greatest sense of burden. Those preferring professional to informal assistance were the most depressed. Among Hispanics, those caregivers most strongly adhering to the filial norms of assistance experienced greater degrees of depression.

These findings suggest that even though caregivers may be willing to use formal services, the decision is not without consequences for their own well-being. By not adhering to cultural norms of responsibility for the elderly, these caregivers jeopardize their own mental health. Rather than relieving the sense of burden associated with caregiving, turning to the formal service network may exacerbate feelings of guilt and depression as the caregiver experiences the utilization as failing to meet expected responsibilities.

The findings further support the continuing influence that ethnicity has on the use of formal services. Although the norms do not deter the use of these services, they may lead to internal conflicts which can affect the caregivers. Ethnicity thus remains a salient factor to be examined and considered in the provision of services to families of the frail.

Because caregivers play such vital roles in assisting the elderly to remain in the community, the ways in which ethnicity may affect their provision of care and decision to use services need to be considered in any model of intervention. As caregiver needs may be the determining factor in the decision to use services, an understanding of the way in which ethnicity may affect these needs is necessary. This is made most salient by the statements of many Hispanic caregivers that they would prefer to institutionalize their relative but were prevented from doing so due to fears of rejection and ridicule from other members of the family.

Strong adherence to norms of filial support to the elderly may in fact be a source of stress to caregivers. Feelings of inadequacy in meeting the needs of the relative can actually exacerbate a sense of incompetence among caregivers. Thus, as needs for care escalate, caregivers themselves may be at particular risk in that they are unable to keep pace with the demands of the impaired relative. Providers of formal services must therefore remain aware of and sensitive to the needs of these individuals and develop interventions that can help them to effectively carry out their traditional roles.

## SUMMARY

Ethnicity is not a buffer from the chronic illnesses and conditions that are conducive to frailty. Although the interpretation of frailty by these individuals may differ, the social, economic, and health impairments that can make frailty a reality are present. As ethnic minority elderly are likely to suffer most from these impairments, they are also at risk of becoming frail. The fact that these individuals are not well-represented in the service system does not imply that they do not require assistance in the community. Moreover, the success of programs such as On Lok in reaching these individuals testifies to their need for services.

Relatives who have traditionally provided care to these elderly are encountering the same demands and burdens as those in non-ethnic groups. As a result, their ability and capacity to continue to provide for the frail is doubtful. However, services and programs to meet the needs presented by these groups are noticeably lacking.

Access is a primary concern with regard to service use. The frail ethnic elderly are among those who may be most isolated in the community and thus be the most lacking in knowledge about existing services. Moreover, information may be difficult to understand and available only in English. Even when literature is printed in other languages, it may not be applicable to the minority elderly who may be functionally illiterate in their native language as well as English. This makes the need for sensitive bilingual staff even more pressing.

The success of indigenous programs in meeting the needs of frail minority individuals is evidence of the importance of access and the acceptability of services for utilization. These programs, located within the ethnic communities and having staff members with the same ethnic backgrounds as the elderly themselves, can have a significant impact on care, which can potentially decrease the risk of frailty in these populations. These programs may also serve to enhance and strengthen the support offered by the family.

The interpretation of need for care by ethnic elderly and their families is basic to both prevention of frailty and to the care that it may require. Interpretation can be attributed to cultural beliefs as well as to experiences with the health care and service systems. At the same time, sensitive outreach programs and professionals can work towards altering behaviors that are responses to years of inadequate and indifferent care. It is also imperative to understand the needs of caregivers and the ways in which their attempts to adhere to traditional values can conflict with their own self-interests and result in stress.

The minority elderly population is growing faster than any other segment of the older population. In order for these individuals to continue to function independently in the community, services that recognize the uniqueness of these populations must be designed. Without appropriate interventions, these elderly and their caregivers will remain vulnerable as services remain underutilized and barriers continue to exist.

*Intervention*

*Chapter Eight*

# Innovations in Community Responses

Meeting the needs of the frail so that they can continue to live as independently as possible in the community requires many areas of intervention. Communities are responding to the needs of the frail on many levels and in many areas. These efforts generally aim at overcoming the fragmentation in existing systems of care. Through state programs, demonstrations, and local efforts, programs that can respond to the many needs of the frail are being developed.

State programs are generally better funded and able to serve a greater proportion of the elderly. They are also able to coordinate and expand the array of services offered while providing consistency throughout the system. Eligibility criteria are uniform and are likely to be strictly adhered to. Under state programs, the ability of local jurisdictions to vary in their services may be restricted. Moreover, continued funding and resources are usually dependent upon the legislature and the availability of funds.

Demonstration projects aim at supporting creative programs that address one specific area such as health care, housing, or community care. These projects receive funding for a designated period from the government; this government funding must be matched by other monies. The demonstrations may also be sponsored by private foundations. Throughout the demonstration period, careful evaluation is maintained to determine the project's effectiveness in meeting its objectives. Successful demonstrations may serve as models for other services.

Services developed through local efforts, often with some government funding, have a greater ability to respond to the specific needs of their populations through their flexibility. These programs are able to target groups of the elderly and to concentrate on programs which may be ignored by larger systems. They, therefore, can be important in filling gaps in programs. However, limited resources and competing local interests can be significant barriers to service development and expansion.

Demonstration programs are able to implement creative programs that can be relatively comprehensive in design. Their weakness is primarily difficulty in securing future funding to maintain the program after the initial funding period. Thus, in some instances, providers may find that they are forced to redirect their energies to locating future funding sources long before the demonstration ends.

Much can also be learned from the experiences of other countries as they wrestle with the challenges of responding to the frail in the community. Britain, Sweden, and Manitoba, Canada, offer models of coordinated systems of care. Although they may not necessarily be adaptable to this country, they do offer further ideas for innovations. The following discussion of programs is not intended to be exhaustive but is designed to illustrate varying approaches to the issue of frailty.

## STATE SYSTEMS OF CARE

Many states have been active in developing their own systems to provide community services for the frail elderly. Common to the programs described here are their efforts to coordinate health and social services at the state and local levels and the provision of comprehensive services.

### Oregon

Oregon reorganized its long-term-care system in 1981, becoming one of the first states to initiate on a statewide basis a program aimed at providing a real alternative to nursing home care for the frail. At that time, all long-term-care programs for the elderly and disabled were reorganized under one state agency, the Senior Service Division. The result has been the doubling of home care services and the development of more adult foster homes (U.S. House Select Committee on Aging, 1990a). In addition, under some of the programs family members may be paid to provide care for their relative.

Oregon's Assisted Living Program is based on a social model of care which builds upon the frail individidual's strengths and capabilities. Individuals live in their own apartments in a complex where 24-hour staff assistance is available as are many of the intermediate care services that are normally available only in a nursing home. Each resident has a care plan uniquely designed to meet individual needs as defined by the resident, family, and staff. The emphasis is on promoting individual choice and independence rather than dependence.

Pilot testing of the model shows an increased level of functioning of the residents and higher levels of satisfaction when compared to persons in intermediate-care nursing facilities. Moreover, the cost of care is only 80 percent of the cost of care in an intermediate facility due to fewer staff requirements and the emphasis on promoting independence.

## Illinois

Illinois has coordinated its long-term-care services under the state's Community Care Program (Justice, 1988). The program aims to meet the needs of the most frail in that participants must meet the criteria for nursing home admission. It is also aimed at low-income elderly in that participants must be Medicaid eligible or have less than $10,000 in liquid assets. The program offers three direct services—adult day-care, homemaker services, and chore services. In addition, care planning and case management are also available.

All assessment and case management is conducted by local Community Care Units under contract to the Department of Aging with a third of these units being home health agencies. The providers are selected based on quality measures designed at the state level. A functional assessment tool, the Determination of Need (DON), operationalizes the level of disability and need for care throughout the system. Scores are derived from 16 items that are assessed in terms of client impairment and the gap between available support and needed support. The total score gives the basis for calculating the monthly service amount of chore/housekeeping or homemaker services.

## Wisconsin

In Wisconsin, the Bureau of Long-term Support has responsibility for administering community long-term-care programs throughout 72 counties (Ball, 1989). The program is built around a care management system that serves all persons requiring long-term-care services. Eligibility is based upon the individual's becoming Medicaid eligible within six months of entering a nursing home.

The state offers guidelines for county agencies, but within these guidelines there is much latitude for care managers to design services to meet individual needs. Care managers may purchase many types of services that would assist their clients to remain independent. This may also involve the hiring of relatives to provide assistance.

Particularly unique to the Wisconsin system is the emphasis on consumer participation. Guidelines mandate that consumers be represented in state and local advisory committees, thus including their opinions and preferences in the design of policy and services.

## Florida

Florida, which has the highest proportion of persons over 60 of any state, seeks to meet the needs of the frail through Community Care Programs for the Elderly administered through the Department of Health and Rehabilitative Services. The intent of the program is to help functionally impaired elderly to live in the community, to reduce nursing home use, and to develop cost-effective service delivery. The overall goal is to avoid unnecessary institutional placement.

Funds for the program are derived from Title III of the Older Americans Act, the State Community Care for the Elderly Act, and Medicaid. Medicaid-eligible clients reimburse the program through the Medicaid funds. Eligibility for the program is based upon being 60 years of age and also being functionally impaired.

Each district in which the program operates is required to have a Community Care Service System comprised of home care, day-care, case management, and other services for the frail elderly. One agency is designated the coordinater for these local services and is responsible for assuring that the clients receive coordinated services. This approach has resulted in diversity among districts as varying types of services are available. In each district, however, the services must include case management and at least three of the following services: homemaker and chore services, respite care, adult day-care, medical transportation, mini day-care, home health aides, home nursing, personal care, and medical therapeutic services.

## Arkansas

Arkansas provides an example of how a state has addressed specific areas of need of its frail population through an innovative approach to funding. In order to provide for the expansion of elder transportation and home-delivered meals, the Arkansas legislature passed in 1991 an excise tax on cigarettes which would go directly to these programs (State Community Care Reporter, 1991).

Passage of the tax was strongly influenced by the lobbying efforts of many organizations for the aged as well as the Arkansas State Unit on Aging and 500 elderly volunteer lobbyists. A one-penny sales tax on each package of cigarettes is allocated to the Area Agencies on Aging for new vans, fuel, van repairs, drivers, kitchen supplies, and more staff for nutrition sites so that more meals can be delivered to the home-bound elderly. Although the program has not restructured services to the elderly, it illustrates how states can address particular concerns using innovative funding mechanisms. Moreover, it underscores the role that the elderly themselves can play as advocates for needed services.

## Pennsylvania

The state's Family Caregiver Support Program is unique in that it responds directly to the needs of family caregivers. The purpose of the program is to reinforce the assistance provided by families so that they can continue to care for frail older relatives at home. It offers a continuum of services to these caregivers as well as financial reimbursement for services such as day-care, home care, and respite care (Pennsylvania Department of Aging, 1991).

The area agencies are the central administering bodies of the program. Staff of the agencies are employed as case managers and make the original needs assessments as well as the subsequent individual care plans.

Families may also receive up to $2,000 to assist in paying for home adaptations or special devices that facilitate caregiving. Financial assistance on a cost-sharing basis is offered to assist with expenses with income guidelines set above the poverty line to enable middle-income families to participate. Families with incomes up to 200 percent of the poverty level qualify for 100 percent of the maximum benefit.

The entry point into the program begins with an assessment of the caregiver and the care receiver that determines the status and needs of each. The assessment form is uniform throughout the state and consists of 160 questions that evaluate the types of caregiving tasks required, the ability of the caregiver to fulfill the tasks, and the caregiver's sense of stress, well-being, and social functioning. An assessment is also made of the home environment with regard to its security, need for repairs, need for assistive devices, and sanitation. The functional status of the care receiver is determined by assessing his or her ability to carry out the activities of daily living, mobility, and cognitive level.

The assessment is followed by the development of a care plan that includes counseling about state, federal, and local benefits. Caregivers are also offered training and education which can improve their coping skills. It is important to also note that the program has received wide support from state aging programs and advocacy groups.

## Minnesota

In January 1992 Minnesota initiated Seniors Agenda for Independent Living (SAIL) as a series of programs to provide community-based alternatives to nursing homes for the frail elderly population (Minnesota Department of Human Services, 1991). The primary objective of SAIL is to enable the elderly to remain in the community through a cost-effective program that reduces the fragmentation of the long-term-care system. In order to achieve this objective, the programs intend to improve access to information, provide a variety of affordable alternatives for living in the community, offer information to encourage consumer preference for low-cost and low-tech options, support informal caregivers, and develop a coordinated system of long-term care.

SAIL is designed to reach its goals in a 20-year period beginning in 1992. During 1992 and 1993 six counties or groups of counties will be selected for the first stage of the implementation. Within each county an integrated access point will provide information and referral, follow-ups, assessment, and preadmission screening for the elderly. The follow-up will monitor health and interventions, while the screening will be required before all nursing home admissions.

A living-at-home/block nurse program will also be established. The nurses acting as case managers will do assessment, provision, and coordination of health and personal care services on a sliding fee scale. They will also train the client and the family and encourage the use of support services.

In order to meet the housing and service needs of the frail, a variety of alternatives will be developed and expanded. Additional funds will be designated for congregate housing, adult foster care, and adult day-care. Efforts will also be made to have home care available for nights and weekends.

A unique aspect of SAIL is its emphasis on public education through the development of a public awareness campaign at the state level. The emphasis will be on educating the public about the aging process and the long-term-care system. Moreover, this campaign will also target individuals already in nursing homes as a means of relocating those who could continue to live more cost-effectively in the community.

Informal caregivers will also be supported under SAIL. Caregiver support and respite projects will be continued or developed with funding provided to establish local coordinated volunteer and paid-respite-worker networks, training, and support groups. Volunteers will be used to provide a wide range of services such as transportation, senior companion, friendly visitor, delivery, chores, and respite care.

A central coordinating agency will be responsible for statewide planning and administration; however, counties will be responsible for developing their own local plans. The state agency will coordinate these efforts and seek to ensure the efficient use of resources throughout the state. Thus, the program seeks to integrate the comprehensiveness of a statewide system while permitting local initiative.

## NATIONAL DEMONSTRATION PROGRAMS

### PACE

The Program of All-inclusive Care for the Elderly (PACE) was initiated in ten sites in 1990 under the Omnibus Budget Reconciliation Act. The demonstration is administered by the Health Care Financing Administration and offers managed care services for the very frail in the community. In 1991 the program existed in Boston; Portland, Oregon; Columbia, South Carolina; Milwaukee; Bronx, New York; Chicago; El Paso; and Denver. Sites are being planned for Webster, New York; Honolulu; Seattle; Sacramento; and Oakland as well as two other locations not yet selected.

PACE replicates the On Lok model of long-term care for the frail elderly through comprehensive services and financing, placing the emphasis on managed care as an alternative to nursing homes. The focus is on the most frail in the community with comprehensive medical and support services managed by a multidisciplinary team of social workers, dietitians, health aides, physicians, and other professionals. Eligibility for PACE is restricted to those meeting Medicaid admission criteria for nursing homes.

Most of the care is provided in adult day health centers and in clients' homes. Clients are entitled to receive both hospital and outpatient medical care, restorative appliances, podiatry, dentistry, grooming, transportation, home care, counseling, recreation therapy, and home-delivered meals. All of the required care is included in one monthly premium with no time limits, additional co-payments, or deductibles.

PACE is financed through Medicare, Medicaid, and individual payments. The sites must apply for Medicare and Medicaid waivers from the Health Care Financing Association. Participants who qualify for both

Medicare and Medicaid do not pay anything. If they qualify for only one program, they must pay a share of the premium. In addition, foundations have also been supportive of PACE with large donations coming from the Robert Wood Johnson Foundation. Eventually, all of the PACE sites will have to assume the entire cost.

The PACE projects are developed in a three-year process which includes a two-stage evaluation. The first evaluation at 18 months studies the implementation of the program in comparison with the On Lok site. The second phase evaluates the site before and after the assumption of full financial risk in order to determine its cost-effectiveness relative to the Medicare and Medicaid systems.

## The Supportive Services Program for Older Adults

The Supportive Services Program, funded by the Robert Wood Johnson Foundation, is a three-year demonstration project operating in 11 home health agencies in different regions of the country (Hereford, 1989). The project's objective is to offer services which complement those tradition-ally provided to the elderly through home health agencies. It thus expands the range of options available to the frail in their homes.

In determining which services to provide in each of the 11 regions, local surveys were conducted of the interests and demands of the well elderly, the frail, and their caregivers. The survey results showed the greatest area of unmet needs was related to home maintenance programs such as housekeeping, yard maintenance, chores, and handyman services. Coin-cidentally, there was little demand for case management by either the elderly or their families. Consequently, unlike many other programs, case management became an ancillary service rather than a core one.

## The Social/HMO Demonstration

The Social/HMO Demonstration Program, established in 1985, was designed to extend the services normally offered by health maintenance organizations to include long-term-care services for the elderly. The program exists in four sites, the Metropolitan Jewish Geriatric Center, Brooklyn, New York; Kaiser Permanente in Portland, Oregon; the Minne-apolis-Ebenezer Society (Seniors Plus); and the Senior Care Action Net-work, Long Beach, California (MacAdam et al., 1991).

The demonstration program is built on the concept that long-term-care services can be insurable under a traditional managed health system of care. Although the sites offer slightly different services, they all provide case management, skilled and intermediate nursing care, home nursing, homemakers, meals, respite, hospice, electronic monitoring, medical transportation, and day-care. These are in addition to the coverage already provided by Medicare. Premiums are paid by Medicare, Medicaid, and participant fees and cover all services.

Enrollment in the plan is through health screening assessments of persons already enrolled in the HMO. Those appearing to meet the criteria for the program are given a more comprehensive assessment. Each site is able to determine its own eligibility criteria. Two of the sites have focused on those most impaired who would meet the admission criteria for nursing homes. These sites offer the widest range of benefits. Sites using only one or two functional impairments in ADLs or the decision of case managers tend to offer fewer services, but these are to a broader group of elderly recipients. These latter programs appear to provide greater access to elderly recipients who are less functionally impaired. Although evaluations of the programs are still being conducted, in theory they provide models for a coordinated and comprehensive system of care.

## COORDINATION THROUGH LOCAL SYSTEMS

In the search to find solutions to the problems confronting the frail elderly and to assist them in remaining in the community, local programs throughout the country have also been developed. By responding to unique geographic and demographic characteristics, these programs illustrate varying ways of helping the elderly to function. The programs described here represent some of these efforts.

### Adult Community Evaluation Services

The Adult Community Evaluation Services (ACES) was begun in 1989 in Howard County, Maryland, consolidating the services provided by the Office of Aging, the Health Department, and Social Services into one program. The purpose of ACES is to reduce fragmentation and facilitate access to the services. Through a cooperative agreement with each of the respective local agencies, ACES offers screening, information and referral, evaluation, case management, and monitoring and licensing of adult day-care programs.

ACES services are provided either by nurses or social workers, who act as the case managers. These professionals make joint assessments of the clients and make the original referrals for assistance. They also provide consultation to the client and the family and arrange for medical and psychiatric consultations and other services.

The consolidation of programs has meant that the time between initial contact and services is noticeably shorter. Calls are responded to within 24 hours, and visits are scheduled within one week of the call. Centralizing client files in one location has also increased the system's accessibility to workers. Consequently, duplication of services is reduced.

The coordinated model of care has attracted the interest of other counties in the state who are also seeking to create a more unified community care system. The single case management system has also received national recognition. In 1991 ACES received a National Achievement Award from the National Association of Counties for its innovativeness in meeting local needs for services.

## Community Health Affiliates

Community Health Affiliates (CHA) is a nonprofit community-based home care agency in the suburbs of Philadelphia. Working with the staff of a residential facility for well elderly individuals with limited incomes, CHA created the Independent Living Program (Flory, 1991). The partnership resulted from concern that without services many of the residents in the facilities were at risk of institutional placement.

Services provided by CHA include personal care, housekeeping, meal planning and preparation, and shopping. These are provided by a home health aide supervised by a registered nurse. Recipients are required to pay $1 per hour for services and receive an average of 2.5 hours per week. Funds are also received from local sources.

In the second year of the project, new services were added, including an assessment of skilled nursing and therapy services and education on nutrition, safety, and medications. Clients are also asked to contribute, if able, $2–$3 per hour for these services. Priority for receiving these services is based on disability, service needs, and the amount of assistance available from family and friends. Funds are also held in reserve for clients in crisis situations. The success of the program in meeting the needs of those in special housing is underscored through its expansion to other communities.

## Bay Area Independent Elders Program

The Bay Area Independent Elders Program (BAIEP) is unique in that it supports the frail by funding local coalitions in the San Francisco Bay Area rather than offering direct services. By supporting coalitions rather than individual agencies, BAIEP, created in 1988, seeks to respond broadly to the needs specified by the community.

The coalitions are composed of professionals, volunteers, businesses, elders, caregivers, and public officials who work together to develop local plans based on local consensus. This enables the program to be flexible and responsive to local concerns. Five principles underlie the program and its critieria for service sponsorship:

1. Empowerment of frail elders and their caregivers;
2. Development of community consensus on frail elders' needs and appropriate responses;
3. Integration of formal and informal sources of care;
4. Expansion of participation and nontraditional resources; and
5. Expansion of the range of choices for the frail elderly and their caregivers.

Based on these principles, funding has been given to 11 coalitions in six counties in the Bay Area to plan and implement strategies that will enable the frail elderly to remain in their own homes. Most coalitions address the needs of ethnically diverse populations with some focused in rural communities. Administrators of the coalitions work jointly with staff from BAIEP in program development, evaluation, and dissemination of results.

Many types of community problems have been addressed. One service initiated a single publicized multilingual information telephone line with agency staff responsible for referrals, in-home assessments, and advocacy for the elderly. Transportation needs were the focus of a coalition that worked with paratransit providers in seven cities to reorganize services for the frail and handicapped. Home rehabilitation, as well as expanded home care services and crime awareness, have also been coalition projects.

An evaluation of the first two years of the program shows that it has made the needs of the frail elderly more visible. With this visibility, services have been expanded. The evaluation also underscored the importance of building on the strengths of each coalition group and of avoiding unrealistic expectations.

## EXPANDING TRADITIONAL SERVICES

### Telephone Reassurance and Friendly Visitors

Telephone reassurance programs have for many years been used as means of providing contact and support to elderly living alone in the community. The program has been expanded in several Canadian communities as a means of providing daily support to the frail elderly living alone (King, 1991).

The service maintains daily telephone contact with its subscribers with the bulk of the work being done by volunteers. Each elderly participant is required to call the central office everyday. These calls are not intended to be long conversations but to provide the older persons with the security of knowing that if there is a problem, professional help is available. If a call is not received by noon, a volunteer calls the individual. If, after several attempts, there is no answer, a contact person is located to make a home visit. All residents over the age of 65 and living alone are eligible for the service, but each must have at least one person who can accept responsibility and act as a contact person.

Although not originally intended to be a social support system, the program has evolved into one which offers emotional support to those living alone. Participants claim that it gives them a sense of well-being, security, and autonomy, particularly with regard to their children. Through these supports it strengthens the ability of the frail in the community.

The social support needs of the frail are also being met through the expansion of a friendly visitors program into a service which seeks to enhance the networks of isolated elderly (Korte and Gupta, 1991). Building upon individuals' needs for intimacy and socialization, the Sunshine Visitors Program was developed in an urban area of North Carolina.

Volunteers in the program receive eight hours of training, which covers the aging process, skills in visiting, community resources, social needs and networks, and strategies for strengthening these networks and relationships. The visitors are carefully matched with clients who, through screening, are found to be socially isolated and lacking a social network. These clients are visited weekly. Program staff maintain monthly contact with the volunteers and review the client action plans.

The program encourages clients to build their networks, with the visitors, acting as advisors, encouraging clients to strengthen existing relationships. The program offers another model for incorporating the skills of volunteers in assisting the elderly in their homes.

## Expanded Health Care

The Over 60 Health Center in Oakland, California, is the first consumer-controlled geriatric health center in the country. Founded in 1991, the center has expanded its services through providing case management, dental care, social work, psychological counseling, and health education. Its focus is on providing comprehensive care to meet the many needs of the frail so that they can remain independent (Over 60 Health Center, 1991).

In order to meet these needs, the center has broadened its scope from medical care to community services. It has begun providing assistance with Durable Power of Attorney to aid elderly patients in deciding upon agents who will be responsible for them in the event that they are unable to make their own decisions. Assisted-living housing for the frail is also being planned. Center staff also screen elderly and provide services in senior centers, community centers, and senior housing. Health education is also offered in these centers.

## SERVING THE MENTALLY FRAIL

Meeting the needs of the cognitively impaired and mentally ill elderly in the community requires particular efforts. Often, these individuals are the most vulnerable to the problems inherent in a fragmented system of care. Without advocates and active outreach, services are likely to be underutilized. The programs described here attempt to respond to the needs of these frail individuals.

### Peer Mental Health Counseling

Peer mental health counseling involves the training of older persons to work as volunteers with community elderly who suffer from emotional problems. Because their ages and life experiences are similar to the clients', these volunteers are able to develop relationships with their clients that are often difficult for professionals to establish.

Unlike friendly visitors, who offer primarily social support to the isolated elder, peer counselors are trained to counsel on a wide array of problems as well as to make referrals. Their roles also provide them with a flexibility frequently lacking in traditional counseling relationships in that they can meet their clients at home or in the community, generally without limits to the number of visits. This flexibility can assist in developing rapport.

The focus of the relationship is on addressing the client's concerns and enabling the client to deal more effectively with these concerns. Skills to do this are taught during special training sessions that encompass aspects of counseling as well as common problems of the elderly such as grief, loneliness, and depression.

A model for peer counseling has been developed and extensively used by the Senior Health and Peer Counseling Center, Santa Monica, California (1988). Through a six-week course, volunteers are trained to work independently with older persons, visiting them in their homes, discussing problems, giving support, and making referrals when necessary. The training involves learning how to listen, observe, and empathize as well as the development of self-awareness. The volunteers are not expected to deal with very complex problems but must be able to make approriate referrals.

Peer counselor programs benefit both the clients and the volunteers. There are no fees for the counseling, although contributions are generally requested. Thus, the program can meet the needs of those who ordinarily could not afford professional help. In addition to counseling, the volunteers are also important links to other community services and can thus truly help to alleviate the isolation often encountered by many elderly. For many elderly, the counselors serve as important role models in that they have successfully endured the same life transitions and losses. As such, they can offer the clients new ways of perceiving and interacting with the world.

## Meeting the Mental Health Needs of the Rural Elderly

The rural elderly face particular problems with regard to mental health services. The availability of programs, as well as access, can be significant barriers to care. The Elderly Outreach Program (EOP), supported by funds from the Administration on Aging, the National Institute of Mental Health, and the State of Iowa, is designed to identify persons in need of mental health care, to provide services, and to initiate and coordinate referrals to other agencies (Buckwalter et al., 1991).

Referrals of potential clients are made from five sources: screenings made by EOP nurses at community sites, an interagency case management network with which the EOP social worker acts as the liaison, mental health outreach specialists, institutions, and gatekeepers. The gatekeepers are those in the community who come into regular contact with the elderly such as mail carriers, veterinarians, grain dealers, extension workers, and utility workers. The program has trained more than 500 of these individuals to locate, identify, and refer isolated elderly believed to be at risk. The training program includes a manual that presents an overview of the gatekeeping role and information on recognizing emotional symptoms with indications for referrals.

Following referral, a multidisciplinary team composed of a part-time psychiatrist, a geriatric nurse practitioner, and two geropsychiatric social workers makes a comprehensive assessment of the potential client in the home. The team also designs the treatment plan, gives the case management responsibility to one of the team members, and assesses progress and determines discharge.

The evaluation of the EOP indicates that it is primarily serving a population that had been functioning well until a crisis such as the loss of a spouse or a physical impairment occurred. The majority are female and living alone and are among those most at risk for not receiving care. One of the main accomplishments of the program, according to its staff, has been educating local people about the mental health needs of the elderly and expanding the outreach sources.

## Coordinated Services

A coordinated approach to meeting mental health needs is used in Baltimore County, Maryland, where the Geriatric Services Program (GSP) has been designed to address several of the problems that are common obstacles to mental health care (DeRenzo et al., 1991). Traditionally, community mental health centers have concentrated on the chronic mentally ill, have not coordinated with aging services, and have given little priority to the elderly with late onset conditions. The GSP, through a cooperative agreement between the Bureau of Mental Health and the Department of Aging, was designed to reduce the gap in existing services, making them more accessible to the elderly.

The GSP team is composed of one full-time psychogeriatric nurse, one part-time geropsychiatrist, and one part-time planner and administrator. This team gives one-third of its staff time to senior centers, one-third to services at the community mental health centers, and one-third to assessment and treatment in the clients' homes.

The work in the senior centers includes support groups, consultation, and training of staff as well as case-finding. In order to overcome potential negative attitudes towards joining the support groups, the groups originated as discussion groups, dealing with topics such as loneliness, relationships, and coping with chronic illness.

Access is facilitated through active outreach, which includes home visits for assessment and therapy, although clients are encouraged to come to the community mental health center in order to save costs. Treatment length varies from only a few months to several years. Funding for the program comes from federal, state, and local sources with clients contributing on a sliding fee scale.

Community mental health centers have also been active in attempting to meet the needs of the mentally frail. Although these centers are drastically underfunded, many have devised innovative and effective methods of reaching the elderly population.

Alexandria Mental Health Center in Alexandria, Virginia, has a geriatric team composed of a psychiatrist, a geriatric/psychiatric nurse, a clinical social worker, and a counselor (Lunardini et al., 1991). Referrals to the team come both from relatives and friends and from professionals.

Upon referral, the older individual is contacted in an informal way to set up a home visit. During the course of two to four visits a treatment plan is developed; this is followed by a care management conference, which includes all involved family and professionals. Therapy is usually one session per week for one year, and the majority of these sessions are not in the office. Fees are based on the client's ability to pay.

The program includes outreach as a major function critical to removing the traditional barriers to mental health care. Visits are routinely made to senior residences, day health, and other community services. In addition, training and consulting are provided to the staff of these services as are support groups for program participants. As well as offering direct services, the program has provided education in mental health needs and the benefits of therapy to both the elderly and service providers.

## Mental Health Outreach

As discussed earlier in the book, tenants of public housing are becoming increasingly older and more frail, and it is frequently their mental functioning that is a deciding factor in their continued residency.

PATTCH (Psychogeriatric Assessment, Treatment, and Teaching in City Housing) is a program of psychogeriatric outreach developed by the departments of psychiatry at the Johns Hopkins Hospital and the Francis Scott Key Medical Center in Baltimore, Maryland. The program has been supported as a demonstration by the National Institute of Mental Health under the local guidance of a community advisory board (Roca et al., 1990).

PATTCH is composed of a team of two nurses and two psychiatrists with a senior geropsychiatrist acting as director. Elderly residents are referred to the team by housing staff. Following the referral, a home visit is made by the nurse, who makes a complete mental health assessment and assessment of physical functioning. Based upon the assessments, recommendations for treatment are made. If residents are unwilling or unable to attend clinics, the team will provide care in the home.

Among the major findings of the project are that housing managers can identify psychiatric symptoms and that such symptoms do not have to lead to eviction. The housing staff are willing to consult with the PATTCH team and to maintain the persons in the buildings. Moreover, very few residents refuse to be visited or to receive interventions.

The project demonstrates the viability and effectiveness of a mobile mental health team for improving accessibility. It also illustrates that this type of program is readily acceptable by both management and residents and that the presence of these services can enable the elderly to remain in their homes.

## INTERNATIONAL MODELS OF COMMUNITY CARE

### Community Care in Britain

With 18 percent of its population over the age of 65 and with an expected growth of 92 percent in the frail elderly population by the year 2010 (Baldock and Evers, 1991), Britain has been increasingly concerned with community care as a means of dealing with the needs of the frail. Current trends and programmatic changes in meeting these needs can provide additional insight relevant to the creation of programs in this country.

Based upon the underlying tenet that remaining in the community is the desire of most older people, while also being less costly than institutional care, the emphasis in the British system is on community care for the frail. The involvement of the government in support of this policy is manifested through both direct financial involvement as well as through plans and guidelines to be enacted by local service systems.

Caregivers are entitled to financial assistance through the Invalid Care Allowances, which provide subsidies for persons providing care to the frail or disabled. The recipients of this care are eligible for their own financial support through Attendance Allowances. These payments, made directly to caregivers and to care recipients by the government, indicate recognition of the needs of these groups as well as providing some support for autonomy and independence.

Further involvement of the public sector in recognizing and meeting the needs of the frail has been rapidly occurring with the reorganization of the community care system. The basis for this reorganization is found in *Community Care Agenda for Action* (Department of Health and Social Security, 1988), a government paper that has revamped the network of services throughout the country. With implementation beginning in 1991, the emphasis in services must be to promote choice and independence among clients, to provide individuals with a wide range of options, to have flexible plans of services, and to concentrate on those with the greatest need. The responsibility for developing plans and services remains with the local governments, but plans must be developed in accordance with national guidelines.

Care managers play pivotal roles in the service system through assessment and formulation of individual care plans that must examine the strengths and living situation of the older person as well as the assistance provided by the informal network. Unlike earlier systems of care that relied primarily on the public sector, the new community care program makes it compulsory for care managers to explore the possibility of using nonstatutory sources of care. In addition, services that can promote independence such as respite services, day-care, and domiciliary help are to be encouraged.

Under these guidelines, each social service department will determine its own service contracts and measures of quality. Each local plan must also include a needs assessment of the population, objectives for community care for the next three years, eligibility procedures, procedures for purchasing services, training provisions, quality assurance, and monitoring systems.

Although the proposals have been criticized—for example, with respect to the coordination of community care plans, the need to improve services for caregivers, and the absence of guidelines for community assessments (Age Concern, 1990)—the intense involvement that the government shows in community care is impressive and exciting.

Local communities have also developed services to meet the needs of the frail. Receiving local subsidies and resources as well as private grants, these programs, like many in the United States, offer innovative ways of offering specific services. Two examples are programs in the City of Liverpool and in Bexley, Kent.

Through joint financing provided by local government and private foundations, the City of Liverpool offers comprehensive services to elderly individuals with dementia who live alone in their own homes. The service is aimed at those at risk for being institutionalized and provides five hours of care a day, seven days a week, through home attendants. Clients are not required to pay for the service, and there is no limit to its duration. The focus is on maintaining these individuals in their homes.

The Bexley Community Care Scheme focuses on strengthening the natural informal network. Rather than providing direct services, the program coordinator works towards empowering the informal caregiver to provide for the frail relative. The role of the professional is to educate the informal caregiver regarding benefits, services, skills and locating assistance with the caregiving tasks.

Care plans are made with the active involvement of the family, who are designated the case managers. As the family caregiver's responsibility increases, the role of the coordinator diminishes into weekly monitoring, which may, in fact, be done by telephone. The emphasis is to have minimal involvement of the formal system while strengthening the abilities of the informal system.

## Sweden

The overall responsibility for the elderly in Sweden resides with the federal government, although local governments are empowered to design their own plans in accordance with federal standards and goals. However, throughout the country social services and health care for the elderly are viewed as being part of the public services to which each citizen is entitled.

The municipalities are directly responsible for institutions and housing for the elderly as well as the health care in these facilities. Underlying all services is the concept that older people should be allowed to remain in their own homes as long as possible. In order to facilitate this type of independent living arrangement, the municipalities can provide for any type of living adaptation, such as adjusting stairs or changing plumbing, that can facilitiate the ability of the older person to remain at home.

Municipal social services are responsible for home helps who assist those elderly living at home and require assistance with shopping, cleaning, cooking, washing, and personal care. The service is provided at night and on weekends with fees for services varying with the municipalities. There are also night patrols composed of home helps and nursing home staff who routinely check on the elderly recipients.

In addition to the home help services, chiropody, meals on wheels, and even hair cutting are generally provided, often through day centers. These centers may be free-standing or a part of a sheltered housing building. The centers act as senior centers in that they also offer activities, meals, and often occupational therapy. These centers are increasingly coming under the direction of the elderly themselves with the idea being that they can best decide on their own activities and interests. Special day centers have also been developed for elderly individuals with dementia who live with their families.

For those unable to remain in their homes, various types of housing are available. Sheltered housing is provided in apartments in buildings with

20 to 100 units. Each apartment has its own kitchen, although a central dining room as well as activity rooms are available to the residents. These buildings also offer home helps to the residents with the fees charged on a sliding scale.

Old-age homes are designed for those elderly who are more functionally impaired. These homes offer complete care to the residents, who live in single rooms. Residents are able to bring their own furniture to these homes and thus retain some degree of independence. Fees for the homes are based on income.

Group housing has become increasingly common for the elderly needing special care as well as for the disabled and those with dementia. Usually six to eight people live in these houses, each with his or her own room. Resident managers both supervise the homes and provide services.

Sweden also has a municipal transportation service that supplements the regular public transit system. This system is for the elderly and handicapped who cannot use other transportation. A particularly innovative program is the use of the postal services to supplement the work of the home helps in rural areas. After consultation with the home helps, these postal employees provide special assistance to the rural elderly who are isolated from neighbors.

Families who care for the elderly can receive payments as well as compensation for up to 30 days a year taken off work to provide care. Efforts are made to support these caregivers, since it is believed that without their assistance the number of home helps would have to be doubled (Swedish Institute, 1991).

There is some doubt as to the ability of services to keep pace with the rising need for care. In order to meet this need, tax increases would be required, and these are unlikely to occur given their present high rate. Furthermore, increased services would require staff increases, and there is limited potential for recruiting more persons into the home help and other caring professions. Thus, although Sweden is committed to a comprehensive system of care, there is some concern that service priorities will have to be set.

## Manitoba, Canada

With increasing attention being paid to the Canadian health care system, the community care program in Manitoba offers an example of a coordinated system of care for the frail in the community. The focus of the system is on maintaining the elderly in their own homes at the highest possible level of functioning. Consequently, community care is perceived as preferential to institutional care, with institutions being used only when support in the community is not feasible.

Representative of the status given to community care in the province is the fact that it is administered through the Ministry of Health with an Office of Continuing Care being a part of the ministry. This office is responsible for policy and planning of services for the ten regions of the province.

Community care is provided through ten regional offices with a coordinator in each who develops, organizes, and administers local plans and services. These activities are carried out in accordance with the plans set at the provincial level. However, coordinators are given some flexibility with regard to staffing and the use of services. Because of the vast geographical differences in the province, ranging from underpopulated rural areas to densely populated urban centers, this capacity for local creativity is essential.

Within each office, nurses and social workers act as care coordinators. In areas such as Winnipeg, they work as a team in assessing the needs of the elderly. In many instances, the coordinator is selected on the basis of the most pressing needs of the frail individual. The coordinators are responsible for the assessments and the arrangement of all services, which can range from home maintenance to intravenous or enterostomal therapy. Services may even involve adaptations to the home to make it more appropriate for the individual. Thus, the program will cover the costs of changing plumbing or fixtures or adding ramps to a house if such improvements will facilitate the frail individual's ability to remain in the commmunity.

Community care is offered without charge to recipients without any time limitation to services. The only restriction is that services, except for temporary periods, must not exceed the cost of care in a nursing home. It is also important to note that referrals can come from any source and do not require medical authorization. Upon referral, the case coordinators make a thorough assessment of the applicant's medical, social, and psychological functioning, as well as the extent of the informal support system. The resulting care plan is designed to meet the needs of the elderly person by supplementing the care that is already being provided.

The systems of care in Britain, Sweden, and Manitoba illustrate strong commitments from the government to maintaining the frail in the community. The comprehensiveness of the systems, the integration of services, and the willingness to consider impairments on the basis of other than purely medical conditions contribute to the responsiveness of these models.

## SUMMARY

The needs of the frail in the community are not going unnoticed. Much creativity and innovation are occurring at state and local levels that address issues of services, coordination, and outreach. The comprehensive scope of services that many of these programs offer provides an effective framework for addressing the types of problems confronted by the frail elderly.

Demonstration programs such as PACE, the Social/HMO, and PATTCH have been particularly important in developing creative and comprehensive ways of meeting the elderly's needs. Findings from the evaluations of these programs as well as the innovative systems initiated in many of the states can provide an essential basis for replication.

In addition, the skillful use of volunteers and teams by community services illustrates the network of resources available in communities as well as the effectiveness of including several professionals in care planning and services. Many of these programs are playing major roles in enabling the frail to continue living in their own homes.

Models of programs outside of the United States further highlight the ways in which government policies can offer a basis for comprehensive services. The programs in Britain, Sweden, and Manitoba offer a vast array of services compatible with the needs of the elderly. In each instance these needs are not dependent upon a medical model that views dependency as resulting from physical problems alone. Consequently, community care for the frail attempts to meet not only the needs of the elderly but also those of caregivers.

Examining the ways in which government policy provides a framework for programs and the ways in which these programs are implemented can provide ideas for service development in the United States. As this country works towards addressing the problems associated with frailty, the approaches used in other countries may assist in the development of broader, more comprehensive community-based care systems.

## Chapter Nine

# Conclusion

The needs of the frail elderly in the community are not going to be met without active responses throughout society. We can anticipate that by the early part of the next century the numbers of elderly people requiring assistance will be far greater than today. Projections from the Urban Institute suggest that in the year 2030 there could be as many as 12 million persons 85 and over and almost 23 million between the ages of 75 and 84 years. It is also projected that the number of elderly who will have ADL limitations may increase by 123 percent between 1990 and 2030 (Zedlewski et al., 1990). With vulnerability to impairment increasing with age, this constitutes a significant number of persons in potential need of assistance.

Addressing the future needs of this population, as well as meeting those of today's elderly, remains a pressing challenge for policy makers and service providers. This book began by depicting frailty as a major public health problem. In its discussion of the scope of frailty and the multitude of responses it requires, it is clear that the problem is not going to be eradicated without varying efforts ranging from prevention to interventions and supports. As with any public health problem, responses and strategies must be implemented in many areas. Moreover, without comprehensive and coordinated efforts, frailty and the problems faced by the frail elderly will continue to mount.

To date, our responses to the needs of the frail have been much less than comprehensive. Shortcomings in both policies and services seriously compromise the ability of the frail elderly to live in the community.

Perhaps basic to these shortcomings is the myopic definition of frailty that has developed through the years coupled with a bias towards institution-alization. Although policy in the 1960s was comprehensive in its concep-tion of frailty and the factors contributing to it, in the last 30 years this definition has become increasingly stringent and based primarily on specific criteria of physical functioning.

Chronic illnesses are major contributors to frailty, although all individ-uals with these illnesses are not necessarily impaired in their functioning. Moreover, many with these illnesses require only minor assistance in order to remain independent. These elderly are perceived and treated as frail only because supports that could sustain them, whether family, friends, grab bars, or transportation, are lacking. Without resources, the independence of these elderly in the community remains threatened.

The stress placed on physical functioning has meant that other problems which can contribute to frailty have been given less weight. Cognitive impairment and mental illness, lack of social resources, and inadequate housing are among the many factors that can severely limit the older person's activities. However, unless these limitations affect the ability to carry out the ADLs or are associated with a specific physical illness, the elderly are unlikely to receive assistance. The social needs, the losses, the isolation, and the economic problems of these individuals are not in themselves criteria for assistance. It is only when a physical problem prohibits the functioning of the older person that he or she becomes eligible for care in the home as well as for many other services.

But a medical emphasis on frailty does not necessarily ensure that all health care needs are addressed. In fact, as viewed by Caplan (1988), the organization of the health care system, the norms guiding health care professionals, and the regulatory and reimbursement schemes for treating illness and disease, as they are based on an acute care model, mean that fewer resources are offered to the frail and chronically ill. These individ-uals, as their problems fail to respond to treatment and most likely cannot be cured, receive far less attention, even with regard to medical care. Consequently, even the health care needs of the frail are likely to remain unmet.

Increased attention is being paid to health education and health promo-tion, and future cohorts of the elderly may live longer without im-pairments. Moreover, the interest being shown on the federal level to the issue of frailty may have a significant impact on the lives of many older persons. These activites are indeed noteworthy but they must not detract from attention to the many other aspects of the elderly's lives that can also impede functioning. Inadequate housing, poverty, and poor services are among the many other phenomena which can affect functioning and which demand attention. But as long as frailty is perceived as being primarily due to physical problems, similar to diseases, its treatment will remain the prerogative of the health care professions.

The basic rights of the frail are also affected by the medicalization of frailty. In that it is perceived as a disease, those with chronic impairments can find their rights to autonomy and self-determination severely threatened. As these rights are juxtaposed with a belief in paternalism or beneficence, the decisions and choices of the elderly are vulnerable to being disregarded. Frailty jeopardizes these basic rights as the impairments are perceived as signs of incapacity.

With limited functioning, whether in hearing, speech, sight, or cognitive ability, advocacy for oneself is extremely difficult. Others who might fill this role are not necessarily available or supportive. Thus the very impairments of the frail jeopardize their ability to defend their own basic rights. On the other hand, as discussed earlier in this book, overlooking these rights can actually lead to more dependence.

Efforts are being undertaken to provide new safeguards to the frail through changes in guardianship proceedings. However, these are not standardized or consistent, so that in many instances, these elderly remain at the mercy of those who hopefully have their "best interest" at heart. Developing more precise means of assessing the ability of the older person to make an informed decision and to act upon the decision and assuring that the individual understands the full meaning and intent of a decision or procedure are essential for assuring the rights of these individuals.

Fundamental to supporting the frail elderly is consistency in what is meant by the term "frail." A global definition referring to all aspects of an individual's life that can limit independence requires inclusive prevention and intervention measures. The more restricted definitions, and particularly the definition limited to three ADLs, obviously call for more limited types of interventions. The ambiguity of what is meant by frailty creates confusion in both the elderly and in service providers. If, instead, services and support were universal, offered on a basis of need for some type of assistance through a coordinated assessment and intervention system, this ambiguity could be greatly reduced.

As discussed in the book, frailty is defined according to varying instruments and measures with wide disparities among programs. Rather than being based on a broad conception of need, assessments of frailty, as resources become scarce, are becoming more stringent and targeted toward the most impaired. The underlying assumption must be that those not meeting these criteria are able to function adequately. However, there is little evidence to support this view, and the status of these elderly individuals remains unclear. Indeed, it would be more humane as well as potentially more cost-effective to support these older persons with a minimal amount of assistance at the time of immediate need rather than to wait until their functioning is more severely impaired.

Consistency and comprehensiveness in assessing frailty are needed to provide a basis for sensitive and appropriate services. Measuring many facets of the older individual's life, the environment, social and psychological supports, income, as well as physical and mental functioning offers a detailed description of needs and consequent areas for specific interventions. With a broad assessment, repeated periodically, it becomes easier to view needs on a continnuum. As needs for assistance fluctuate, a continuum is essential for responsive support. At the same time, it is essential that the elderly individual's concerns also be recognized so that those not defining themselves as frail are not coerced into unwanted support or services.

Overall, policy makers at the federal level have remained reticent and perhaps anxious about the extent of interventions required by the elderly in the community. These hesitations, coupled with the fact that programs for the elderly must compete with those for other population groups, have meant that policy at the federal level has evolved very slowly. Changes that have occurred have been incremental, without any real alterations in either policies or services. But, as has been indicated, structural changes may be warranted if comprehensive services and a continuum of community care are to be offered.

With the medical orientation to frailty, it is particularly disturbing that the health care needs of the frail are largely unmet through the current system. Acute care and its related services remain the focus of Medicare. In the continued absence of an affordable system of long-term care, even the health care needs of many of the frail remain unanswered. However, as long-term care legislation continues to be proposed, there is reason to be optimistic that proposals cognizant of the needs of these elderly, such as the need for continued home care, will be enacted and the bias towards institutionalization finally removed.

The Older Americans Act provides a framework for meeting the needs of the elderly in the community, but its effectiveness is severely compromised through a lack of resources. Moreover, as it remains enmeshed in the political process, its ability to offer preventive and supportive services to all elderly individuals in the community is difficult. Services such as home repair programs, nutrition, and transportation, which can have a major impact on the ability of the elderly to remain in the community, continue to struggle for existence. Depending on local resources and priorities, services are frequently curtailed or discontinued. For many elderly, the loss of such programs can be a major assault on their ability to remain independent.

Adequate financing is basic to the implementation of the services supported by the Older Americans Act and to the fulfillment of its original goals of meeting the needs of all elderly in the community. However, restricted funding has forced policy makers to rethink these original aims and to begin targeting those most in need. As with other services based on eligibility criteria, this focus risks leaving the needs of many other elderly individuals who could benefit from programs, unmet. Those who do not fit specific criteria may be ineligible for services. Moreover, targeting only those with the greatest needs may be a source of stigmatization as they are identified as having particular problems which require the greatest help.

Offering adequately funded programs, in keeping with the original intent of the Older Americans Act, is essential to maintaining the act's integrity. The act offers a framework for both comprehensive services and for a continuum of care in the community as it provides the basis for both preventive and supportive services. However, the role of the Older Americans Act in fulfilling its objectives remains seriously hampered.

Although the federal government may be slow in responding to the needs of the frail, states are becoming increasingly active. Policies regarding the care of the frail in the community are being developed throughout the country. States are becoming increasingly active and responsive to the needs of these individuals. In contrast to the reticence at the federal level, many states have drastically altered their policies, resulting in new and expanded services. Although the majority of these efforts are targeted at the poor or near poor, they offer important models for the development of responsive systems of care.

A particular policy concern exists regarding the role of government services vis-à-vis the family. The traditional reluctance to interfere in the realm of the family must be tempered with the realization that the demographics of society and of families themselves are changing. Increases in life expectancy coupled with the decline in the availability of caregivers necessitate a more active role by services in caring for the frail elderly.

This notwithstanding, the myth that introducing formal services necessarily reduces family involvement must be dispelled. A failure to do so will mean that family caregivers will be forced to meet the demands of their relatives without support. Moreover, it is essential to view the problems of frailty as pertaining not only to the elderly but also to their support systems. The needs of caregivers remain largely unattended in the current system of care. Yet without their interventions and support, the ability of the majority of frail to remain in the community would be significantly affected.

As the book has discussed, families provide the majority of assistance to the frail elderly. Yet there remains little formal recognition of the needs of these caregivers. Interventions to assist them remain limited and are often available only when the caregivers themselves have reached a point of crisis. Moreover, access to many services, particularly respite and home care, remain beyond the economic means of the majority of families.

Elderly spouses are in particular jeopardy with regard to the care they provide to the frail. Concerns over assets and eligibility criteria and norms stressing responsibility for the spouse serve as further barriers to assistance. Having services accessible to these individuals that provide both emotional and important instrumental support as well as linking them to other services is greatly needed. Without such assistance, the well-being of these caregivers may be as vulnerable as the person for whom they are providing care.

Legislative efforts to assist employed caregivers have met with opposition due to concerns over costs and productivity. But, as discussed the struggles that these caregivers encounter in their efforts to meet the demands of their frail relatives in conjunction with those of work are also affecting productivity. Official recognition must be given to the strains and needs of these caregivers so that they can continue to fulfill their roles and meet expectations. Permitting them to take leave and offering counseling, respite, and even day-care for their frail relatives are among the many alternatives that can relieve the burden on these individuals. With increasing numbers of adults beginning to encounter the strain of juggling these multiple demands, interventions to assist them through elder-care programs must be developed.

The confusion with regard to frailty, its definition, and whose responsibility it remains contributes to the fragmentation of the service system. With varying eligibility criteria, overlap, and duplication of services, those most in need are frequently those most in danger of being ignored. Navigating through the maze of services requires an expertise even professionals frequently lack. Poor coordination, accessibility, and linkage between services only accentuates the vulnerability of the frail elderly as they attempt to deal with an incoherent system of care.

Case management is being promoted as a service that can overcome these systemic problems. As such, it is assuming a pivotal role in many community programs and in proposed legislation. Rather than attempting to restructure the system, case management is being promoted as a remedy for its deficiencies. However, this is occurring without sufficient research on its process or outcomes. Case management may in fact pose a particular threat to many frail elderly as it assumes a paternalistic stance with regard to their needs. The lack of guidelines and standards for case management, in conjunction with its rapid proliferation, must be an area of concern for both policy makers and service providers. Without appropriate safeguards, there is a risk that case management will lead to further dependency.

A prerequisite to the frail elderly's remaining in the community is having an environment and services that offer support congruent with individual needs. However, by virtue of their impairments the frail are often limited in their options. Choices with regard to living arrangements as well as the availability of assistance in the home are affected by the level of resources available. These resources are, predominantly, the informal support network and the financial ability to purchase services. Frailty places the greatest hardship on and poses the most signficant threat to those without these resources. Consequently, the effects of frailty are most strongly determined not by any specific physical or mental impairment but by the availability of family or income.

The book has described the many types of community services that can assist the frail in the community. Many of these services can enhance independence while also relieving the burden on families. But barriers continue to exist which jeopardize utilization. A lack of availability and accessibility are dominant problems with these services. Regional variations in services means that in many communities supports essential to community living do not exist. The rural elderly remain particularly vulnerable to isolation from the service network, particularly from essential health care services. Creating accessible services for these individuals is essential for assisting them to remain independent.

However, as discussed earlier in book, even available services may be underutilized. Many elderly and their caregivers do not understand the role of specific programs or are not even aware of their existence. Using local networks can be important in increasing public awareness regarding programs. Providers should assure that intended clients and their families are able to associate services with their specific needs. Moreover, it is essential that any stigma associated with utilization be removed. A prerequisite to utilization is engendering the feeling that services are a right and not a symbol of failure. Finally, services for the frail should not unnecessarily segregate them. To do so may result in the further fragmentation of services as well as in unnecessary discrimination.

Of all services required by the frail elderly, none is of greater importance than home care. Evidence of its significant role in the independence of the elderly is found in its inclusion in all major legislative proposals for long-term-care reform. Having assistance in the home with routine chores, domestic tasks, and personal care can be the determining factor in preventing institutionalization. Often the required assistance is minimal, such as help in getting out of bed or preparing a meal, but without it, the ability to remain in the community is threatened. The result can often be far more expensive and restrictive care, which meets the needs of neither society nor the elderly. Expanding home care coverage is a critical component in the continuum of services for the frail.

Mental health programs are noticeably absent in the continuum of services. Yet the effects of the interaction of mental, social, and physical problems on the well-being and functioning of the elderly is well-documented. Unfortunately, bias on the part of professionals as well as the attitudes of the elderly themselves contribute to this lack of appropriate services. Expectations that symptoms of stress and depression will be more prevalent in the elderly mean that these conditions are not aggressively addressed or even necessarily recognized as problematic. The outcome is that these frail individuals remain vulnerable to being untreated, which can have major implications for their ability to remain in the community. As described in the book, several innovative programs are demonstrating the ways in which these individuals can be reached and in which care can be provided. Replicating these models in other communities can lead to the development of increased mental health services for these at-risk elderly.

Adequate housing and services to assist elderly frail home owners are greatly needed. Frequently these individuals have no alternative but to move due to a lack of services or an inability to maintain their homes. Home maintenance programs are limited and are often the first programs to be curtailed in times of budget restraints. Affordable home adaptations that can maximize the ability of the frail individual to remain in the home, such as by adjusting stairs or widening doorways, are difficult to obtain in many communities in the country.

The frail elderly, in order to remain in the community, must have housing appropriate to their needs and limitations. However, for those without resources, options in housing are severely limited. Even though most prefer to remain in their own homes, curtailment in home repair programs and limited funds for home adaptations mean that this option is often not available. As with other community services, the system for making existing housing suitable for the elderly is fragmented, uncoordinated, inadequately funded, and full of gaps in coverage (Pynoos, 1992). Moreover, the absence of available community options may actually exacerbate costs as individuals are compelled to accept a more restrictive environment than they actually need.

The demand for housing far outweighs its availability meaning that many frail elderly are forced to live in housing that is not suitable to their needs. Congregate housing programs and 202 housing for the elderly are needed if many are to be able to remain in the community. Although legislation for these programs has been enacted, appropriations have not kept pace with rising needs. The lack of resources has, in fact, placed the elderly in competition with other subgroups who also have pressing housing problems.

Responses to the housing needs of the frail elderly have at best been sporadic. Programs which could assist in keeping these individuals in the community are developed but not expanded, even when their effectiveness is demonstrated. Support services and home adaptations that can enhance independence are not universally available. The elderly with mental health problems are particularly vulnerable in all types of senior housing. However, the success of innovative responses suggests that even the needs of these frail elderly can be successfully addressed enabling them to remain in their homes.

Due to histories of discrimination and poverty and lifetimes of poor health care, minority elderly are at increased risk of impairment and frailty. However, the needs of these individuals often go unnoticed as they are underrepresented in the formal service system. This lack of utilization must not be used as evidence that services are not needed. Both health care and community programs that are designed to be both accessible and culturally acceptable are used by these elderly and their caregivers. The fact that individuals do not use services must not be taken to signify an absence of need. Instead, it should cause service providers to examine their programs, their outreach, and the ways in which services are offered.

Interventions for ethnic and minority populations are necessary but must be designed with attention to specific cultural values and traditions. An understanding of the backgrounds of these populations and their towards frailty attitudes as well as the formal service system must be incorporated into the design of services. Without a sensitivity to the needs of these groups, frailty will remain a major problem.

The final chapter of this book reviews several of the innovative efforts being undertaken throughout this country as well as abroad as responses to the needs of the frail elderly. Coordinated service delivery and planning, comprehensive services, and a knowledge of local needs and priorities are basic to many of these programs. Many states are implementing prototypes that can serve as models for future long-term-care systems. In addition, model programs in many areas of the country that are attempting to deal with specific needs and populations of elderly merit particular attention as they respond to the needs of the frail.

The programs in Manitoba, Sweden, and Britain illustrate the way in which a broad interpretation of need offers a basis for comprehensive and universal systems of care which are responsive to the many needs of the frail. Although the wholesale transfer of these programs to the United States may not be feasible, certain elements of these programs such as assessment tools, strategies for strengthening families, and service houses may provide ideas for replication that could help in reducing our present fragmentation.

Developing appropriate responses to the needs of the frail is essential for the elderly, their families, and those aspiring to old age. Efforts to develop these responses are occurring throughout our society as well as in many others. Care must now be taken to assure that these efforts are not wasted. Although the federal government can provide the basis for major structural changes, both state and local programs can offer creativity and often flexibility in the design of systems and progams. It is through these innovative responses and the replication of sensitive and successful programs that today's elderly and the frail of tomorrow can begin to feel secure in their ability to remain independent in the community.

# References

Advisory Panel on Alzheimer's Disease (1989). *Report of the Advisory Panel on Alzheimer's Disease*. DHHS Pub. No. (ADM)89–1644. Washington: U.S. Government Printing Office.

Age Concern (1990). *Caring for People: Draft Implementation Guidance Age Concern Comments*. Ref: ACECCI 1. London: Age Concern.

Ailinger, R. L. (1989). Functional capacity of Hispanic elderly immigrants, *Journal of Applied Gerontology* 8(1), 97–109.

Alperin, D., and Richie, N. (1990). Continuing/life care facilities and the continuum of care. *Journal of Housing for the Elderly*, 6, 125–130.

American Association of Retired Persons (1989). *Empowerment of Minority Elderly, Conference and Roundtable Discussion*, Minority Affairs Initiative. Washington: AARP.

_____. (1992). *Product Report: PERS*. Consumers Affairs Department, AARP. Washington: AARP.

American Association of Retired Persons and The Travelers Foundation (1989). *A National Survey of Caregivers*. Washington: AARP.

Andersen, R., and Newman, J. (1973). Societal and individual determinants of medical care utilization in the United States. *Milbank Memorial Fund Quarterly* 51, 95–124.

Antonnucci, T., and Depner, C. (1982). Social support and informal helping relationships. In T. A. Wills (ed.), *Basic Processes in Helping Relationships*. New York: Academic Press.

Archbold, P. (1982). An analysis of patient caring by women. *Home Health Care Services Quarterly* 3, 5–26.

Arling, G. (1976). The elderly widow and her family, neighbors, and friends. *Journal of Marriage and the Family* 38, 757–768.

Aronson, M., and Gaston, P. (1986). Excess morbidity in spousal caregivers of patients with Alzheimer's disease. Paper presented at the 39th Annual Meeting of the Gerontological Society of America, November, Chicago.

Atchley, R. C. (1989). A continuity theory of normal aging. *The Gerontologist* 29, 183–90.

Baldock, J., and Evers, A. (1991). Innovations and care of the elderly: The front line of change for social welfare services. *Aging International* XVIII, 8–22.

Ball, C. (1989). *Long Term Care Management: A Policy Analysis of Four Exemplary Models.* Public Policy Institute, American Association of Retired Persons. Washington: AARP.

Barker, J. C., Mitteness, L. S., and Wood, S. J. (1988). Gatekeeping: Residential managers and elderly tenants. *The Gerontologist* 28, 625–631.

Barush, A., and Spaid, W. (1989). Gender differences in caregiving: Why do wives report greater burden. *The Gerontologist* 29, 667–677.

Bay Area Independent Elders Program (1991). *Foundation Report.* San Francisco: author.

Belgrave, L. L. (1990). The relevance of chronic illness in the everyday lives of elderly women. *Journal of Aging and Health* 24, 475–500.

Bengston, V. (1976). *The Social Psychology of Aging.* Indianapolis: Bobbs Merrilll.

Berg, R., and Cassells, J., eds. (1990). The Second Fifty Years: Promoting Health and Preventing Disability. Washington: National Academy Press.

Birkel, R., and Jones, C. (1989). A comparison of the caregiving networks of dependent elderly individuals who are lucid and those who are demented. *The Gerontologist.* 29, 114–120.

Blazer, D., and Williams, C. (1980). Epidemiology of dysphoria and depression in an elderly population. *American Journal of Psychiatry* 137, 430–444.

Blume, L., Persily, N., Mirones, M., Swaby-Thorne, A., and Albury, S. (1990). Anatomy of the Alzheimer's respite care program (ARCP). *Home Health Care Services Quarterly* 11, 75–90.

Branch, L., Horowitz, A., and Cain, C. (1989). The implications for everyday life of incident self-reported visual decline among people over age 65 living in the community. *The Gerontologist,* 29 359–365.

Brody, E. (1985). Parent care as a normative family stress. *The Gerontologist* 25, 19–29.

Brody, E., Kleban, M., Johnson, P., Hoffman, C., and Schoonover, C. (1987). Women's changing roles and help to elderly parents: Attitudes of three generations of women. *Journal of Gerontology* 38, 597–607.

Brody, E., Hoffman, C., Kleban, M., and Schoonhover, C. (1989). Caregiving daughters and their local siblings: Perceptions, strains, and interactions. *The Gerontologist* 29, 529–538,

Brody, J., Brock, D. B., and Williams, T. F. (1987). Trends in the health of the elderly population. In L. Breslow, J. E. Fielding, and L. B. Lave (eds.),

*Annual Review of Public Health*, No. 8, 211–234. Palo Alto, California: Annual Reviews, Inc.

Buckwalter, K., Smith, M., Zevenbergen, P., Russell, D. (1991). Mental health services of the rural elderly outreach program. *The Gerontologist* 31, 408–413.

Bulcroft, K., Lielkoph, M., and Tripp, K. (1991). Elderly wards and their legal guardians: Analysis of county probate records in Ohio and Washington. *The Gerontologist* 31, 156–165.

Butler, R., and Hyer, K. (1989). Reimbursement reform for the frail elderly. *Journal of the American Geriatrics Society* 37, 1097–1098.

Callahan, J.. (1989). Case management for the elderly: A panacea? *Journal of Aging and Social Policy* 1(1/2), 181–195.

Callahan, J., and Lansprey, S. (1991). *Supportive Services in Senior Housing: Lessons from the Robert Wood Johnson Foundation Demonstration.* Waltham: Policy Center on Aging, Heller School, Brandeis University.

Callahan, J., and Warach, S. (1981). *Reforming the Long Term Care System.* Lexington: D.C. Heath and Co.

Cantor, M. H. (1979). Social and family relationships of black aged women in New York City. *Journal of Minority Aging* 4, 50–61.

————. (1983). Strain among caregivers: A study of experience in the United States. *The Gerontologist* 23(4), 597–664.

Caplan, A. (1988). Is medical care the right prescription for chronic illness? In S. Sullivan and M. Lewin (eds.), *The Economics and Ethics of Long-Term Care and Disability.* Washington: American Enterprise Institute.

Caring for People (1989). *Community Care in the Next Decade and Beyond.* Presented to Parliament by the Secretaries of State for Health, Social Security, Wales and Scotland. London: Her Majesty's Stationery Office.

Caserta, M., Lund, D., Wright, S., Redburn, D. (1987). Caregivers to dementia patients: The utilization of community services, *The Gerontologist* 27, 209–215.

Cattanach, L., and Tebes, J. (1991). The nature of elder impairments and its impacts on family caregivers' health and psychosocial functioning. *The Gerontologist* 31, 246–256.

Chapko, M., Weissert, W., Ehreth, J., Hedrick, S., and Kelly, J. (1990). A model for reducing the cost of care in VA medical centers that offer adult day health care. *Journal of Aging and Health* 2, 501–513.

Chapleski, E. (1989) Determinants of knowledge of services to the elderly: Are strong ties enabling or inhibiting? *The Gerontologist* 29, 539–545.

Charmaz, K. C. (1983). Loss of self: A fundamental form of suffering in the chronically ill. *Sociology of Health and Illness* 5, 168–195.

Chenoweth, B., and Spencer, B. (1986). Dementia: the experience of family caregivers. *The Gerontologist* 26, 267–272.

Cherry, D., and Rafkin, M. (1988). Adapting day care to the needs of adults with dementia. *The Gerontologist* 28, 116–120.

Chodorow, N. (1978). *The Reproduction of Mothering: Psychoanalysis and the Sociology of Gender.* Berkeley: University of California Press.

Christenson, M. (1990). *Aging in the Designed Environment.* New York, London: Haworth Press.

Clipp, E., and George, L. (1990). Caregiver needs and patterns of social supports, *Journal of Gerontology* 45, 102–112.

Cohen, E. (1988). The elderly mystique: Constraints on the autonomy of the elderly with disabilities. *Gerontologist* 28, 24–32.

Cohen, M., Tell, B., Batten, H., and Larson, M. (1988). Attitudes towards joining a continuing care retirement community. *The Gerontologist* 28, 637–644.

Cohen, S. (1982). Arthritis—but what part? *Geriatrics* 37, 49–51.

Collopy, B. (1988). Autonomy in long-term care: some crucial distinctions. *The Gerontologist* 28, 10–18.

The Commonwealth Fund Commission (1987). *Medicare's Poor, Filling the Gaps in Medical Coverage for Low-Income Elderly Americans.* Baltimore: The Commonwealth Fund Commission.

_____ . (1989). *Poverty and Poor Health Among Elderly Hispanic Americans.* Baltimore: The Commonwealth Fund Commission.

Conrad, K., and Guttman, R. (1991). Characteristics of Alzheimer's versus non-Alzheimer's adult day care centers. *Research on Aging* 13, 96–116..

Conrad, K. J., Hanrahan, P., and Hughes, S. L. (1990). Survey of adult day care in the United States. *Research on Aging* 12(1), 36–55.

*Consumer Reports* (1991). *Review of long term care insurance*, June.

Cook, C. (1989). Statement before the Select Committee on Aging, House of Representatives, *Hearing on Hispanic and Indian Elderly: America's Failure to Care,* Comm. Pub. 101–730. Washington: U.S. Government Printing Office.

Coombs, S, Lambert, T., and Quirk, D. (1982). *An Orientation to the Older Americans Act.* Washington: National Association of State Units on Aging.

Coordinated Care Management Corporation (1989). *Personal Emergency Response System Demonstration Project.* Buffalo: author.

Coulton, C., and Frost, A. (1983). Use of health services by the elderly. *Journal of Health and Social Behavior* 23, 230–236.

Cox, C. (1986). Physician utilization by three groups of ethnic elderly. *Medical Care* 24, 667–676.

_____ . (1991). A comparison of the use of Alzheimer's services by minority and non-minority caregivers. Paper presented at the 44th Annual Meeting of the Gerontological Society of America, San Francisco, November.

_____ . (1992a). Reaching African American staff and patients. Paper presented at the Alzheimers Association Annual Conference: Alzheimer

Care Strategies: Practical Approaches, Professional Alliances, Chicago, July, 1992.

_____. (1992b). Supports and well-being: A comparison of black and white caregivers of dementia victims. Paper presented at the 45th Annual Meeting of the Gerontological Society of America, Washington, November, 1992.

Cox, C., and Gelfand, D. (1987). Familial assistance, exchange, and satisfaction among Hispanic, Portuguese, and Vietnamese elderly. *Journal of Cross-Cultural Gerontology* 2, 241–255.

Cox, C., and Monk, A. (1989). Measuring the effectiveness of a health education program for older adults. *Educational Gerontologist* 15, 9223.

_____. (1990a). Minority caregivers of dementia victims: A comparison of Black and Hispanic families. *Journal of Applied Gerontology* 9, 340–355.

_____. (1990b). Integrating the frail and well elderly: The experience of senior centers. *Journal of Gerontological Social Work* 15, 131–144.

_____. (1992a). The burden of caregiving among Puerto Rican families. Paper presented at the Annual Meeting of the American Society on Aging, San Diego, March.

_____. (1992b). Black and Hispanic caregivers: Their needs and implications for services. In C. Baressi and D. Stull (eds.), *Ethnic Elderly and Long Term Care*. New York: Springer.

Crook, T., and Cohen, G. (1983). *Physicians Guide to the Diagnosis and Treatment of Depression in the Elderly*. Center for the Study of Mental Health and Aging, National Institute of Mental Health. Washington: U.S. Government Printing Office.

Curley, L. (1990). Strategies for implementation: The American Indian perspective in minority affairs Initiative, *Aging and Old Age in Diverse Populations,* Amercian Association of Retired Persons. Washington, D.C.: AARP.

Danigelis, N., and Fengler, A. (1990). Homesharing: How social exchange helps elders live at home. *The Gerontologist* 20, 162–170.

Dawson, D., Hendershot, G., and Fulton, J. (1987). *Aging in the Eighties: Functional Limitations of Individuals Age 65 Years and Over*. U.S. Department of Health and Human Services, Vital and Health Statistics, Number 133, June.

Department of Health and Human Services (1991). *Physical Frailty: A Reducible Barrier to Independence for Older Americans, Report to Congress*, NIH Publication No. 91–197. Washington: National Institutes of Health.

Department of Health and Social Security (1988). *Community Care Agenda for Action: A Report to the Secretary for Social Services by Sir Roy Griffiths*. London: Her Majesty's Stationery Office.

DeRenzo, E., Byer, V., Grady, H., Matricardi, E., Lehmann, S., and Gradet, B. (1991). Comprehensive community based mental health outreach services for suburban seniors. *The Gerontologist* 31, 836–841.

Des Harnais, S., Kobrinski, J., and Chesnev, J. (1987). The early effects of the prospective payment system on inpatient utilization and the quality of care. *Inquiry* 24, 7–16.

Dibner, A. (1990). Personal emergency response systems: Communication technology aids elderly and their families. *Journal of Applied Gerontology* 9, 504–510.

Diemling, G. T., and Bass, D. M. (1986). Symptoms of mental impairment among aged and their effects on family caregivers. *Journal of Gerontology* 41, 778–784.

Dobrish, C. M. (1987). Private practice geriatric care management: a new social work speciality. *Journal of Gerontological Social Work* 11(1/2), 159–172.

Dowd, J. (1975). Aging as exchange: A preface to theory. *Journal of Gerontology* 30, 584–594.

———— . (1980.) *Stratification Among the Aged.* Monterey: Wadsworth.

Duffy M., and MacDonald, E. (1990). Determinants of functional health of older persons. *The Gerontologist* 30, 503–510.

Duke University Center for the Study on Aging (1978). *Multidimensional functional assessment: The OARS methodology* (2nd ed.). Durham: Duke University Press.

Edelman, P. (1986). The impact of community care to the homebound elderly on provision of informal care. *The Gerontologist* 26, Special Issue, 263–274.

Ekert, J., and Lyons, S. (1992). Board and care homes: From the margins to the mainstreams in the 1990's. In M. Ory and A. Duncker (eds.), *In-Home Care for Older People: Health and Supportive Services.* Newbury Park: Sage.

Feinstein, A., Josephy, B., and Wells, C. (1986). Scientific and clinical problems in functional disability. *Annals of Internal Medicine* 105, 413–420.

Fengler, A. and Goodrich, N. (1979). Wives of elderly disabled men: The hidden patients. *The Gerontologist* 12(2), 175–183.

Fillenbaum, G. (1985). Screening the elderly: A brief instrumental activities of daily living measure. *Journal of the American Geriatrics Society* 33(10), 698–706.

Fitting, M., Rabins, P., Lucas, M., and Eastham, J. (1986). Caregivers of dementia patients: A comparison of husbands and wives. *The Gerontologist* 26, 248–259.

Flemming, A., Buchanan, J., Santos, J., and Richards, L. (1984). *Mental Health Services for the Elderly: Report of a Survey of Community Mental Health Centers.* Washington: The Action Committee to Implement the Mental Health Recommendations of the 1981 White House Conference on Aging.

Flory, C. (1991). The independent living program: An alternative to institution-alization. *Caring* January, 42–46.

Folstein, M. (1983). The mini–mental status examination. In T. Crook, S. Ferris, and R. Bartus (eds.), *Assessment in Geriatric Psychopharmacology.* New Canaan: Mark Powley Associates.

Folstein, M., Folstein, S., and McHugh, P. (1975). Mini-Mental Status. A Practical Method for Grading the Cognitive State of Patients for the Clinician. *Journal of Psychiatric Research* 12, 189–198.

Folstein, M., Anthony, J., and Parhad, I. (1985). The meaning of cognitive impairment in the elderly. *Journal of the American Geriatric Society* 33, 228–235.

Ford, A., Folmar, S., Salmon, R., Medalie, J., Roy, A., and Galazka, S. (1988). Health and function in the old and very old. *Journal of the American Geriatrics Society* 33, 246–252.

Fujii, S. M. (1976). Elderly Asian Americans and use of public services. *Social Casework* 57, 202–207.

Gaberlavage, G. (1987). *Social Services to Older Persons Under the Social Services Block Grant,* American Association of Retired Persons, Public Policy Institute. Washington: AARP.

Gadow, S. (1980). Medicine, ethics, and the elderly. *The Gerontologist* 20, 680–688.

Gatz, M., and Pearson, C. (1988). *Evaluation of an emergency alert response system from the point of view of subscribers and family members.* Unpublished manuscript, University of Southern California, Los Angeles.

Gelfand, D. (1984). *The Aging Network.* New York: Springer.

Gelfand, D., and Barresi, C. (1987). Current perspectives in ethnicity and aging. In D. Gelfand and C. Barresi (eds.), *Ethnic Dimensions of Aging.* New York: Springer.

Gelfand, D., and Fandetti, D. (1980). Urban and suburban white ethnics: Attitudes toward care of the aged. *Gerontologist* 20, 588–594.

_____ . (1986). The emergent nature of ethnicity: Dilemmas in assessment. *Social Casework* 67, 542–550.

George, L. (1988). Social participation in later life. In J. Jackson (ed.), *The Black American Elderly.* New York: Springer.

George, L. K., and Gwyther, P. (1986). Caregiver well-being: A multidimensional examination of family caregivers of demented adults. *The Gerontologist* 26(3), 253–259

German, P., Rover B., Burton L., Brandt, L, and Clark, R. (1992). The role of mental morbidity in the nursing home experience. *The Gerontologist* 32, 152–159.

German, P., Shapiro, S., and Skinner, E. (1985). Mental health of the elderly. *Journal of the American Geriatrics Society* 33, 246–252.

Gerontological Society (1978). *Working with Older People: A Guide to Practice.* Rockville: U.S. Department of Health, Education, and Welfare.

Gibson, R. (1982). Blacks at middle and late life: Resources and coping. *Annals of the American Academy of Political and Social Science* 464, 79–90.

_____ . (1983). *Coping in the 80's: New Research Findings from the National Survey of Black Americans.* Richmond: Virginia Union College, Black Family Institute.

Gibson, R. C., and Jackson, J. S. (1988). The health, physical functioning and informal supports of the black elderly. *Milbank Quarterly* 65 (Supplement 2), 421–454.

Gonyea, J. G. (1987). The family and dependency: Factors associated with institutional decisionmaking. *Journal of Gerontological Social Work* 12, 61–73.

Gonyea, J., and Silverstein, N. (1991). The role of Alzheimer's disease support groups in families' utilization of community services. *Journal of Gerontological Social Work* 16, 43–55.

Gonyea, J., Hudson, R., and Seltzer, G. (1990). Housing preferences of vulnerable elders in suburbia. *Journal of Housing for the Elderly* 1(2), 79–95.

Goodman, C. C. (1987). The elderly frail: Who should get case management? *Journal of Gerontological Social Work* 11(3/4), 99–113.

Gould, K. (1989). A minority–feminist perspective on women and aging. *Journal of Women and Aging* 1, 195–216.

Gozali, J. (1971). The relation between age and attitudes toward disabled persons. *The Gerontologist* 4, 289–291.

Greene, R. (1986). Countertransference issues in social work with the aged. *Journal of Gerontological Social Work* 9, 79–87.

Greene, V., and Monahan, D. (1987). The effect of a professionally guided caregiver support and education group on institutionalization of care receivers. *The Gerontologist* 27, 716–722.

Guralnik, J. M. (1991). Prospects for the compression of morbidity: The challenge posed by increasing disability in the years prior to death. *Journal of Aging and Health* 3(2), 138–154.

Guralnik, J. M., LaCroix, A. Z., Everett, D. F., and Kovar, M. (1989). Aging in the eighties: The prevalence of comorbidity and its association with disability. *Advance Data*, 170. Hyattsville, Md.: National Center for Health Statistics.

Gurland, B. J., Kurlansky, J., Sharpe, L., Simon, R., Stiller, P., and Berkett, P. (1978). The comprehensive assessment and referral evaluation (CARE): Rationale, development and reliability. *International Journal of Aging and Human Development* 8, 9–41.

Gurland, B., Cross, P., and Golden, R. (1980). The epidemiology of depression and dementia in the elderly: The use of mutiple indicatiors in these conditions. In J. Cole and J. Barnett (eds.), *Psychopathology of the Aged.* New York: Raven.

Haley, W., Brown, S., and Levine, E. (1987). Family caregiver appraisals of patient behavioral disturbance in senile dementia. *Clinical Gerontologist* 6, 25–34.

Hansen, A., Melma, H., Buckspan, L., Henderson, B., Helbig, B., and Fair, S. (1978). Correlates of senior center participation, *The Gerontologist* 18, 193–199.

Hare, P. (1991). The Echo housing/granny flat experience in the U.S. *Journal of Housing for the Elderly* 7, 57–70.

Harel, Z. (1985). Nutrition site service users: Does racial background make a difference. *The Gerontologist* 23, 500–504.

―――. (1987). Older Americans Act related homebound aged: What difference does racial background make? *Journal of Gerontological Social Work* 10, 133–143.

Harel, Z., Noelker, L., and Blake, B. (1985). Comprehensive services for the aged: Theoretical and empirical perspectives. *The Gerontologist* 25, 644–649.

Harel, Z., McKinney, E., and Williams, M. (1987). Aging, Ethnicity, and Services. In D. Gelfand and C. Baressi (eds.). *Ethnic Dimensions of Aging*. New York: Springer.

Harper, M., and Alexander, C. (1990). Profile of the black elderly. In M. Harper, (ed.), *Minority Aging, Essential Curricula Content for Selected Health and Allied Professions*. Health Resources and Services Administration, DHHS Pub. No. HRS (P–DV–90–4). Washington: U.S. Government Printing Office.

Hasler, B. (1991). *Report on the Characteristics of Clients Receiving Community-based Long Term Care*. Washington: National Association of State Units on Aging.

Hawes, C. (1990). Selecting eligibility criteria for individuals with dementia. In M. Keenan (ed.), *Issues in the Measurement of Cognitive Impairment for Determining Eligibility for Long Term Care Benefits*. Washington: American Association of Retired Persons.

Hendrickson, M. (1988). State tax incentives for persons giving informal care to the elderly. *Health Care Financing Review, Annual Supplement* 123–128.

Hereford, R. (1989). The market for community services for older persons. *Pride Institute Journal of Long Term Home Health Care* 8, 44–51.

Hofland, B. (1988). Autonomy in long term care: Background issues and a programmatic response. *The Gerontologist* 28, 3–10.

Hogstel, M., and Kashka, M. (1989). Staying healthy after 85. *Geriatric Nursing* 5, 16–18.

Horowitz, A. (1985). Family caregiving to the frail elderly. *Annual Review of Gerontology and Geriatrics* 5, 194–246.

Hunt, M., and Gunter-Hunt, G. (1985). Naturally occurring retirement communities. *Journal of Housing for the Elderly* 3, 3–21.

Iris, M. (1988). Guardianship and the elderly: A multi-perspective view of the decision-making process. *Gerontologist* 28, 39–45.

Isensee, L., and Campbell, N. (1987). *Dependent Care Tax Provisions in the States: An Opportunity for Reform.* Washington: National Women's Law Center.

Jaffe, D., and Howe, E. (1988). Agency assisted shared housing: The nature of programs and matches. *The Gerontologist* 20, 162–170.

———. (1989). Case management for homesharing. *Journal of Gerontological Social Work* 14, 91–110.

Jecker, N. (1990). The role of intimate others in medical decision making. *The Gerontologist* 30, 65–71.

Jette, A., Branch, L., and Berlin, J. (1990). Musculoskeletal impairments and physical disablement among the aged. *Journal of Gerontology* 45, 203–208.

Johnson, H., Gibson, R., and Lucky, I. (1990). Health and social characteristics: Implications for services. In Z. Harel, E. Mckinney, and M. Williams (eds.), *Black Aged: Understanding Diversity.* Newbury Park: Sage.

Johnson, C. (1983). Dyadic family relations and social support. *The Gerontologist* 2, 377–383.

Johnson, C., and Baher, B. (1990). Families and networks among older inner city blacks. *Gerontologist* 30, 726–733.

Justice, D. (1988). *State Long Term Care Reform: Development of Community Care Systems in Six States.* Washington: National Governors Association.

Kane, R., and Kane, R. (1981). *Assessing the Elderly: A Practical Guide to Measurement.* Lexington: Lexington Books.

Kannel, W., and Gordon, T. (1978). Evaluation of cardiovascular epidemiology from Framingham. *American Journal of Cardiology* 37, 269–282.

Kashner, T., Magaziner, J., and Pruitt, S. (1990). Family size and caregiving of aged persons with hip fracture. In D. Biegel and A. Blum (eds.), *Aging and Caregiving.* Newbury Park: Sage.

Katz, S., Ford, A. B., Moskowitz, R. W., Jackson, B., and Jaffe, M. (1963). Studies of illness in the aged—the index of ADL. *Journal of the American Medical Association* 185 (12), 94–99.

Kaufman, A. (1990). Social network assessment: A critical component in case management for functionally impaired older persons. *International Journal on Aging and Human Development* 30 (1), 63–75.

Kay, D. (1977). The epidemiology and identification of brain deficit in the elderly. In C. Eisdorfer and R. Friedel (eds.), *Cognitive and Emotional Disturbance in the Elderly.* Chicago: Year Book Medical Publishers.

Kemper, P. (1990). Case management agency systems of administering long-term care: Evidence from the Channeling Demonstration. *The Gerontologist* 30, 817–824.

Kemper, P., Applebaum, R., and Harrigan, M. (1987). Community care demonstrations: What have we learned? *Health Care Financing Review* 8, 87–100.

King, H. (1991). A telephone reassurance service: A natural support system for the elderly. *Journal of Gerontological Social Work* 16(1/2), 159–175.

Korte, C., and Gupta, V. (1991). A program of friendly visitors as network builders. *The Gerontologist* 31, 404–408.

Krout, J. (1988). Senior center linkages with community organizations. *Research on Aging* 10, 258–274.

_____ . (1989). *Senior Centers in America*. Westport: Greenwood.

Krout, J., Cutler, S., and Coward, R. (1990). Correlates of senior center participation: A national analysis. *The Gerontologist* 30, 70–79.

Kuriansky, J. B., Gurland, B. J., Sleiss, M., and Cowan, D. M. (1976). The assessment of self-care capacity in geriatric psychiatric patients by objective and subjective methods. *Journal of Counseling Psychology* 32, 95–102.

Kusserow, Richard, U.S. Inspector General (1990). *Cost-Sharing For Older Americans*. OEI–02–90–01010. Washington: Office of the Inspector General.

Lacayo, C. G. (1982). Triple jeopardy: Underserved Hispanic elderly. *Generations* 6 (3).

Lawton, M., and Brody, E. (1969). Assessment of older people: Self-maintaining and instrumental activities of daily living. *The Gerontologist* 9 (3), 179–186.

Lawton, M., Moss, M., Fulcomer, M., and Kleban, M. (1982). A research and service oriented multilevel assessment instrument. *The Journal of Gerontology* 37, 91–99.

Lawton, M., Brody, E., Saperstein, A., and Grimes, M. (1989). Respite services for caregivers: Research findings for service planning. *Home Health Care Services Quarterly* 10, 5–32.

Lazarowich, N. (1991). Summary of the Echo Housing experience. *Journal of Housing for the Elderly* 7, 71–74.

Lebowitz, B., Light, E., and Baily, R. (1987). Community mental health center services for the elderly: The impact of coordination with Area Agencies on Aging. *The Gerontologist* 27, 699–702.

Lee, J. (1987). Asian American elderly: A neglected minority group. *Journal of Gerontological Social Work* 10, 103–116.

Lee, P. (1985). Theoretical perspectives on social networks. In W. Sauer and R. Coward (eds.), *Social Support Networks and the Care of the Elderly*. New York: Springer.

Lee, P., and Ellithorpe, E. (1982). Intergenerational exchange and subjective well-being among the elderly. *Journal of Marriage and the Family* 44, 217–224.

Leon, J., and Lair, T. (1990). *Functional status of the noninstitutionalized elderly: Estimates of ADL and IADL Difficulties,* Research Findings 4 (DHHS Publication No. (PHS) 90–3462) Rockville: Public Health Service.

Light, E., Lebowitz, B., and Baily, F. (1986). CHMC's and elderly services: An analysis of direct and indirect services and service delivery sites. *Community Mental Health Journal* 4, 294–302.

Lipson, L., and Laudicina, S. (1991). *State Home and Community-Based Services for the Aged Under Medicaid.* American Association of Retired Persons, Public Policy Institute. Washington: AARP.

Litwak, E. (1985). *Helping the Elderly: The Complementary Roles of Informal Networks and Formal Systems.* New York: Guilford.

Liu, K., and Manton, K. (1988). *Effects of medicare hospital prospective payment system (PPS) on disabled medicare beneficiaries.* Final report to the U.S. Department of Health and Human Services, Office of the Assistant Secretary for Planning and Evaluation and the Health Care Financing Administration (18C–9864).

Liu, K., and Cornelius, E. (1989). *ADLs and Eligibility for Long Term Care Services.* Report prepared for the Commonwealth Fund Commission on Elderly People Living Alone. Background Paper Series No. 14. Baltimore: The Commonwealth Commisssion.

Lockery, S. (1991). Caregiving among racial and ethnic minority elders: Family and social supports. *Generations* (Fall/Winter), 58–63.

Lombardo, N. (1990). Issues in the Measurement of Cognitive Impairment for Determining Eligibility for Long-term Care Benefits. In *Issues in the Measurement of Cognitive Impairment for Determining Eligibility for Long-Term Care Benefits.* Report to the Public Policy Institute, American Association of Retired Persons. Washington: AARP.

Lonergan, Edmund T., ed. (1991). *Extending life: A national research agenda on aging.* Washington: National Academy Press.

Longino, C., Jackson, D., Zimmerman, R., and Bradsher, J. (1991). The second move: Health and geographic mobility. *Journal of Gerontology* 46, S218–S225.

Lopez, C., and Aguilera, E. (1991). *On the Sidelines: Hispanic Elderly and the Continuum of Care.* Washington: National Council of La Raza.

Luehrs, J., and Ramthun, R. (1989). *State Experience with ADL's.* Background Papers Series: No. 17. Baltimore: The Commonwealth Fund, Commission on Elderly People Living Alone.

Lum, D., Cheung, L., Cho, E., Tang, T., and Yau, H. (1980). The psychosocial needs of the Chinese elderly. *Social Casework* 61, 100–105.

Lunardini, S., Cunningham, T., and Warren, D. (1991). Health comes of age. *Aging.* No. 362, 15–21.

Lyman, S. (1976). *Chinese Americans.* New York: Random House.

MacAdam, M., Greenberg, J., Greenlick, M., Gruenberg, L., and Malone, J. (1991). Targeting long-term care for the frail elderly: Models from the social/HMO demonstration. *The Journal of Applied Gerontology* 10 (4), 389–405.

Macken, C. (1986). A profile of functionally impaired elderly persons living in the community. *Health Care Financing Review* 7, 33–42.

Maier, S., and Seligman, M. (1976). Learned helplessness: Theory and evidence. *Journal of Experimental Psychology: General* 105, 3–46.

Malozemoff, I. K., Anderson, J. G., and Rosenbaum, L. V. (1978). *Housing for the Elderly: Evaluation of the Effectiveness of Congregate Residences.* Boulder, Colorado: Westview.

Manson, S., and Callaway, D. (1990a). Older American Indians: Status and issues in income, housing, and health. In *Aging and Old Age in Diverse Populations,* Minority Affairs Initiative, American Association of Retired Persons. Washington: AARP.

_____. (1990b). Health and aging among American Indians: Issues and Challenges for the Geriatric Sciences. In M. Harper (ed.), *Minority Aging: Essential Curricula Content for Selected Health and Allied Health Professions.* Health Resources and Services Administration, DHHS Pub. No. HRS (P–DV–90–4). Washington: U.S. Government Printing Office.

Manton, K. G. (1988). A longitudinal study of functional change and mortality in the U.S. *Journal of Gerontology* 43, S153–S161.

Markides, K., Liang, J., and Jackson, J. (1990). Race, ethnicity, and aging: Conceptual and methodological issues. In L. George and R. Binstock (eds.), *Handbook of the Social Sciences,* 3rd Edition. New York: Academic Press.

Maslow, K. (1990). Linking persons with dementia to appropriate services: Summary of an OTA study. *Pride Institute Journal of Long Term Care* 9, 42–50.

Matsuoka, J. (1990). Differential acculturation among Vietnamese refugees. *Social Work* 35, 341–345.

McCaslin, R. (1989). Service utilization by the elderly: The importance of orientation to the formal system. *Journal of Gerontological Social Work* 14(1/2), 153–174.

McCoy, J., and Conley, R. (1990). Surveying board and care homes: Issues and data collection problems. *The Gerontologist* 30, 147–154.

McCulloch, S. (1990). The relationship of intergenerational reciprocity of aid to the morale of older parents: Equity and exchange theory comparisons. *Journal of Gerontology* 45, S150–S155.

Mead, G. (1934). *Mind, Self and Society.* Chicago: The University of Chicago.

Meltzer, J. (1982). *Respite Care: An Emerging Family Support Service.* Washington: The Center for the Study of Social Policy.

Merrill, J., and Hunt, M. (1990). Aging in place: A dilemma for retirement housing administrators. *Journal of Applied Gerontology* 9, 60–76.

Mikelsons, M., and Turner, M. (1991). *Housing Conditions of the Elderly in the 1980's, A Data Book.* Washington: Urban Institute.

Miller, C. (1978). Survival and ambulation following hip facture. *Journal of Bone and Joint Surgery* 60-A, 930–934.

Miller, D., and Goldman, L. (1989). Perceptions of caregivers about special respite services for the elderly. *The Gerontologist* 29, 408–410.

Mindel, C., and Wright, R. (1982). The use of social services by black and white elderly: The role of social support systems. *Journal of Gerontological Social Work* 4, 106–125.

Minnesota Department of Human Services (1991). *A Strategy for Long-Term Care in the State of Minnesota, Developed in Response to the SAIL Report.* St. Paul: Department of Human Services.

Mitchell, J., and Register, J. C. (1984). An exploration of family interaction with the elderly by race, socioeconomic status and residence. *The Gerontologist* 24, 48–54.

Monk, A. (1990). Gerontological social services: Theory and practice. In A. Monk (ed.), *Handbook of Gerontological Services,* 2nd edition. New York: Columbia University Press.

Monk, A., and Cox, C. (1991). *Home Care for the Elderly: An International Perspective.* Westport: Auburn House.

Montgomery, R. (1988). Respite care: Lessons from a controlled design study. *Health Care Financing Review,* Supplement, 133–138.

Montgomery, R., and Borgatta, E. (1989). The effects of alternative support strategies on family caregiving. *The Gerontologist* 29, 457–464.

Montgomery, R., and Kamo, Y. (1987). Differences between sons and daughters in parental caregiving. Paper presented at the Annual Meeting of the Gerontological Society of America, November, Washington, DC.

Morris, J., Sherwood, S., and Mor, V. (1984). An assessment tool for use in identifying functionally vulnerable persons in the community. *The Gerontologist* 24(4), 373–379.

Morycz, R. K. (1985). Caregiving strain and the desire to institutionalize family members with Alzheimer's disease. *Research on Aging* 7, 329–361.

Motenko, A. K. (1989). The frustrations, gratifications and well-being of dementia caregivers. *The Gerontologist* 29(2), 166–172.

Mutran, E., and Reitzes, D. (1984). Intergenerational support activities and well-being among the elderly: A convergence of exchange and symbolic interaction perspectives. *American Sociological Review* 49, 117–130.

National Association of Nutrition and Aging Services (1989). *The role of congregate nutrition providers in emerging long-term care strategies. A position statement.* National Association on Nutrition and Aging Services, Grand Rapids, Michigan.

National Center for Health Statistics (1987). *Health Statistics on Older Persons, United States 1986.* DHHS Publication No. (PHS) 97–1409. Washington: U.S. Government Printing Office.

———. (1988). *Utilization of Short Stay Hospitals, U.S. 1985, Annual Summary.* Vital and Health Statistics, Series 13, No. 96. Hyattsville: Public Health Service.

———. (1989). *The National Nursing Home Survey: 1985, Summary for the United States.* Vital and Health Statistics, Series 14, No. 97. Washington: U.S. Government Printing Office.

_____. (1990). *Health of Black and White Americans, 1985–87*. Vital and Health Statistics, 10 (171) Series 10., DHHS Pub. No. 90–1599. Hyatts-ville: Public Health Service.

National Council of La Raza (1990). *Anciano Network News* 1, March-April, 4–5.

National Indian Council on Aging (1981) *American Indian Elderly: A National Profile*. Albuquerque: National Indian Council.

National Institute on Adult Daycare (1984). *Standards for ADC*. Washington: The National Council on the Aging.

National Resource Center on Health Promotion (1991). *Perspectives in Health Promotion and Aging*. Washington, American Association of Retired Persons.

Neal, M., Chapman, N., and Ingersoll-Dayton, B. (1987). Work and eldercare: A survey of employees. Paper presented at the Annual Meeting of the Gerontological Society, November, Washington, DC.

Nelson, G. (1980). Contrasting services to the aged. *Social Service Review* September, 376–389.

_____. (1982). A Role for Title XX in the Aging Network, *The Gerontologist* 22, 18–25.

Neugarten, B., and Gutman, D. (1968). Age-sex roles and personality in middle age. In B. Neugarten (ed.), *Middle Age and Aging*, Chicago: University of Chicago Press.

New York State Office for the Aging (1990). *Respite Guide: Running a Respite Care Program in the 1990's*. Albany: New York State Office on Aging.

Noelker, L., and Bass, D. (1989). Home care for elderly persons: Linkages betweeen formal and informal caregivers. *Journal of Gerontology* 44, 563–570.

Noelker, L., and Wallace, R. (1985). The organization of family care for im-paired elderly. *Journal of Family Issues* 6, 23–44.

Norris, V., Stephens, M., and Kinney, J. (1990). The impact of family interac-tions on recovery from stroke: Help or hindrence. *The Gerontologist* 30, 535–543.

O'Donnell, R. M. (1989). Functional disability among the Puerto Rican elderly. *Journal of Aging and Health* 1(2), 244–264.

Oktay, J. S., and Palley, H. A. (1988). The frail elderly and the promise of foster care. *Adult Foster Care Journal* 2(1), 8–24.

Osako, M. M., and Liu, W. T. (1986). Intergenerational relations and the aged among Japanese Americans. *Research on Aging* 8(1), 128–155.

Over 60 Health Center: (1991). *Annual Report*, Berkeley: author.

PACE, *Program of All-Inclusive Care for the Elderly*. San Francisco: On-Lok, Inc.

Penning, M. (1990). Receipt of assistance by elderly people: Hierarchical selec-tion and task specificity. *The Gerontologist* 30, 220–228.

Pennsylvania Department of Aging (1991). *Family Caregiver Support Pro-gram: Final Evaluation Report*. Harrisburg: Pennsylvania Department on Aging.

Phillips, B., Stephens, S., Cerf, J., Ensor, W., McDonald, A., Moline, C., Stone, R., and Wooldridge, J. (1986). *The Evaluation of the National Long Term Care Demonstration Survey Data Collection Design, and Procedures*. New Jersey: Mathematica Policy Research Inc.

Poulshock, S. W. and Diemling, G. T. (1984). Families caring for elders in residence: Issues in the measurement of burden. *Journal of Gerontology* 39, 230–239.

Prosper, V. (1987). *A Review of Congregate Housing in the U.S.* New York: State Office for the Aging.

Pruchno, R., and Resch, N. (1989). Aberrant behaviors and Alzheimer's disease: Mental health effects on spouse caregivers. *Journal of Gerontology* Social Sciences, 44, S177–S182.

Pynoos, J. (1992). Strategies for home modification and repair. *Generations* XVI, 21–25.

Pynoos, J., Hamburger, L., and June, A. (1990). Supportive relationships in shared housing. *Journal of Housing for the Elderly* 6, 1–24.

Rabins, P. (1990). Defining the population and its problems. In *Issues in the Measurement of Cognitive Impairment for Determining Eligibility for Long Term Care Benefits*. Report to the Public Policy Institute, American Association of Retired Persons. Washington: AARP.

Rabins, P., Mace, N., and Lucas, M. (1982). The impact of dementia on the family. *Journal of the American Medical Association* 248, 333–335.

Ralston, P. (1984). Senior center utilization by black elderly adults: Social, attitudinal and knowledge correlates. *Journal of Gerontology* 39, 224–229.

———. (1991). Senior centers and minority elderly: A critical review. *The Gerontologist* 31, 325–332.

Randolph, S. (1990). Health care problems of the black elderly, testimony before the Select Committee on Aging, U.S. House of Representatives. Comm. Pub. No.101–743. Washington: U.S. Government Printing Office.

Regan, J. J. (1990). *The Aged Client and the Law*. New York: Columbia University Press.

Reisberg, B., and Ferris, S. H. (1983). A clinical rating scale for symptoms of psychosis in Alzheimer's disease. *Psychopharmacology Bulletin* 21, 101–104.

Reschovsky, J., and Newman, S. (1990). Adaptations for independent living by older frail households. *The Gerontologist* 30, 543–552.

Rivlin, A. M., and Weiner, J. M. (1988). *Caring for the Disabled Elderly*. Washington: The Brookings Institution.

Roberto, K. (1988). Women with osteoporosis: The role of the family and service community. *The Gerontologist* 28, 224–233.

Roberts, R., and Bengston, V. (1990). Is intergenerational solidarity a unidimensional construct? A second test of a formal model. *Journal of Gerontology* 45, S12–S20.

Roca, R., Storer, D., Robbins, B., Tlasek, M., and Rabins, P. (1990). Psychogeriatric assessment and treatment in public housing. *Hospital and Community Psychiatry* 41, 916–920.

Rosenthal, C. (1986). Family supports in later life: Does ethnicity make a difference. *The Gerontologist* 26, 19–24.

Rovner, B., Kafonek, S., Filipp, L., Lucas, M., and Folsteing, M. (1986). Prevalence of mental illness in a community nursing home. *American Journal of Psychiatry* 143, 11.

Rowland, D., (1989). *Help at Home: Long Term Care Assistance for Impaired Elderly People.* The Commonwealth Commission on Elderly People Living Alone, Baltimore: The Commonwealth Fund Commission.

Rowland D., and Lyons P. (1987). *Medicare's Poor: Filling the Gaps in Medical Coverage for Low Income Elderly Americans.* Baltimore: The Commonwealth Fund Commission.

Rowland, D., Lyons, P., Neuman, P., Salganicoff, A., and Taghavi, L. (1988). *Defining the Functionally Impaired Elderly Population.* Report to the American Association of Retired Persons, Public Policy Institute. Washington: AARP.

Ruchln, H. (1988). Continuing care retirement communities: An analysis of financial viability and health care coverage. *The Gerontologist* 28, 156–162.

Safilios-Rothschild, C. (1970). *The Sociology and Social Psychology of Disability and Rehabilitation.* New York: Random House.

Salcido, R. M. (1980). The use of formal and informal health and welfare services of the Asian–American elderly: An exploratory study. *California Sociologist* 3(3), 213–229.

Sauer, W., and Coward, R. (1985). The role of social support networks in the care of the elderly. In W. Sauer and R. Coward (eds.), *Social Support Networks and the Care of the Elderly.* New York: Springer.

Scharlach, A. E., and Boyd, S. (1989). Caregiving and employment: Results of an employer survey. *The Gerontologist* 29(3), 382–387.

Scharlach, A., and Frenzel, C. (1986). An evaluation of institutional-based respite. *The Gerontologist* 26, 77–82.

Schurman, R., Kramer, P., and Mitchell, J. (1985). The hidden mental health network: Treatment of mental illness by non-psychiatric physicians. *Archives of General Psychiatry* 42, 89–94.

Seligman, M. (1975). *Helplessness.* San Francisco: W.H. Freeman.

Senior Health and Peer Counseling Center (1988). *Manual for Developing Peer Counseling Programs.* Santa Monica: author.

Sharp, K., Ross, C., and Cocherhan, W. (1983). Symptoms, beliefs, and use of physician services among the disadvantaged. *Journal of Health and Social Behavior* 24, 255–263.

Sheehan, N. (1986). Aging of tenants: Termination policy in public senior housing. *The Gerontologist* 26, 505–509.

Sheehan, N., and Wisensale, S. (1991). Aging in place: Discharge policies and procedures concerning frailty among senior housing tenants. *Journal of Gerontological Social Work* 16, 109–123.

Shephard, R. (1987). *Physical Activity in Aging,* 2nd ed. London: Croom Helm.

Sherman, S., and Newman, E. (1988). *Foster Families for Adults: A Community Alternative in Long Term Care.* New York: Columbia University Press.

Shibutani, T., and Kwan, K. (1965). *Ethnic Stratification.* New York: Macmillan.

Sillman, R., and Strasberg, J. (1988). Family caregiving: Impact on patient functioning and underlying causes of dependency. *The Gerontologist* 28, 377–382.

Skinner, J. (1990). Federal programs for the vulnerable aged. In Z. Harel, P. Ehrlich, and R. Hubbard (eds.), *The Vulnerable Aged: People, Services and Policies.* New York: Springer.

Smith, G., Smith, M., and Toseland, R. (1991). Problems identified by family caregivers in counseling. *The Gerontologist* 31, 15–23.

Soldo, B., and Longino, C. (1988). Social and physical environments for the vulnerable aged. In *America's Aging, the Social and Built Environments.* Institute of Medicine and National Research Council. Washington: National Academy Press.

Soldo, B., Wolf, D., and Agree, E. (1990). Family, households, and care arrangements. *Journal of Gerontology* 45, Social Sciences, S238–S249.

Spector, W. (1991). Cognitive impairment and disruptive behaviors among community-based elderly persons: Implications for targeting long-term care. *The Gerontologist* 31, 51–60.

Spector, W., Katz, S., Murphy, J., and Fulton, J. (1987). The hierarchical relationship between activities of daily living and instrumental activities of daily living. *Journal of Chronic Diseases* 40(65), 481–489.

Stafford, J., and Dibner, A. (1984). *Lifeline Programs in 1984: Stability and Growth.* Watertown: Lifeline Systems, Inc.

Stanford, E., Peddecord, K., and Lockery, S. (1990). Variations among the elderly in Black, Hispanic and White families. In T. Brubaker (ed.), *Family Relationships in Later Life.* Newbury Park: Sage.

Stanley, B. (1983). Senile dementia and informed consent. *Behavioral Sciences and the Law* 1, 57–71.

Stanley, B., Stanley, M., Guido, J., and Garvin, L. (1988). The functional competency of elderly at risk. *The Gerontologist* 28, 53–58.

State Community Care Reporter (1991). "Supported services in federally-assisted housing for the elderly: Arkansas." Washington: National Association of State Units on Aging, 3(3), 1–2.

Statement of Recommended Judicial Practices (1986). E. Wood (ed.). The Commission on Legal Problems of the Elderly, American Bar Association. Washington, D.C. and the National Judicial College, Reno, Nevada.

Stearns, L., Netting, F., Wilson, C., and Branch, L. (1990). Lessons from the implementation of CCRC regulations. *The Gerontologist* 30, 154–162.

Steinmetz, S. (1988). *Duty Bound: Elder Abuse and Family Care.* Newbury Park: Sage.

Stoller, E. (1985). Exchange patterns in the informal networks of the elderly: The impact of reciprocity on morale. *Journal of Marriage and the Family* 47, 335–342.

_____. (1989). Formal services and informal helping: Myth of service substitution. *Journal of Applied Gerontology* 8, 37–52.

_____. (1990). Males as helpers: The role of sons, relatives, and friends. *The Gerontologist* 30, 228–236.

Stone, R. (1986). *Aging in the eighties, Age 65 and over—use of community services, preliminary data from the Supplement on Aging to the National Health Interview Survey.* Advance data for Vital and Health Statistics, No.124, DHHD Pub. No. (PHS) 86–1250. Hyattsville: Public Health Service.

Stone, R., and Kemper, P. (1990). Spouses and children of disabled elders: How large a constituency for long-term care reform. *The Milbank Quarterly* 67, 485–506.

Stone, R., and Murtaugh, C. (1990). The elderly population with chronic functional disability: Implications for home care eligibility. *The Gerontologist* 30, 491–496.

Stone, R., Cafferata, G., and Sangl, J. (1987). Caregivers of the frail elderly: A national profile, *The Gerontologist* 27, 616–626.

Struyk, R. (1987). Housing adaptations: Needs and practices. In V. Bengston and J. Pynoos (eds.), *Housing the Aged: Design Directives and Policy Considerations.* New York: Elsevier Science Publications.

Struyk, R., Page, D., Newman, S., Carroll, M., Ueno, M., Cohen, B., and Wright, P. (1989). *Providing Supportive Services to the Frail Elderly in Federally Assisted Housing.* Washington: Urban Institute Press.

Suchman, E. A. (1965). Social patterns of illness and medical care. *Journal of Health and Human Behavior* 6 (Spring), 2–16.

Swan, J., Fox, P., and Estes, C. (1986). Community mental health services and the elderly: Retrenchment or expansion. *Community Mental Health Journal* 22, 275–285.

Swedish Institute (1991). *Fact Sheets on Sweden: Health and Medical Care in Sweden.* October. Stockholm.

Talbott, M. (1990). The negative side of the relationship between older widows and their adult children: The mothers' perspective. *The Gerontologist* 30, 595–603.

Task Force on Long-Term Health Care Policies (1987). Report to Congress and the Secretary of Health and Human Services, September. Washington: U.S. Government Printing Office.

Taub, H. (1980). Informed consent, memory, and age. *The Gerontologist*, 20, 686–694.

Taub, H., Kline, G., and Baker, M. (1981). The elderly and informed consent: Effects of vocabulary level and corrected feedback. *Experimental Aging Research* 7, 137–146.

Taylor, R. (1985). The extended family as a source of support to elderly Blacks. *The Gerontologist* 25, 488–495.

Taylor, R., and Chatters, L. (1986). Patterns of informal support to elderly Black adults: Family, friends and church members. *Social Work* 432–438.

Teitelman, J. L., and Priddy, J. M. (1988). From psychological theory to practice: Improving frail elders' quality of life through control-enhancing interventions. *Journal of Applied Gerontology* 7(3), 298–315.

Tennstedt, S., McKinlay, J., and Sullivan, L. (1989). Informal care for frail elders: The role of secondary caregivers. *The Gerontologist* 29, 677–684.

Thomas, P., Hunt, W., Garry, P., Hood, R., Goodwin, J., and Goodwin, J. (1983). Hearing activity in a healthy elderly population: Effects on emotional, cognitive, and social status. *Journal of Gerontology* 38, 321–25.

Timberlake, E., and Cook, K. O. (1984). Social work and the Vietnamese refugee. *Social Work* 29(2), 108–113.

Tinker, A. (1984). *The Elderly in Modern Society*. London: Longman.

Tobin, S., and Toseland, R. (1990). Models of services for the elderly. In A. Monk (ed.), *Handbook of Gerontological Social Services*, 2nd edition. New York: Columbia University Press.

Toseland, R. W., Rossiter, C. M., and Lebreque, M. S. (1989). The effectiveness of peer led and professionally led groups to support family caregivers. *The Gerontologist* 29(4), 465–471.

Trela, J., and Simms, L. (1971). Health and other factors affecting membership and attrition in a senior center. *Journal of Gerontology* 6, 46–51.

U.S. Bipartisan Commission on Comprehensive Health Care (1990). *A Call for Action: The Pepper Commission Final Report*. Washington: U.S. Government Printing Office.

U.S. Bureau of the Census (1980). *Persons of Spanish Origin by State: Supplementary Report*. Washington: U.S. Government Printing Office.

———. (1984). *Characteristics of the Population Below the Poverty Level, 1982*. Current Population Reports. Series P–60/ No. 144. Washington: U.S. Government Printing Office.

———. (1990). *The Need for Personal Assistance with Activities*. Washington: U.S. Government Printing Office.

U.S. Congress, Office of Technology Assessment (1990). *Confused Minds, Burdened Families: Finding Help for Alzheimer's Disease and Other Dementias*. OTA–BA–403. Washington, D.C.: U.S. Government Printing Office.

U.S. Department of Health, Education, and Welfare (1978). *Public Policy and the Frail Elderly*, DHEW Publication No. (OHDS) 79–20959, Washington: Federal Council on Aging.

U.S. Department of Health and Human Services (1985). *Report of the Secretary's Task Force on Black and Minority Health.* V.1, Executive Summary. Washington: U.S. Government Printing Office.

———. (1988). *Income of the Population 55 or Older, 1986*, SSA Pub. No. 13–11871. Washington: U.S. Government Printing Office.

———. (1989). *The National Nursing Home Survey, 1985 Summary for the United States*, data from the National Health Survey. Series 13, No. 97 DHHS Publication No. (PHS) 89–1758. Washington: U.S. Government Printing Office.

U.S. Department of Housing and Urban Development (1988). *American Housing Survey for the United States in 1985.* Current Housing Reports, Series H–150–185. Washington: U.S. Government Printing Office.

U.S. Department of Labor (1986). *Facts on U.S. Working Women.* Fact Sheet No. 86–4. Washington: U.S. Department of Labor.

U.S. General Accounting Office (1989). *Board and Care: Insufficient Assurances that Residents' Needs Are Identified and Met.* (GAO/HRD–89–50). Washington: U.S. Government Printing Office.

U.S. House Select Committee on Aging (1988a). *Dignity, Independence, and Cost-effectiveness: The Success of the Congregate Housing Services Program*, A report by the Chairman of the Subcommittee on Housing and Consumer Interests. Comm. Pub. No. 100-650. Washington: U.S. Government Printing Office.

———. (1988b). *Demographic Characteristics of the Older Hispanic Population.* Comm. Pub. No. 100–696. Washington: U.S. Government Printing Office.

———. (1989a). *Board and Care: A Failure in Public Policy.* Pub. No. 101–174. Washington: U.S. Government Printing Office.

———. (1989b). *Health Care Problems of the Black Elderly.* Comm. Pub. No. 101–743. Washington, D.C.: U.S. Government Printing Office.

———. (1990a). *Foundation for Aging Policy in the 90's: The 1987 Older Americans Act Amendments*, House of Representatives, Comm. Pub., No. 101–749. Washington: U.S. Government Printing Office.

———. (1990b). *Elder Abuse: A Decade of Shame and Inaction.* Comm. Put. No. 101–752. Washington: U.S. Government Printing Office.

———. (1990c). *Housing for the Frail Elderly*, Hearing before the Select Committee on Aging, House of Representatives. Comm. Pub. No. 101–757. Washington: U.S. Government Printing Office.

———. (1990d). *Sharing the Caring: Options for the 90s and Beyond.* Pub. No. 101–750. Washington: U.S. Government Printing Office.

U.S. Senate Special Committee on Aging (1989). *Aging America: Trends and Projections.* Washington: U.S. Government Printing Office.

———. (1990). *Long-Term Care for the Nineties: A Spotlight on Rural America.* Serial No. 101–27. Washington: U.S. Government Printing Office.

———. (1991). *Developments in Aging: 1990* V.1, S. Res. 66, Sec.19, Feb., 1990. Washington: U.S. Government Printing Office.

Uhlmann, R. F., Pearlman, R. A., and Cain, K. A. (1988). Physicians' and spouses' predictions of elderly patients' resusitation preferences. *Journal of Gerontology* 43, M115–121.

VandenBos, G., Stapp, J., and Kilburg, R. (1981). Health services providers in psychology. Results of the 1978 APA Human Resources Survey. *American Psychologist* 36, 1395–1418.

Verbrugge, L. M., Lepkowski, J. M., and Imanaka, Y. (1989). Comorbidity and its impact on disability. *The Milbank Quarterly* 67 (3–4), 450–481.

Vicente, L., Wiley, J., and Carrington, A. (1979). The risk of institutionalization before death. *The Gerontologist* 19, 361–368.

Volland, P. (1988). Foster care for the frail elderly: Implications of the Johns Hopkins experience. *Adult Foster Care Journal* 2(1), 72–81.

Wallace, S. (1990). The no-care zone: Availability, accessibility, and acceptability in community based long term care. *The Gerontologist* 30, 254–262.

Weiner, J., Hanley, R., Spence, D., and Murray, S. (1988). We can run, but we can't hide: Toward reforming long-term care. In *Proceedings of the Commonwealth Fund Commission on Elderly People Living Alone.* Background Papers No. 11. Baltimore: Commonwealth Fund.

Weiner, J., Hanley, R., Clark, R., and Van Nostrand, J. (1990). Measuring the activities of daily living: Comparisons across national surveys. *Journal of Gerontology* 45, S229–237.

Weinstein, B., and Ventry, I. (1982). Hearing impairment and social isolation in the elderly. *Journal of Speech and Hearing Review* 25, 593–599.

Weissert, W. G., Elston, J. M., Bolda, E. J., Cready, C. M., Zelma W. N., Sloane, P. D., Kalsbee, W. D., Mutran, E., Rice, T. H., and Koch, G. G. (1989). Models of adult day care: Findings from a national survey. *The Gerontologist* 5, 640–649.

Wells, K., Stewart, A., Hays, R., Burman, M., Rogers, W., Daniels, M., Berry, A., Greenfield, S., and Ware, J. (1989). The functioning and well-being of depressed patients—results from the medical outcomes study. *Journal of the American Medical Association* 262, 914–919.

White, J. (1992). The federal refocusing on long term care. *Caring* XI, 32–40.

White-Means, S., and Thornton, M. (1990). Ethnic differences in the production of informal home health care. *The Gerontologist* 30, 778–758.

Williams, J., Drinka, T., Greenberg, J., Ferrekk-Holton, J., Euhardy, R., and Schram, M. (1991). Development and testing of living skills and resources (ALSAR) in elderly community dwelling veterans. *The Gerontologist* 31, 84–92.

Wolfson, C., Barker, J., and Mitteness, L. (1990). Personalization of formal social relationships by the elderly. *Research on Aging* 12(1), 94–112.

Wolinsky, F., Aguirre, B., Fann, L., Keith, V., Arnold, C., Niederhauer, J., and Dietrich, K. (1989). Ethnic differences in the demand for physician and hospital utilization among older adults in major American cities: Conspicuous evidence of considerable inequalities. *The Milbank Quarterly* 67, 412–449.

Work, J. (1989). Strength training: A bridge to independence for the elderly. *The Physician and Sports Medicine* (November), 134–140.

World Health Organization (1980). International Classification of Impairments, Disabilities, and Handicaps. In *A Manual of Classification Relating to the Consequences of Disease*. Geneva: WHO.

Yeatts, D., Crow, T., and Folts, E. (1992). Service use among low-income minority elderly: Strategies for overcoming barriers. *The Gerontologist, 32*, 24–31.

Young, R., and Kahana, E. (1989). Specifying caregiver outcomes: Gender and relationship aspects of caregiving strain. *The Gerontologist* 29, 660–666.

Zarit, S., Reeves, S., and Bach-Peterson, J. (1980). Relatives of the impaired elderly: Correlates of feelings of burden. *The Gerontologist* 20, 649–655.

Zawadski, R., and Ansak, M. (1983). Consolidating community-based long term care: Early returns from the On Lok demonstration. *The Gerontologist* 23, 364–370.

Zborowski, M. (1952). Cultural components in response to pain. *Journal of Social Issues* 8, 16–30.

Zedlewski, S., Barnes, R., Burt, M., McBride, T., and Meyer, J. (1990). *The Needs of the Elderly in the 21st Century*. Washington: Urban Institute.

Zola, I. (1973). Pathways to the doctor: From person to patient. *Social Science and Medicine* 7, 677–689.

Zweibel, N., and Cassel, C. (1989).Treatment choices at the end of life: A comparison of decisions by older patients and their physician-selected proxies. *The Gerontologist, 29*, 615–621.

# Index

Volunteers: as counselors, 157, 158;
   for friendly visiting, 76; for telephone services, 156

Wallace, S., 63, 135
Weiner, J., 23
Weissert, W. G., 72
White-Means, S., 139
Wisconsin, Bureau of Long-term
   Support, 147–48

Wisensale, S., 92
Women: caregiving role of, 111,
   113; and osteoporosis, 119; risks
   for, 4–5; self-perceptions of, 11
World Health Organization, 20

Young, R., 107

Zola, I., 127

## About the Author

CAROLE COX, DSW, is Associate Professor in the School of Social Service at The Catholic University of America in Washington, D.C. She is co-author (with A. Monk) of *Home Care for the Elderly: An International Perspective* (Auburn House, 1991) and has contributed many chapters and articles on gerontology to various books and journals.